UNHCR and the Struggle for Accountability

Despite the key importance of accountability for the legitimacy of humanitarian action, inadequate academic attention has focused on how the concept of accountability is evolving within the *specific* branches of the humanitarian enterprise. Up to now, there exists no comprehensive account of what we label the 'technologies of accountability', the effects of their interaction, or the question of how the current turn to decision-making software and biometrics as both the means and ends of accountability may contribute to reshaping humanitarian governance.

UNHCR and the Struggle for Accountability explores the UNHCR's quest for accountability by viewing the UNHCR's accountability obligations through the web of institutional relationships within which the agency is placed (beneficiaries, host governments, implementing partners, donors, the Executive Committee and UNGA). The book takes a multidisciplinary approach in order to illuminate the various layers and relationships that constitute accountability and also reflect on what constitutes *good enough* accountability.

This book contributes to the discussion regarding how we construct knowledge about concepts in humanitarian studies and represents a valuable resource for academics, researchers and professionals in the areas of anthropology, history, international relations, international law, science, technology studies and socio-legal studies.

Kristin Bergtora Sandvik is a senior researcher at PRIO and the director for the Norwegian Centre for Humanitarian Studies, Norway. She holds an SJD from Harvard Law School (2008).

Katja Lindskov Jacobsen is assistant professor at Metropolitan University College, Denmark and external lecturer at Copenhagen Business School, Denmark. She holds a PhD in International Relations from Lancaster University (2011).

Routledge Humanitarian Studies Series

Series editors: Alex de Waal and Dorothea Hilhorst
Editorial Board: Mihir Bhatt, Dennis Dijkzeul, Wendy Fenton,
Kirsten Johnson, Julia Streets, Peter Walker

The Routledge Humanitarian Studies series in collaboration with the International Humanitarian Studies Association (IHSA) takes a comprehensive approach to the growing field of expertise that is humanitarian studies. This field is concerned with humanitarian crises caused by natural disaster, conflict or political instability and deals with the study of how humanitarian crises evolve, how they affect people and their institutions and societies and the responses they trigger.

We invite book proposals that address, amongst other topics, questions of aid delivery, institutional aspects of service provision, the dynamics of rebel wars, state building after war, the international architecture of peacekeeping, the ways in which ordinary people continue to make a living throughout crises and the effect of crises on gender relations.

This interdisciplinary series draws on and is relevant to a range of disciplines, including development studies, international relations, international law, anthropology, peace and conflict studies, public health and migration studies.

Disaster, Conflict and Society in Crises
Everyday politics of crisis response
Edited by Dorothea Hilhorst

Human Security and Natural Disasters
Edited by Christopher Hobson, Paul Bacon and Robin Cameron

Human Security and Japan's Triple Disaster
Responding to the 2011 earthquake, tsunami and Fukushima nuclear crisis
Edited by Paul Bacon and Christopher Hobson

The Paradoxes of Aid Work
Passionate professionals
Silke Roth

UNHCR and the Struggle for Accountability

Technology, law and results-based management

Edited by Kristin Bergtora Sandvik and Katja Lindskov Jacobsen

Routledge
Taylor & Francis Group
LONDON AND NEW YORK

earthscan
from Routledge

First published 2016
by Routledge
2 Park Square, Milton Park, Abingdon, Oxon OX14 4RN

and by Routledge
711 Third Avenue, New York, NY 10017

First issued in paperback 2017

Routledge is an imprint of the Taylor & Francis Group, an informa business

British Library Cataloguing-in-Publication Data
A catalogue record for this book is available from the British Library

Library of Congress Cataloging-in-Publication Data
Names: Sandvik, Kristin Bergtora, editor. | Jacobsen, Katja Lindskov,
editor.
Title: UNHCR and the struggle for accountability : technology, law and
results-based management / edited by Kristin Bergtora Sandvik and
Katja Lindskov Jacobsen.
Other titles: United Nations High Commissioner for Refugees and the
struggle for accountability
Description: New York, NY : Routledge, 2016. |
Series: Routledge humanitarian studies
Identifiers: LCCN 2015034708| ISBN 9781138911529 (hb) |
ISBN 9781315692593 (ebook)
Subjects: LCSH: Office of the United Nations High Commissioner for
Refugees—Evaluation. | Office of the United Nations High Commissioner
for Refugees—Management. | Refugees—International cooperation.
Classification: LCC HV640.3 .U425 2016 | DDC 362.87/58—dc23LC
record available at http://lccn.loc.gov/2015034708

ISBN 13: 978-0-8153-5506-9 (pbk)
ISBN 13: 978-1-138-91152-9 (hbk)

Typeset in Baskerville
by diacriTech, Chennai

Contents

Notes on contributors

Kristin Bergtora Sandvik is a senior researcher at PRIO and the director for the Norwegian Centre for Humanitarian Studies. She holds an SJD from Harvard Law School (2008). Her research takes a socio-legal approach to international law, war and humanitarian action, with an ethnographic focus on UNHCR, Uganda and Colombia. Her work has appeared in *Disasters*, the *International Journal of Refugee Law, Refugee Survey Quarterly*, the *Political and Legal Anthropology Review (PoLAR)* and *Millennium: Journal of International Studies* and *ICRC World Disasters Report*.

Miriam Bradley is an assistant professor at the Institut Barcelona d'Estudis Internacionals. Her research interests lie at the intersection of international relations, international security and humanitarian policy. She has written on the protection of civilians in armed conflict, with a particular focus on the work of the United Nations High Commissioner for Refugees and the International Committee of the Red Cross. She holds a doctorate in International Relations from the University of Oxford.

Ashley Brooke Rockenbach is a doctoral candidate in History at the University of Michigan-Ann Arbor, United States. Her dissertation project, 'An Uncertain Order of Things: Banyarwanda Settlers and the Making of the Ugandan State, 1911–Present', focuses on the history of Ugandan refugee management.

Marion Fresia is an assistant professor at the Institute of Anthropology, University of Neuchâltel, Switzerland. Her research has focused on West African refugee camps as spaces of governance and social change, and more recently, she has explored the role of UNHCR headquarters and UNHCR Turkey in circulating and universalizing the refugee label as well as the institutional fabric and circulation of refugee experts, norms and policies. Her work has appeared in the *Refugee Survey Quarterly, Development and Change, Revue Européenne des Migrations Internationales* and the *Oxford Handbook of Refugee and Forced Migration Studies*, among others.

Adèle Garnier is a postdoctoral fellow at the Interuniversity Research Centre on Globalization and Work (CRIMT) and the Faculty of Law, Université de Montréal, Canada. She holds a PhD in Politics from Macquarie University, Australia, and the University of Leipzig, Germany. Her research adopts an institutionalist approach to investigate continuity and change as well as knowledge diffusion in refugee policy in national and international perspectives, focusing currently on Canada and UNHCR. She has published in *Refugee*, the *Journal of Ethnic and Migration Studies* and *WeltTrends* and is associated with the development of the International Migration Law and Policy Analysis (IMPALA) database.

Maja Janmyr (PhD) is a postdoctoral researcher at the Faculty of Law, University of Bergen, currently working on refugee homeland activism in the Middle East. She has previously studied the United Nations High Commissioner for Refugees' (UNHCR) international responsibility in relation to insecurity in refugee camps and human rights issues related to the forced return of failed asylum seekers.

Niamh Kinchin joined the School of Law at the University of Wollongong (UOW), Australia, as a lecturer in January 2015. From 2008 to 2014, she was a casual lecturer at the UOW and University of NSW (UNSW). Prior to teaching, she was employed for a number of years at the Commonwealth Administrative Appeals Tribunal as a legal officer. In 2002, she was admitted as a legal practitioner in NSW. Niamh holds a PhD from UNSW. Her primary research interests are in global accountability and administrative justice, global administrative law and public law within the Australian and international contexts. Niamh's PhD, which she completed in 2014, is titled 'Accountability in the Global Space: Plurality, Complexity and UNHCR'.

Katja Lindskov Jacobsen (PhD) is an assistant professor at Metropolitan University College, Copenhagen, in the Department of Risk and Disaster Management, and external lecturer at Copenhagen Business School. She holds a PhD in International Relations from the University of Lancaster. She combines insights from International Relations, Humanitarian Studies and Science and Technology Studies in her research on humanitarian uses of new technology. Her work has appeared in journals such as *Security Dialogue* and *The Journal of Citizenship Studies*. Her recent book is titled *The Politics of Humanitarian Technology* (Routledge 2015).

Andreas von Känel is a PhD candidate at the Institute of Anthropology, University of Neuchâtel, Switzerland. Von Känel conducted his master thesis' research on UNHCR refugee status determination in Mauritania and is currently undertaking a PhD on education in a Congolese refugee camp in Tanzania, under 'Education in Spaces of Exception' directed by Marion Fresia.

1 Introduction: quest for an accountability cure

Katja Lindskov Jacobsen and Kristin Bergtora Sandvik[1]

The Office of the United Nations High Commissioner for Refugees (UNHCR) was established in 1950 to oversee the international protection of refugees, with emphasis on the estimated 1 million refugees who had been displaced in the wake of World War II. From that period, the scope of UNHCR's activities and responsibilities has grown significantly, in addition to the size of its staff. Equally important, changes have occurred in the UNHCR's approaches towards refugee protection (including, for example, biometric identity management and digital mapping technologies) and in its mandate interpretation (Betts 2012, p. 121). Meanwhile, the need for UNHCR's services is greater than ever: by 2015, UNHCR had warned that 'wars, conflict and persecution have forced more people than at any other time since records began to flee their homes and seek refuge and safety elsewhere' (UNHCR 2015a). In 2015, UNHCR had more than 9,300 staff members working in more than 125 countries, assisting 42.9 million refugees and other people of concern (UNHCR 2015b).

Both internal and external changes inevitably present questions regarding accountability. In the case of UNHCR, however, accountability concerns stem from a different source: Despite decades of protection work, designed and conducted with the best of intentions, the agency continues to be dogged by a legacy of scandals involving mismanagement, financial waste and illegal or unethical behaviour on the part of staff. This history, combined with the task of protecting an unprecedentedly large number of refugees in an increasingly complex political landscape, renders questions regarding accountability more acute than ever – not only for UNHCR but for its donors and, most importantly, for the people whom UNHCR is mandated to protect.

Accountability production occurs at UNHCR in a uniquely complex environment: UNHCR's work affects, and is affected by, various actors (including beneficiaries, host governments, implementing partners, donors and the UNHCR Executive Committee) and contextual factors (from everyday practices to historical contingencies and political dynamics). Moreover, accountability is not simply a technical or neutral aspect of management; the accountability measures that UNHCR has implemented since the mid-1990s have given rise to new relationships. For example, because UNHCR has expanded its protection and relief activities, accountability cannot be understood apart from the emergence of new stakeholder relationships, legal frameworks and protection challenges.

The existing literature on UNHCR and accountability is voluminous and appears to be associated with one of four fields of study. First, UNHCR has been studied from an international relations perspective, as a global security actor (Betts and Loescher 2010; Hammerstad 2014), and in relation to the politics of UNHCR's protection work – with a specific focus on institutional dynamics, relations with donor and host states and changes in the contours of the global political landscape, all of which have implications for accountability (Loescher 2001; Steiner, Gibney and Loescher 2003; Betts, Loescher and Milner 2012). Second, scholars in international law have analysed UNHCR's mandate, as well as the agency's role in the production of legal norms, in relation to accountability (Wilde 2005; Pallis 2006; Lewis 2012; Simeon 2013; Druke 2014). Finally, UNHCR's accountability has been addressed by scholars in the fields of migration studies (e.g. *Journal of Ethnic and Migration Studies* 2014) and refugee studies (Harrell-Bond 1986; Verdirame and Harrell-Bond 2005; Hilhorst 2002; Kagan 2006).

No one volume, however, has attempted to demonstrate how our understanding of this complex issue can be enhanced by allowing different perspectives and approaches to enter into the conversation. To address this gap, we propose a conception of accountability as consisting of various types and layers of initiatives, which are best described from a multidisciplinary and interdisciplinary approach. By incorporating case studies, historical narratives and legal analyses, in addition to a range of geographical, topical and temporal perspectives, we hope to emphasize those aspects of accountability that defy disciplinary boundaries.[2]

This volume assembles perspectives from anthropology, critical security studies, international law, international relations, political science and sociolegal studies. The contributions are based on fieldwork in Australia, Colombia, Mauritania, Turkey, Uganda and the European Union. Thematically, the chapters deal with the complexity of accountability in the global space; the application of the law of international responsibility to UNHCR; UNHCR's deployment of accountability narratives in refugee resettlement; UNHCR's efforts to hold the state accountable for responding to internal displacement; the struggle for accountability in the determination of refugee status; use of historical contingency and multiple meanings of the 'refugee' label to stimulate critical thinking on UNHCR's efforts to apply result-based management (RBM) to the construction of a more legible refugee population; the use of rights-based approaches and results-based management as 'accountability technologies'; and finally, use of biometric identity management in reshaping accountability in refugee management. Broadly speaking, the time frame addressed in the volume dates from the mid-1990s to the present, that is, it begins in the period immediately after the Cold War, when initial optimism regarding the new potential for international collaboration on disasters and emergencies began to give way to concerns regarding the inadequacies and failures of the growing humanitarian enterprise.

In addition to juxtaposing a range of inter- and multidisciplinary insights into accountability at UNHCR, the volume moves beyond investigating accountability from the perspective of gap studies – that is, as a problem of normative deficiency and implementation failure – to exploring accountability as a social, political and ethical practice. We are interested not only in who is accountable for what and but also in how concepts and duties of accountability are negotiated and distributed as UNHCR engages with various actors.

This introductory chapter explores accountability in the context of the 'humanitarian accountability revolution', that is, the struggle to improve accountability across the humanitarian sector, and in relation to the specific practice of UNHCR. It is important to note at the outset, however, that it is occasionally difficult to fully separate UNHCR accountability from the broader issue of UN accountability. UNHCR often collaborates closely with – and indeed often depends on – the work of other UN organizations. Hence, several accountability initiatives described in this chapter are specific to UNHCR, whereas other initiatives have been pursued more generally by UN agencies as reform efforts. Our principal focus, however, is on the relationship between humanitarian action and accountability as it has evolved within UNHCR.

The remainder of this chapter offers a broad-brush account of UNHCR's struggle for accountability; the purpose is to set the stage for the more specific considerations presented in the individual chapters. The chapter is divided into four main parts: (1) a description of UNHCR's overarching accountability narrative, focusing on the evolving interpretations of the agency's mandate; (2) an overview of several UNHCR's key accountability initiatives; (3) a consideration of criticisms levelled against UNHCR with respect to accountability; and (4) a reflection on the current state of accountability at UNHCR, which argues that the absence of perfection in accountability should not be observed to be detrimental. The chapter is followed by a summary of each of the remaining chapters in the volume.

UNHCR's mandate: evolving interpretations of accountability

According to UNHCR's website, the agency is mandated to 'lead and co-ordinate international action to protect refugees and resolve refugee problems worldwide' (UNHCR n.d.c); to strive 'to ensure … the right to seek asylum' (UNHCR n.d.c); and to 'help find durable solutions' (UNHCR n.d.a) to refugee situations, principally through repatriation, local integration or third-country resettlement.

The provision of international protection to refugees was originally intended to be a set of supervisory humanitarian tasks, including obtaining information from the states regarding refugees, assisting with repatriation or admission to third countries and ensuring the implementation of international conventions. Challenged by long-term refugee crises, however, UNHCR began to provide direct protection to refugees, which included running refugee camps and determining refugee status (see Rockenbach in this volume); through such expansions of activities and responsibilities, UNHCR gradually evolved into the organization that we know today.

When UNHCR was established, an important element of its role was to hold states accountable for the obligations that they had committed to as signatories of the 1951 Convention relating to the Status of Refugees (see Kinchin in this volume). Under that convention, UNHCR was assigned the 'task of supervising international conventions providing for the protection of refugees, and recognizing that the effective co-ordination of measures taken to deal with this problem will depend upon the co-operation of states with the High Commissioner' (OHCHR n.d.; see also Kälin 2003).

In practical terms, UNHCR was responsible for either monitoring the states' compliance with international law (occasionally referred to as 'passive accountability') or setting the standards for their conduct (referred to as 'active accountability') (Valticos 1998, p. 461). However, the relationship between UNHCR and the states was never easy or uncomplicated, and it was clear from the outset that UNHCR's ability to ensure protection to refugees was inseparable from the states' willingness to cooperate (Garvey 1985).

UNHCR's accountability efforts play out against a complex and evolving backdrop. In this regard, four circumstances are of particular note: First, although UNHCR still 'struggles to hold states accountable for respecting their obligations' (UNHCR 2012, p. 11), current discussions of UNHCR and accountability largely neglect this aspect of the agency's mandate, tending to focus instead on how UNHCR can become more accountable to its donors, specifically with regard to how funds are used.

Second, as an agency operating as the interface between persons of concern in the Global South and donors in the Global North, UNHCR is in a difficult position. On the one hand, it is a critic of the asylum policies and resettlement decisions of countries in the North; on the other hand, UNHCR serves as a gatekeeper and governance actor in the South and, as such, engages in activities that are of considerable interest to donors. The ambiguity of its position unavoidably affects UNHCR's relationship with powerful donor states, particularly in the realm of accountability.

Third, much of the existing literature tends to assume that upward accountability (e.g. to donors and to the UNHCR Executive Committee) and downward accountability (to persons of concern) is somehow an either-or choice. Although this assumption may occasionally be true (as is illustrated by several chapters in this volume), the situation is more complex than an either-or model might suggest. Certainly, UNHCR's struggles to meet complicated and occasionally conflicting accountability demands warrant more nuanced attention.

Finally, UNHCR's accountability efforts are affected by not only its relationship to donor states but also its relationship to host states. One issue is the tendency, on the part of host states, to take a more assertive stance towards UNHCR (and other humanitarian actors), which may necessitate negotiations and compromises with relevance to accountability. For example, if a host state were to insist on camp closures and the only alternative were repatriation or relocation to areas where refugee safety could not be assured, UNHCR would need to come to an agreement with the host state.

Another area of concern is refugee status determination (RSD). Although UNHCR has 'encouraged governments to re-assume responsibility for RSD', the agency operates in an environment where 'states do not always do every-thing they are supposed to' (Kagan 2014). UNHCR occasionally must assume responsibility for key functions, such as RSD, simultaneously attempting to pres-sure states to take responsibility for those very tasks. As might be expected, the host governments may in several cases 'prefer to shift responsibility for refugee policy to UNHCR' (Kagan 2014; see also Kagan 2006). Given UNHCR's origi-nal mandate to hold the states accountable for their obligation to protect the refugees, this situation is hardly ideal (see Janmyr; and Fresia and von Känel in this volume).

Finally, another important dimension of UNHCR's relationship to the host states concerns the responsibility for internally displaced persons (IDPs). Because internal displacement raises sensitive questions regarding state sover-eignty, achieving international consensus concerning the legal status of IDPs has proven to be difficult (Cohen 2004). In 1998, the UN Commission on Human Rights adopted the Guiding Principles on Internal Displacement, which is the most authoritative statement from the international community.[3] The principles reiterate the responsibilities of the states before, during, and after displacement, in accordance with the relevant human rights and humanitarian law. Despite the principles' focus on the responsibility of the states, UNHCR's IDP protection practices bear witness to the political sensitivity of internal displacement and to the types of challenges that the agency confronts to offer protection to IDPs (see Bradley in this volume).

If UNHCR succeeds in its effort, articulated in 2012, to design 'new prac-tices and approaches', specifically for the purpose of improving its ability to 'hold states accountable for their obligations under the 1951 convention' (UNHCR 2012, p. 1), we may note a renewed focus on UNHCR's initial role in relation to state accountability. Whether UNHCR can bring new life to that role depends, however, on several factors. Although the influence of global political dynamics and the power of individual states on UNHCR's work should not be underes-timated, one should not conclude that institutions, such as UNHCR, 'are com-pletely without power or influence' (Steiner, Gibney and Loescher 2003, p. 4). In an analysis of the development of UNHCR's mandate, for example, Betts pointed out that despite the states' influence, changes in UNHCR's mandate have 'fre-quently contradicted, rather than complied with, the preferences of major donors' (Betts 2012, p. 136). In other words, UNHCR has previously demonstrated its ability to assert a certain degree of autonomy (Loescher 2001), which could be relevant to the task it currently faces, namely, accountably providing protection to an unprecedentedly large number of displaced persons.

To complement this overarching narrative of the changing relationship between UNHCR's mandate and the focus of its accountability efforts, the fol-lowing section presents a number of key transitions in UNHCR's struggle for accountability, which altogether create a backdrop for detailed discussions presented in subsequent chapters.

Mapping the trajectories of UNHCR's accountability efforts

Post-Cold War demands for financial and managerial accountability

The first turning point in UNHCR accountability efforts was sparked by the convergence of two factors: the rapid growth of the humanitarian enterprise; and post-Cold War challenges to humanitarian action. During the 1980s and 1990s, the number of nongovernmental organizations (NGOs) grew rapidly, especially in the Global South; this growth was fuelled, in part, by the belief on the part of donors that NGOs were better able to reach the poor and could more cost effectively provide basic social services than governments. This growth was accompanied, however, by a number of high-profile scandals, which led to a greater focus on financial accountability. In response, NGOs borrowed conceptions of accountability (along with accounting language) from business-sector discussions of responsibility and ethics (Edwards and Hulme 1996).

Several observers have suggested that during the 1980s, the Cold War political landscape made life easy, in a sense, for UNHCR (Trinh 2005). Discussions of global governance or the roles and activities of international organizations tended not to centre on accountability. Not only did UNHCR's activities receive little scrutiny but in 1981, the agency was awarded the Nobel Peace Prize for helping refugees flee Communism. The environment in which UNHCR operated changed significantly, however, with the end of the Cold War. Whereas the refugees who had fled Communism had been perceived in a heroic light, this view had begun to shift by the 1980s: Under pressure from donor and host states, increasing emphasis was placed on repatriation and assisting refugees to remain within their countries of origin.[4]

In UNHCR policy documents, the earliest references to accountability concerned the financial aspects of UNHCR activities, particularly the cost-effective use of public funds (UNHCR 1980, 1986). Accompanying this focus on finances was an emphasis on effective management.

The idea of equipping UNHCR with modern managerial structures and working tools was first suggested by High Commissioner Poul Hartling in the early 1980s (Chaulia 2002). Not until 1995, however, did UNHCR embark on project Delphi, which was designed to improve 'delivery, accountability and performance' and transform UNHCR into 'a slimmer, trimmer organization' (UNHCR 1996, p. 1). The legacy of Project Delphi has been contested (Goodwin-Gill 1999); meanwhile, the broader challenges persisted: As UNHCR continued to grow, the international media noted the donor countries' discontent with the agency's accounting practices, which yielded headlines, such as 'Refugees' agency lost in wilderness of bungling and waste' (Burns and Williams 1998).

In the late 1990s and early 2000s, UNHCR suffered serious budget cuts, in part, as a consequence of donors' lack of confidence in the quality of UNHCR's management and accountability mechanisms (Lawry-White 2000). Notably, a report from the UNHCR Evaluation and Policy Analysis Unit pointed to a 'steady upward-moving staff cost structure' as one of 'the root causes' of repetitive financial crisis in UNHCR (UNHCR 2003, as quoted in Kelley, Sandison and Lawry-White 2004, p. 6). As will be discussed later in the chapter, these negative trends were eventually addressed through a series of initiatives, dating from the mid-2000s, which led to what can be considered a new start for UNHCR.

Failures to prepare, protect and navigate: rwanda and Kosovo

Beginning in the mid-1990s, UNHCR shifted its focus to a different type of account-ability, namely, the potential for political dynamics to undermine UNHCR's protection mandate. The following two examples illustrate such dynamics and the agency's failure to pay sufficient attention to them: (1) local power relations in the context of the Rwandan genocide and (2) global power relations in the context of ethnic cleansing in Kosovo.

In the wake of the humanitarian community's failure to respond to the Rwandan genocide, UNHCR and the rest of the relief sector recognized that humanitarian accountability was more than a matter of finance and slim, trim managerial structures. Although humanitarian accountability had first emerged as a concern in the 1980s and had been institutionalized through the 1994 Code of Conduct for the International Red Cross and Red Crescent Movement and NGOs in Disaster Relief, the findings of the 1996 Joint Evaluation of Emergency Assistance to Rwanda represented a defining moment in the understanding of UNHCR accountability (Eriksson 1996). Specifically, the findings raised questions that extended beyond the financial and managerial issues and addressed the fun-damental humanitarian ideals, for example, whether UNHCR had failed to be accountable to the victims of genocide, including whether the agency could be held accountable for inadvertently feeding génocidaires. In the wake of the Rwandan genocide, UNHCR was also criticized for 'harping solely on the precarious exter-nal environment that hampers its performance' (Chaulia 2002; Power 2008).

In its early phases, UNHCR's response to the humanitarian accountability revolution focused on human resources, technical standards and the quality of humanitarian assistance, specifically, greater attention to the needs of persons of concern.[5]

Whereas in Rwanda, the political dynamics that compromised UNHCR's protection work were local, in Kosovo external political dynamics undermined UNHCR's ability to offer protection to those affected by the crisis. Critics have observed that UNHCR's response to the events in Kosovo exposed a number of weaknesses, including the agency's 'inability to rapidly meet its own standards of response' (ECHCPSC 2000, para. 4). In addition to suffering from a critical lack of coordination,[6] however, UNHCR was subject to donor pressures, policies and national security concerns that complicated its ability to deliver protection to refu-gees (Booth 2005; Gibney 1999). As Hammerstad had noted, under pressure from key donors, such as the United States, important decisions – such as where to place refugee camps – were taken out of UNHCR's hands, as expressed in the following manner: 'in reality its influence over core assistance and protection decisions … was minimal' (2014, p. 243).

More generally, UNHCR's response to the Kosovo crisis generated debates concerning whether UNHCR's close relations with major donors interfered with its ability to fulfil its protection mandate (Trinh 2005) and concerning the politicization of humanitarianism more generally (Chandler 2006). Indeed, UNHCR itself acknowledged that 'the Kosovo case … brought out some fundamental questions of policy facing UNHCR' (ECHCPSC 2000, para. 4); the agency was concerned, for example, 'that contingency planning which assumes that states will not comply with their responsibilities to receive and host new arrivals … runs the risk of becoming a self-fulfilling prophecy' (ECHCPSC 2000, para. 4).

Thus, the events in Kosovo revealed state failures to help protect the refugees. An independent evaluation observed, for example, that 'donors appeared to have unreasonable expectations that UNHCR was solely responsible for camp security' (ECHCPSC 2000, para. 2). By exposing how the relationship between UNHCR and both donor and host states can complicate the fulfilment of UNHCR's protection mandate, the Kosovo crisis highlighted the question of accountability.

Altogether, the events in Rwanda and Kosovo led UNHCR to recognize the need for a broader view of accountability, i.e. one that acknowledged that the agency's work could not be viewed in isolation from either local or global political dynamics. Thus, Rwanda and Kosovo helped move discussions of accountability beyond a narrow focus on financial matters to embrace accountability to people of concern, including accountability for failing to offer protection or for the unintended consequences of well-meaning humanitarian practices.

Protection from humanitarians and the emerging focus on downward accountability

Whereas the events in Rwanda and Kosovo had demonstrated how local and global power dynamics could undermine UNHCR's ability to fulfil its protection mandate, subsequent accountability scandals (examples of which will be discussed later in the chapter) pointed to types of harm that had been inflicted on people of concern by UNHCR's own staff and implementing partners.

Two key events brought attention to the issue: In 1999, it was discovered that as many as 70 people were involved in a complex conspiracy to extort money from the refugees at the regional UNHCR hub in Nairobi, Kenya (Browne 2006). Investigations conducted by the UN Office of Internal Oversight Services (OIOS) in October 2000 revealed that the refugees were obliged to pay UNHCR staff between 0.50 and 0.100 Kenyan shillings (US$0.60–US$1.28) merely to access the offices (OIOS 2001) and that those who wanted resettlement to a third country were asked to pay bribes ranging from US$1,500 to US$6,000 each (OIOS 2001, p. 5). The investigations led to the arrest and dismissal of a number of UNHCR staff (OIOS 2001).

The second event occurred in 2002, with the publication of a joint UNHCR/ Save the Children-UK report on the sexual exploitation and abuse of refugee children in Guinea, Liberia and Sierra Leone by the staff of 42 agencies. More specifically, the report noted the following: 'The agencies that are possible implicated in some way include UN peacekeeping forces, international and local NGOs, and government agencies responsible for humanitarian response' (2002, p. 2). In the wake of these revelations that included instances, for example, in which the staff had 'traded humanitarian commodities and services ... for sex with girls under 18' (UNHCR and Save the Children-UK 2002, p. 4), UNHCR initiated additional investigations and acknowledged the need for immediate 'remedial measures' (UNHCR and Save the Children-UK 2002, p. 2).

Scandals, such as these, powerfully demonstrated that for UNHCR, downward accountability was not simply a matter of protecting refugees from external threats; UNHCR must also be held accountable for failing to protect persons of concern from harms stemming from the agency's own activities. UNHCR's efforts to address intentional harm (including criminal activity) (Sandvik 2011) have been complicated, however, by the web of immunities and privileges within which international organizations operate, as well as by the high number of implementing partners that contract with the agency (Janmyr 2014). More broadly, accountability to persons of concern is an aspect of protection to which UNHCR still struggles to observe. In 2012, after many years of discussing downward accountability, UNHCR observed in *The state of the world's refugees*, which the agency regards as a flagship publication, that the agency had '*increasingly recognized* that their principal accountability is to the people they serve' (UNHCR 2012, p. 5, italics added).[7]

In sum, since the initial conceptualization of accountability as a financial and managerial issue, UNHCR has experienced two turning points that have implications for accountability: first, the difficulty of providing refugee protection in highly politicized contexts where UNHCR's activities cannot be isolated from the local or global power dynamics; second, the failure to protect refugees from harm stemming from UNHCR's own activities. Each of the events described in this section sparked severe criticism from various actors, including donors. Ultimately, these events and the resulting criticism led to calls for radical reforms within UNHCR; initiated in 2006, these reforms sought to address not only the financial and management issues but also the normative aspects of what it means to provide accountable international protection.

A new start? Accountability through organizational change

Between 2006 and 2012, UNHCR embarked on an ambitious programme of structural and management reform, which in 2011 led the United Kingdom Department for International Development (DFID) to observe that the Structural and Management Change Process, as it was known, had yielded an unprecedented increase in productivity (DFID 2011, p. 47; see also Garnier in this volume). The key components of the initiative were the Comprehensive Needs Assessment, the Global Strategic Priorities and the Focus software. New budgeting models were introduced; and in 2012, UNHCR completed the transition to international public sector accounting standards. Finally, the reform process entailed a shift in the direction of decentralization and regionalization. A revised resource allocation framework, issued in 2007, transferred significant responsibility and authority from the headquarters to the field; and in 2009, the agency introduced a global learning hub to support decentralized training for UNHCR staff.

Two elements of UNHCR's reform initiative are particularly relevant to accountability. First, the notion of accountability as a managerial issue can be addressed through organizational change. We see this situation, for example, in the integration of results-based management (RBM) into UNHCR practice (see Sandvik in this volume). Although UNHCR had embarked on a piecemeal adoption of RBM in the late 1990s, as part of its response to demands for greater financial and managerial accountability, the reforms undertaken in 2006 substantially accelerated the pace at which RBM was implemented throughout the agency. Despite loosely defining RBM as 'a philosophy that emphasizes the achievement of results as the essential task of management' (UNHCR 2010, p. 1), the agency felt that it offered significant potential. In a speech to the 64th session of the UNHCR Executive Committee, Volker Türk, UNHCR's director of international protection, argued that RBM could help UNHCR realize its protection mandate and that accountability was 'being strengthened through an emphasis on global coherence, transparency, participation, impact, and performance measurement and analysis' (Türk 2013).

The second accountability-related aspect of the 2006–2012 reforms concerns the introduction of specific accountability initiatives that were intended to address criticisms. In 2007, responding, in part, to the 2002 UNHCR/Save the Children-UK report on sexual abuse by the NGO staff, as well as to the increasing attention given to sexual violence on the international agenda, UNHCR established an accountability system for age, gender and diversity (AGD), which UNHCR partners are required to implement.[8] According to a synthesis report prepared by the DFID, the primary focus of the AGD initiative was to improve downward accountability by ensuring 'that all staff see their responsibility for mainstreaming age and gender' and pay explicit attention to 'the different protection needs of each group' (Groves 2005, p. 16).

In 2008, UNHCR established a fully independent ethics office to oversee whistle-blowing and financial disclosure programmes. In 2010, it introduced the global management accountability framework, aimed to map 'accountabilities, responsibilities and authorities across UNHCR, at the country, regional and headquarters levels' (Türk and Eyster 2010, p. 168). That same year, UNHCR introduced a policy on information classification, handling and disclosure. In 2011, UNHCR established the Independent Audit and Oversight Committee, 'in order to mitigate the risks associated with gaps in the current oversight structure and mechanisms' (Executive Committee of the High Commissioner's Programme 2011). In May 2015, the agency introduced the Biometric Identity Management System and published the *Policy on the protection of personal data of persons of concern to UNHCR* (UNHCR 2015c), a document that various actors had called for, for some time, given that UNHCR had been engaging in sporadic, pilot deployment of biometrics since the early 2000s (Lindskov Jacobsen 2016). Only recently, however, has UNHCR referred to the use of biometrics as a 'strategic decision' and as something to be included 'as a regular and routine feature of its registration processes' (UNHCR 2013, p. 1).

Altogether, these initiatives might seem to counter the notion that UNHCR suffers from a lack of accountability. However, it is important to note that UNHCR tends to label a wide range of practices 'accountability initiatives'. Moreover, as a consequence of its broad understanding of accountability, UNHCR engages in little elaboration or critical reflection regarding how accountability is defined in any given instance, who the relevant stakeholders are or to what ends accountability mechanisms are addressed. In 2002, for example, UNHCR launched the Standards and Indicators Initiative to structure planning, assessment and implementation of operations; this framework has since been updated and expanded. Dunlop (2011) argued that more critical scrutiny is needed when an initiative can be deemed an accountability mechanism. With respect to indicators, Dunlop observed that the 'perceived benefits of indicators turn on their capacity to improve assessment and accountability within organizations, and to provide key data capable of improving project development and implementation' (Dunlop 2011, p. 3). However, she noted that caution is warranted with respect to the ability to provide participatory accountability to persons of concern, who in this scheme have been assigned an important role as providers of data for UNHCR's consumption. We believe that this insight has more general applications.

Technology and accountability: automatic results?

Growth in the number and variety of UNHCR accountability efforts has been accompanied by the proliferation of technological accountability tools that are intended to support institutional reorganization and measurement of results. Increasingly, UNHCR has viewed the introduction of new information technologies as a means of realizing the promise of accountability inherent in RBM. One important aspect of this emphasis on technology, however, is the broader political landscape within which it occurs (Lindskov Jacobsen 2015; Sandvik *et al.* 2014): several technologies that UNHCR has introduced, under the aegis of improving accountability, have also been used by various donors to boost the post-9/11 security.

Technologically based accountability efforts also raise provocative questions with regard to upward and downward accountability. Specifically, there is this question: Are UNHCR's new accountability technologies capable of improving *both* upward *and* downward accountability (which is what the agency seems to expect) (see Lindskov in this volume)? UNHCR appears to assume, for example, that biometric registration will yield more accurate refugee population figures. Because these figures constitute the basis for the agency's call for funding, improving their accuracy should improve accountability to donors. Similarly, UNHCR seems to assume that by speeding up registration, biometric technology will allow more rapid access to assistance and thereby improve downward accountability.

Such assumptions concerning how new technology, in this case, biometric registration, might strengthen both upward and downward accountability need more careful attention, however. First, in view of UNHCR's having turned away from its early focus on holding states accountable, it remains to be seen whether the shift to digital technologies will instigate or support a renewed interest in state accountability. Certainly, the addition of new technologies to UNHCR's refugee protection practices does not render state accountability for asylum, refugee protection and funding practices any less important. Second, the introduction of a new technology, such as biometrics, is not necessarily a solution to concerns regarding downward accountability; instead, it should be thought of as potentially adding new dimensions to UNHCR's accountability to those who register their biometric data with the agency.

Finally, the ability of new digital technologies to improve downward accountability cannot be taken for granted. Technology does not always work as intended, and technical failures can potentially undermine UNHCR's ability to provide protection (Lindskov Jacobsen 2010; Hosein 2011; Hosein and Nyst 2013). For example, UNHCR's efforts to collect biometric data, as a means of better protecting particularly vulnerable groups, carry some risk: Critics have already observed that such sensitive data could end up in the hands of actors who have no interest in protecting vulnerable refugees. In addition to potentially harming the refugees, such an outcome would undermine UNHCR's reputation as a global guardian of refugee populations.

In 2008, when UNHCR asked two biometric technology experts to assess a new fingerprinting system, the experts 'recommended wholesale changes to the way UNHCR assessed and handled the technology, and … urged a radical shift in the way it viewed the security risks to the people whose safety was its responsibility'. Instead of following this recommendation, UNHCR decided not to publish the findings. Four years later, one of the experts who had been consulted chose to reveal this story, despite being 'in breach of a confidentiality agreement with the UN' (Davies 2012).

Collecting more detailed information and plugging it into software that can aggregate and disaggregate the data for potentially unforeseen uses in unforeseen contexts introduce risks that we have yet to fully grasp. Indeed, instead of simply assuming that new digital technologies can help improve accountability, it would seem more promising to take seriously, rather than to silence, findings concerning the risk of harmful consequences, for which UNHCR could arguably be held accountable.

Our consideration of the complexities in UNHCR's quest for accountability showed that the agency's understanding of accountability has shifted a number of times. Before offering several reflections on UNHCR's search for perfection in accountability, we must first examine the types of criticisms that have been directed against the agency's accountability efforts.

Enduring and new points of critique

Since the mid-1990s, UNHCR's struggle for accountability has been animated by both internal and external criticism, and the agency has introduced various initiatives in response. Despite the implementation of numerous accountability efforts, however, complaints and criticism remain rampant. At least five areas of dispute can be identified: Some concern new issues, such as the addition of technology, and others concern long-standing matters that have either assumed new forms or that, in the eyes of critics, simply remain unresolved.[9]

Accountability and expansion of responsibilities

The first question is to what extent the expansion of UNHCR's activities and areas of responsibility can be regarded as a move towards improved accountability. Within UNHCR, there seems to be an assumption that as the agency's activities expand to include an ever-burgeoning number of persons in need of protection, the agency's accountability, in relation to its protection mandate, will automatically increase. As noted earlier, UNHCR's purview has grown steadily since its inception; as Betts, Loescher and Milner noted, 'even while UNHCR was preoccupied with refugee problems in Europe, the Office was taking initial steps to lay the groundwork for an expansion of its activities to the developing world' (2012, p. 24). Most recently, in 2005, as part of the Humanitarian Reform Project (HRP), UNHCR was designated as a global cluster lead for protection, which effectively made the agency responsible not only for the protection of refugees who cross internationally recognized borders but also for IDPs.

UNHCR itself has argued that the reforms of the humanitarian system conducted under the aegis of the HRP 'made international humanitarian action more efficient, accountable and predictable' (UNHCR 2012, p. 5). However, the expansion of UNHCRs may not necessarily translate into greater accountability. Although it is indeed laudable to strive to protect an increasing number of people, the expansion of UNHCR's sphere of action should not overshadow a fundamental principle of international protection, namely, that the states have the ultimate and primary responsibility for leading humanitarian responses within their borders. In other words, if expanding UNHCR's purview risks weakening its ability to hold the states accountable, then such an expansion cannot be assumed to improve accountability for the protection of those whose security states have failed to ensure (Janmyr and Bradley both in this volume).

Neither UNHCR nor its critics, however, have addressed the likelihood that to improve accountability, UNHCR may occasionally need to 'do less' rather than more. A number of chapters in this volume invite us to consider more carefully this viewpoint. As was noted in the context of the Kosovo crisis, UNHCR functions in a complex political landscape in which it must simultaneously (1) meet immediate needs for protection and (2) ensure that the solutions it offers do not aggravate the very problems that made protection necessary in the first place. These conflicting demands warrant more critical attention in debates concerning the presumed accountability gains from the expansion of UNHCR's activities and responsibilities. Indeed, when acting in a complex political landscape characterized by conflicting demands, we should be careful not to expect that better refugee protection will automatically ensue if only UNHCR does more.

Lack of improvement in downward accountability

Despite the institutional perception that UNHCR has placed accountability towards persons of concern at the heart of its accountability framework, critical gaps remain. In addition to the authors of other chapters in this volume (Bradley, Fresia and von Känel; Rockenbach; and Lindskov Jacobsen), we would suggest that UNHCR continue to struggle with downward accountability. For instance, *UNHCR has yet to develop a sufficient theoretical underpinning, or appropriate formats and processes, for ensuring downward accountability* (Dunlop 2011). Indeed, this criticism could be applied beyond UNHCR; arguably, UNHCR is not the only organization in the humanitarian realm that has yet to achieve radical improvements in accountability to persons of concern.

In the wake of its failures in Rwanda and Kosovo, the agency attempted in different ways to increase its emphasis on downward accountability. Critics, meanwhile, began to call attention to other issues, shifting from a focus on the normative accountability gap (i.e. the dissonance between what UNHCR was claiming to do and what it was actually doing) to UNHCR's increasingly technical and depoliticized approach to downward accountability, under which important political issues (e.g. eligibility for assistance) were viewed as technical matters that could be resolved through the 'accuracy' of biometric registration and recognition technology. Among the critiques, for example, was that a focus on standards risked transforming humanitarian action into a technocratic endeavour, at the expense of addressing the ethical and political dimensions of crises (for example, see Morris 2014).

One new dimension of long-standing accountability criticisms concerns the notion that participation – for example, the use of various evaluation procedures, for which people of concern are encouraged to supply data – can improve downward accountability by engaging beneficiaries in new ways. Early notions of achieving accountability through participation had been subject to critiques of participation as a panacea for underdevelopment and injustice (Hilhorst 2002). Christopher Morris, in a critique of the current focus on participation and evaluation, has observed that 'affected communities were not able to use evaluation to influence decisions that affect them' (Morris 2014).

A recently articulated and relevant critique is that evaluation practices intended to engage people of concern, thereby improving downward accountability, may be unrepresentative, particularly in certain areas. For example, UNHCR (along with other humanitarian actors) has had significant difficulty conducting outreach in urban areas (e.g. sites receiving refugees from Syria or the Philippines). If the evaluations are conducted only with 'easy to access' refugees, UNHCR cannot fully grasp, let alone address, the concerns perceived by affected populations, which calls into question UNHCR's claims to have improved downward accountability through evaluation. Moreover, difficulty conducting outreach leaves broader questions unanswered, if, among the increasing populations of urban refugees, many choose not to register with UNHCR, what is preventing these refugees from registering? And if they do not register, are there strategies that UNHCR can use to identify their needs?

In environments in which current methods for seeking input from persons of concern do not work, accountability is undermined. Wigley (2015) made the following remarks: 'If we put "accountability mechanisms" in place, but fail to ensure that the most vulnerable and marginalised can access them, or if we speak only to those with political and social power, we risk strengthening social exclusion and marginalisation'.

UNHCR and states: more than a matter of 'upward accountability'

Another issue concerns UNHCR and the states and the point that if we define too narrowly the role of the state in relation to debates regarding UNHCR and accountability, then there are certain limits to what can be achieved by continuously refining accountability mechanisms. In other words, despite the framing offered by the upward/downward accountability discourses in which upward accountability can too easily come to be understood as a matter of how UNHCR can improve its accountability to the states, we should not to forget to raise a set of more critical questions regarding the role of the state. Indeed, as we had suggested at the beginning of this chapter, this is only one dimension of the difficult question of accountability in the relationship between the states and the mandate of UNHCR. Indeed, in current accountability discussions, it would seem crucial not to overlook the likelihood of UNHCR playing a more prominent role in holding states accountable when they fail to live up to their responsibilities vis-à-vis the protection of refugees globally.

Voluntary nature of accountability

The voluntary nature of humanitarian accountability mechanisms has been the subject of ongoing concerns. For the most part, NGOs and UN agencies are free to come and go as they wish and provide those services that they deem appropriate in ways that they see fit. In the case of NGOs, no official sanctions result from failure to comply with self-imposed responsibilities nor are UN agencies' formal mandates matched by equally formal accountability requirements (Darcy 2013). We would argue that adherence to internal, self-imposed standards is a necessary but insufficient approach to improving accountability and should accordingly be viewed only as one item in a broader accountability agenda.

Since the creation, in 2012, of the Task Team on Accountability to Affected Populations, voices from within UNHCR have claimed to find evidence of the emergence of a 'culture of accountability' in humanitarian relief. Indeed, UNHCR has in recent years replaced talk regarding a weak 'accountability climate' (Lawry-White 2000, p. 3), with proclamations of the need to go beyond 'a menu of accountability activities' to embrace 'approaches to work' that are 'more a process than an end state' and that require a culture of accountability (SCHR 2010, p. 50).

However, even if UNHCR aims to develop such a culture, it seems important to acknowledge – and perhaps even problematize – the fact that the state is not external to this culture but is, in fact, a key actor to ensure protection to the burgeoning number of refugees in the contemporary political landscape. In other words, no matter how committed NGOs and intergovernmental organizations are to accountability, failing to address the role of the state leaves an important dimension of the accountability issue unaddressed.

Standardization, technology and accountability

Critics have observed that the general standardization and codification of humanitarian aid that have occurred since the mid-1990s, along with the attendant emphasis on technology, risk being regarded as an end in itself, leading UNHCR to pay too little attention to the effects of such initiatives on both upward and downward accountability (Sandvik 2010; Wigley 2015; see also Lindskov Jacobsen in this volume). For example, whereas UNHCR perceives new technology as a means of boosting accountability, observers have argued that an increasing emphasis on, and faith in, the ability of new technologies to 'solve' a variety of challenges risks overshadowing the political dynamics that can affect UNHCR's work, a consequence that has potentially important implications for accountability. In a similar vein, Wigley, who wrote the influential mid-2000 review of UNHCR's organizational culture (Wigley 2006), expressed the following concern:

> an attraction to the functional and structured language of tools and mechanisms has been accompanied by a drift away from the primary purpose of a culture of accountability that seeks to make accountability to the people we seek to assist 'the way we do things around here' …. Somewhere along the way in the struggle to get the humanitarian system on board with new ways of thinking and doing, the tools and the mechanisms have become an 'as if' primary purpose, where the ultimate goal is rewritten as if it is the regulation of organisations, having certain processes in place, ticking certain boxes and even mobilising certain technology. (Wigley 2015)

Looking to the future: is perfection in accountability possible – or even necessary?

It has been suggested that UNHCR's ability to provide protection declined in the 2000s (Hammerstad 2014). We would argue instead that UNHCR's trajectory has taken a new turn in this period because the organization has struggled to remake itself to meet the demands of the twenty-first-century needs. Accountability has been a central component of these efforts; nevertheless, UNHCR continues to face significant criticism in that realm. For UNHCR's supporters, critics and other observers alike, the question is how best to respond.

In a UNHCR accountability report issued in 2014, the following was noted regarding the agency's 'system of accountability is not captured in a single document or tool. Rather, the Office's mandate and a vast collection of policies, rules, procedures and guidelines constitute UNHCR's system of accountability' (UNHCR 2014, p. 7).

This comprehensive approach marks a considerable evolution since the mid-1990s, not only in terms of how UNHCR sees itself but also in terms of how it operates and in the role it assigns to accountability concepts and mechanisms.

At the same time, the elasticity of UNHCR's conception of accountability allows the agency to categorize various undertakings, whether the implementation of RBM or expansions in the categories of protected individuals, as 'accountability initiatives'; this conceptual elasticity can make it difficult to assess their effects. More generally, it seems that instead of paying close attention to the (occasionally conflicting) accountability demands of its various constituencies, UNHCR exhibits a tendency to wish for a single, all-encompassing accountability solution, as reflected, for example, in the expectations surrounding the introduction of biometric registration technologies (Lindskov Jacobsen in this volume).

An alternative response is to acknowledge that given the constant state of change in political contexts and refugees' circumstances, it is impossible to find one encompassing mechanism that can 'resolve', once and for all, the variety of accountability challenges that confront UNHCR in its refugee protection practices. This conclusion need not be discouraging; instead, it should foster appreciation of the need for constant striving, not for perfection but for continuous improvement, which should always be accompanied by an awareness that changing accountability practices towards one group (e.g. donors) can affect accountability to other groups (e.g. persons of concern).

Understanding that one will search in vain for an 'all-encompassing accountability system' (Hilhorst 2002, p. 369) can be useful for several reasons. First, this understanding can counterbalance the current faith in the ability of new technologies to solve a vast range of accountability problems. Second, a focus on all-encompassing accountability solutions risks obscuring different, but equally important, dimensions of accountability. As noted earlier, for example, it is important to distinguish between – rather than conflate – accountability for protection against external threats, and accountability for protection failures that stem from UNHCR's own practices. Certainly, the two call for a different response from UNHCR.

In sum, we suggest replacing the dream of an all-encompassing accountability solution with the recognition that accountability cannot be ensured, once and for all, by any means, including the implementation of a fancy new system, mechanism or technology. Most importantly, we must acknowledge that many dimensions of accountability do not necessarily and certainly do not automatically add up.

Indeed, conflicts between accountability requirements are inevitable. It is thus important to address the different dimensions of accountability that necessarily characterize the work of UNHCR. This volume seeks to present these different dimensions, particularly as they apply to various constituent groups. Several chapters, for example, focus on UNHCR's accountability towards beneficiaries, whereas others focus on its ability to hold donor states accountable for the consequences of their actions, and still others focus on the relationship between

UNHCR and host states. In collecting a range of perspectives in a single volume, our goal was not only to illustrate the value of each viewpoint but also to bring varying perspectives into conversation with each other.

Overview of chapters

Chapter 2: Niamh Kinchin's chapter, 'UNHCR and the complexity of accountability in the global space', takes a pluralistic approach to global accountability. Drawing its analytical framework from political science and legal scholarship, the chapter argues that UNHCR's accountability obligations are determined by its unique legal and organizational characteristics and the ways in which those characteristics define its relationships. UNHCR is a subsidiary organ of the United Nations; however, it retains significant functional autonomy. At the same time, UNHCR's supervisory mandate has been compromised by the self-interest of states, by increasingly restrictive asylum policies and by the role of states as voluntary contributors to UNHCR's funding. Crucially, the agency is one of the only global decision-making bodies that makes administrative decisions, namely, refugee status determinations that directly affect the rights and obligations of individuals. Each of these characteristics shapes UNHCR's relationships, which can be classified as institutional, state-based or participatory, in ways that produce unique accountability obligations. Kinchin argues that without insight into the complexity of UNHCR, accountability solutions risk becoming aspirational tools that 'say the right thing' yet remain ineffectual because they fail to understand and respond to their subject.

Chapter 3: Maja Janmyr's chapter, 'Advancing UNHCR accountability through the law of international responsibility', explores UNHCR accountability from the perspective of international law. The chapter starts from the notion that there is a normative gap, with respect to accountability, between UNHCR's international protection mandate and its actions. Janmyr argues that this gap might be addressed by recourse to the law of international responsibility. To that end, Janmyr examines the International Law Commission's 2011 Articles on the Responsibility of International Organizations (ARIO), detailing the circumstances under which UNHCR can be held accountable under the ARIO, and reflecting on the potential and practical limitations of applying the ARIO to UNHCR. On the one hand, for example, individual refugees would not be able to sue UNHCR for human rights violations under the ARIO, and the imposition of extensive responsibilities on UNHCR may lead the agency to withdraw from particularly challenging protection environments. On the other hand, one of the most welcome impacts of the ARIO would be to tighten UNHCR's management of its implementing partners.

Chapter 4: Adèle Garnier's chapter, 'Narratives of accountability in UNHCR's refugee resettlement strategy', takes as its starting point UNHCR's post-2006 commitment to accountability. Adopting an institutionalist perspective, Garnier assesses to what extent the narrative of UNHCR accountability with regard to refugee resettlement reflects the overarching accountability framework that the agency has promoted since 2006. She then investigates the relationship of accountability to resettlements in Australia and in the European Union (EU).

Drawing on core UNHCR policy documents on resettlement, Garnier finds that the agency's post-2006 accountability commitments have not been fully embraced in the field; the result is a layered narrative of accountability that is more closely aligned with the understanding of accountability reflected in the EU's recently established joint resettlement programme than with Australia's long-standing refugee resettlement policy. The chapter thus contributes to discussions of the potential and limits of policy diffusion within UNHCR and highlights variability in policy diffusion among the agency's key partners.

Chapter 5: Miriam Bradley's chapter, 'UNHCR and accountability for IDP protection in Colombia', examines UNHCR's role in offering protection to internally displaced people (IDPs) in the absence of a specific protection mandate. Drawing on fieldwork in Colombia, Bradley uses international relations theory to explore the interplay between UNHCR's accountability to different stakeholders (states and beneficiaries) and its ability to hold other actors (states) accountable. Bradley identifies a tension between UNHCR's formal, legalistic framing of IDP protection as the responsibility of the Colombian state and the reality of UNHCR's protection efforts, which focus on supporting the state and helping other actors to hold the state accountable. Arguing that overall this approach impedes accountability to people of concern, Bradley offers an innovative account of how downward accountability is undermined: first, because UNHCR allows the Colombian government to set the prevention of displacement as the agency's primary objective; second, through restrictions on the types of activities UNHCR can undertake (specifically with regard to contact with armed actors); third, through restrictions on UNHCR's relationships with host states; and fourth, through the particular ways in which UNHCR partners with the Colombian state.

Chapter 6: Marion Fresia's and Andreas von Känel's chapter, 'Universalizing the refugee category and struggling for accountability: the everyday work of eligibility officers within UNHCR', examines the effect of UNHCR's quest for accountability in the realm of refugee status determination (RSD). Starting from an anthropological perspective and building on ethnographic fieldwork in UNHCR offices in Mauretania and Turkey, Fresia and von Känel demonstrate how everyday accountability efforts are shaped by the need to adapt to the local political context and engage with states. Both UNHCR's organization of RSD and its lack of accountability mechanisms for RSD procedures have been sharply criticized. Although UNHCR has put significant effort into universalizing norms and procedures, the authors observe that the work of meaning making and application remains profoundly local. At the same time, the sorting of migrants and refugees is also a deeply political project, in the context of which 'accountability' is not only about sorting individuals according to correct procedures but about strengthening and globalizing the rationalities and logics of a specific, Northern bureaucratic model of migration management.

Chapter 7: Ashley B. Rockenbach's chapter, 'Accounting for the past: a history of refugee management in Uganda, 1959–64', takes a historical approach to the categorization of refugees. The analysis builds on a case study of Rwandans who came to Uganda just as the post-colonial Ugandan state was beginning to develop its population management practices. The chapter provides insights into

UNHCR's early role in managing the 'African refugee problem'. Rockenbach proposes that the historical contingency and multiple meanings of the 'refugee' label raise critical questions regarding contemporary efforts to improve accountability by constructing a more legible refugee population through results-based management, including the use of registration technology. Rockenbach criticizes the assumption that displaced people want to be registered as such, thereby revealing the limitations of registration technology as a vehicle for downward accountability. Moreover, renewed efforts to identify 'refugees' will not serve a self-settled population that is neither recognized nor recognizable as refugees, thus potentially undermining claims regarding upward accountability. Rockenbach links the early refugee movements from Rwanda to Uganda with the 1994 Rwandan genocide, which was among the events that sparked the humanitarian accountability movement.

Chapter 8: Kristin Bergtora Sandvik's chapter, 'How accountability technologies shape international protection: results-based management and rights-based approaches revisited', uses a sociolegal prism to explore how results-based management (RBM) and rights-based approaches (RBA) work as 'accountability technologies'. Although RBA and RBM are intended to improve accountability through managerial and moral improvements, respectively, implementation is characterized by inconsistencies and has been the subject of legitimate criticism. One difficulty, in particular, is the likelihood that RBA and RBM skew the content of protection efforts: RBA because it is conceptualized in overly broad ways that are difficult to effectively operationalize, and RBM because it can impede the programming of activities and objectives that are not easily measurable, including RBA. These initiatives also impact the direction of protection efforts. Sandvik argues that UNHCR's accountability efforts, as articulated through RBA and RBM, contribute to fixing international protection as an object with value. UNHCR increasingly presents RBM as instrumental to downward accountability, whereas the agency's view of RBA, as an expansive concept with a minimalist legalistic core, may function as a form of upward accountability. The chapter concludes by observing that the complex roles played by RBM and RBA in accountability production reveal these initiatives to be a form of humanitarian governance.

Chapter 9: Katja Lindskov Jacobsen's chapter, 'UNHCR, accountability and refugee biometrics', emphasizes as its starting point the individualized refugee data in the context of the war on terror and the securitization of humanitarian practices. Drawing on insights from international relations and science and technology studies, Lindskov Jacobsen examines how the adoption of biometric technology affects upward and downward accountability. In UNHCR's view, biometric registration automatically improves accountability by making registration faster and more efficient, making distribution more fair (and thereby reducing fraud) and providing a more accurate accounting of the use of donor resources. For donors, biometrics promises more accurate population data and a greater likelihood of distinguishing 'worthy' recipients (i.e. individuals who are both genuine refugees and not terrorists) from others. Critics, however, are increasingly concerned about the potential safety risks associated with technological failures (including data loss), which could wrongfully exclude people of concern from protection or otherwise put them at risk. By unpacking UNHCR practice with respect to biometric registration procedures and the use of biometric data, Lindskov Jacobsen provides an important critique of the emerging notion that competent technology management is a sufficient and dependable route to accountability.

Notes

1 The title was inspired by Thea Hilhorst (2002).
2 There is a rich literature discussing and typologizing forms of accountability and their function. For accounts of accountability in world politics and public accountability in modern-day governance, see Grant and Keohane (2005) and Dowdle (2006).
3 The text of the principles is available online at www.brookings.edu/about/projects/ idp/gp-page.
4 For example, see Robinson (2004) on the repatriation of Vietnamese boat refugees.
5 Within the humanitarian sector as a whole, the most well-known initiative is the Sphere Project, launched in 1997, which focused on both humanitarian ethics through the Humanitarian Charter and technical regularization of humanitarian action through the Minimum Standards in Disaster Response (Dufour *et al.* 2004; Tong 2004).
6 One result of this lack of coordination was a wasteful duplication of resources (Hammerstad 2014, p. 244).
7 UNHCR's thinking about downward accountability has been significantly intertwined with its thinking regarding human rights (Sandvik 2010). Although human rights protection has long been an implicit and explicit part of UNHCR's portfolio, the notion of refugees as rights holders is inherently complex and is, therefore, difficult to implement. In the late 1990s, when UNHCR first turned to rights-based approaches (RBA) as a means of improving accountability, the complexities and ambiguities of RBA quickly became apparent. For example, RBA assumes that persons of concern are not simply 'beneficiaries' but rights holders who can exercise their rights, including the right to participation (UNHCR 2006, p. 17). When UNHCR's conception of its role in relation to rights-holders is subjected to close scrutiny, however, it becomes clear that UNHCR sees itself as a facilitator and capacity builder, rather than as an entity that is duty bound to enable persons of concern to realize their rights. Despite this significant and unresolved conundrum, UNHCR continues to insist that its assistance and protection activities are 'rights-based' (see Sandvik in this volume). The downward accountability, human rights nexus, exemplifies the complexities that must be considered to understand UNHCR's downward accountability efforts.
8 In the wake of the 2002 UNHCR/Save the Children-UK report, there was growing consensus within UNHCR that sexual exploitation and abuse of persons of concern by humanitarian workers was a real and widespread problem that required remedying. Reports from 2008, nevertheless, concluded that exploitation and abuse continued to be chronically underreported and poorly dealt with institutionally (Lattu 2008).
9 On the notion that UNHCR has failed, for decades, to attend to long-standing downward accountability problems, see, for example, Verdirame and Harrell-Bond (2005).

References

Betts, A. (2009) *Protection by Persuasion: International Cooperation in the Refugee Regime*. Ithaca, NY: Cornell University Press.
Betts, A. (2012) 'UNHCR, autonomy and mandate change', in J. E. Oestreich (ed.), *International Organizations as Self-Directed Actors: A Framework for Analysis*. New York: Routledge.
Betts, A. and G. Loescher, (2010) *Refugees in International Relations*. Oxford, UK: Oxford University Press.
Betts, A., G. Loescher, and J. Milner, (2012) *The United Nations High Commissioner for Refugees (UNHCR): The Politics and Practice of Refugee Protection into the 21st Century*, 2nd edition. London and New York: Routledge.

Booth, K. (2005) *The Kosovo Tragedy: The Human Rights Dimensions*. London: Psychology Press.

Browne, P. (2006). *The Longest Journey, Resettling Refugees from Africa* (Briefings). Sydney: UNSW Press.

Burns, J. and F. Williams, (1998) 'United Nations High Commissioner for Refugees: special report; refugees' agency lost in wilderness of bungling and waste', *Financial Times*, 29 July, p. 7.

Chandler, D. (2006) *From Kosovo to Kabul and Beyond: Human Rights and International Intervention*. London: Pluto Press.

Chaulia, S. S. (2002) 'UNHCR's relief, rehabilitation and repatriation of Rwandan refugees in Zaire (1994–1997)', *Journal of Humanitarian Assistance*. http://reliefweb.int/report/burundi/unhcrs-relief-rehabilitation-and-repatriation-rwandan-refugees-zaire-1994-1997.

Cohen, R. (2004) 'The guiding principles on internal displacement: an innovation in international standard setting', *Global Governance*, 10(4): 459–480.

Darcy, J. (2013) *Have We lost the Plot, Humanitarian Accountability Report*, URL: www.hapinternational.org/pool/files/2013-har.pdf.

Davies, S. (2012) 'How a United Nations agency buried a security report that warned of potential genocide'. Available online at www.privacysurgeon.org/blog/incision/how-a-united-nations-agency-buried-a-security-report-that-warned-of-potential-genocide/ (accessed 15 September 2015).

DFID. (2011) *Multilateral Aid Review: Ensuring Maximum Value for Money for UK Aid through Multilateral Organisations*. London: DFID.

Dowdle, M. (ed.) (2006) *Public Accountability: Designs, Dilemmas and Experiences*. Cambridge: Cambridge University Press.

Druke, L. (2014) *Innovations in Refugee Protection: A Compendium of UNHCR's 60 Years Including Case Studies on IT Communities, Vietnamese Boatpeople, Chilean Exile, and Namibian Repatriation*. Frankfurt: Peter Lang International Academic Publishers.

Dufour, C., V. Geoffroy, H. Maury, and F. Grünewald, (2004) 'Rights, standards and quality in a complex humanitarian space: is Sphere the right tool?', *Disasters*, 28(2): 124–141.

Dunlop, E. (2011) 'Indications of progress? Assessing the use of indicators in UNHCR operations', UNHCR Research Paper No. 214.

ECHCPSC (Executive Committee of the High Commissioner's Programme Standing Committee) (EC/50/SC/CRP.12). (2000) 'The Kosovo refugee crisis: an independent evaluation of UNHCR's emergency preparedness and response'. 9 February. UNHCR: Geneva. Available online at www.unhcr.org/3ae68d19c.html (accessed 15 September 2015).

Edwards, M. and D. Hulme, (eds.) (1996) *Beyond the Magic Bullet: NGO Performance and Accountability in the Post-Cold War world*. West Hartford, CT: Kumarian Press.

Eriksson, J. (1996) *The International Response to Conflict and Genocide: Lessons from the Rwandan Experience: Synthesis Report*. Copenhagen: Steering Committee of the Joint Committee Evaluation of Emergency Assistance to Rwanda.

FMR. (2010) 'Disability and displacement', *Forced Migration Review*, 35: 1–60.

European Union Agency for Fundamental Rights (FRA). (2009) 'Developing indicators for the protection, respect and promotion of the rights of the child in the European Union'. Available online at fra.europa.eu/sites/default/files/fra_uploads/358-RightsofChild_summary-report_en.pdf (accessed 15 September 2015).

Garvey, J. I. (1985) 'Toward a reformulation of international refugee law', *Harvard International Law Journal*, 26(2): 483–500.

Gibney, M. (1999) 'Introduction: learning from Kosovo', *Forced Migration Review*, August 1999, 5. p. 5.

Goodwin-Gill, G. (1999) 'Refugee identity and protection's fading prospect', in F. Nicholson and P. M. Twomey (eds.), *Refugee Rights and Realities*. Cambridge: Cambridge University Press.

Grant, R. W. and R. O. Keohane, (2005) 'Accountability and abuses of power in world politics', *American Political Science Review*, 99(1): 29–43.

Groves, L. (2005) 'UNHCR's age and gender mainstreaming pilot project 2004: synthesis report', EPAU/2005/03. Available online at http://globalag.igc.org/armedconflict/countryreports/africa/ageandgender.pdf (accessed 15 September 2015).

Hammerstad, A. (2014) *The Rise and Decline of a Global Security Actor: UNHCR, Refugee Protection and Security*. Oxford: Oxford University Press.

Harrell-Bond, B. (1986) *Imposing Aid: Emergency Assistance to Refugees*. Oxford: Oxford University Press.

Hilhorst, T. (2002) 'Being good at doing good? Quality and accountability of humanitarian NGOs', *Disasters*, 26(3): 193–212.

Hosein, G. (2011) 'Why we work on refugee privacy', *Privacy International*. 8 July. Available online at www.privacyinternational.org/?q=node/300 (accessed 15 September 2015).

Hosein, G. and C. Nyst, (2013) 'Aiding surveillance: an exploration of how development and humanitarian aid initiatives are enabling surveillance in developing countries'. International Development Research Centre and Centre de recherches pour le développement international.

Janmyr, M. (2014) 'Attributing wrongful conduct of implementing partners to UNHCR', *Journal of International Humanitarian Legal Studies*, 5(1–2): 42–69.

Journal of Ethnic and Migration Studies 40(6), special issue on international migration management edited by Martin Geiger and Antoine Pecoud.

Kagan, M. (2006) 'The beleaguered gatekeeper: protection challenges posed by UNHCR refugee status determination', *International Journal of Refugee Law*, 18(1): 1–29.

Kagan, M. (2014) 'When UNHCR does the state's job: coping with the reality of mandate status determination'. Available online at blog.unhcr.org/globalviews/author/mkagan/ (accessed 15 September 2015).

Kälin, W. (2003) 'Supervising the 1951 Convention relating to the status of refugees: article 35 and beyond', in E. Feller, V. Türk and F. Nicholson (eds.), *Refugee Protection in International Law: UNHCR's Global Consultations on International Protection*. Cambridge: Cambridge University Press.

Kelley, N., P. Sandison, and S. Lawry-White, (2004) 'Enhancing UNHCR's capacity to monitor the protection, rights and well-being of refugees'. United Nations High Commissioner for Refugees Evaluation and Policy Analysis Unit. EPAU/2004/06.

Krueger, S. and E. Sagmeister, (2014) 'Real time evaluation of humanitarian assistance revisited: lessons learned and the way forward', *Journal of Multi-Disciplinary Evaluation*, 10(23): 59–72.

Lattu, K. (2008) *To complain or not to complain: still the question; consultations with humanitarian aid beneficiaries on their perceptions of efforts to prevent and respond to sexual exploitation and abuse*. Geneva, Switzerland: Human Accountability Partnership.

Lawry-White, S. (2000) *Improving the effectiveness of UNHCR's evaluation function*. Geneva, Switzerland: The Evaluation and Policy Analysis Unit (EPAU), UNHCR.

Lewis, C. (2012) *UNHCR and International Refugee Law: From Treaties to Innovation*. New York: Routledge.

Lindskov Jacobsen, K. (2010) 'Making design safe for citizens: a hidden history of humanitarian experimentation', *Citizenship Studies*, 14(1): 89–103.

Lindskov Jacobsen, K. (2015) *The Politics of Humanitarian Technology: Good Intentions, Unintended Consequences and Insecurity*. Abington and New York: Routledge.

Lindskov Jacobsen, K. (2016) 'More than a decade of humanitarian refugee biometrics', Unpublished.

Loescher, G. (2001) 'The UNHCR and world politics: state interests vs. institutional autonomy', *International Migration Review*, 35(1): 33–56.

Loescher, G., A. Betts, and J. Milner, (2012) *The United Nations High Commissioner for Refugees (UNHCR): The Politics and Practice of Refugee Protection into the 21st Century*, 2nd edition. Abingdon: Routledge.

Morris, C. (2014) 'Investigating evaluation as an accountability mechanism by international non-governmental organizations working in humanitarian relief'. MA thesis, the University of British Columbia.

OHCHR. (n.d.) 'Convention relating to the status of refugees'. Available online at www.ohchr.org/EN/ProfessionalInterest/Pages/StatusOfRefugees.aspx (accessed 15 September 2015).

OIOS. (2001) *Investigation into Allegations of Refugee Smuggling at the Nairobi Branch Office of the United Nation High Commissioner for Refugees* – Doc A/56/733.

Pallis, M. (2006) 'The operation of UNHCR's accountability mechanism', *The New York University Journal of International Law and Politics*, 37 N.Y.U. J. Int'l. L. & Pol. 869–918.

Power, S. (2008) *Chasing the Flame: One Man's Fight to Save the World*. New York: Penguin Press.

Robinson, W. C. (2004) 'The comprehensive plan of action for Indochinese refugees, 1989–1997: sharing the burden and passing the buck', *Journal of Refugee Studies*, 17(3): 319–333.

Sandvik, K. B. (2010) 'Framing accountability in refugee resettlement accountability for human rights violations of international organisations', in J. Wouters, E. Brems, S. Smis and P. Schmitt (eds.), *Accountability for Human Rights Violations of International Organizations*. Cambridge, UK: Intersentia.

Sandvik, K. B. (2011) 'Blurring boundaries: refugee resettlement in Kampala – between the formal, the informal, and the illegal', *PoLAR: Political and Legal Anthropology Review*, 34(1): 11–32.

Sandvik, K. B., M. Gabrielsen Jumbert, J. Karlsrud, and M. Kaufmann, (2014) 'Humanitarian technology: a critical research agenda', *International Review of the Red Cross*, 96(893): 219–242.

Simeon, J. C. (ed.) (2013) *The UNHCR and the Supervision of International Refugee Law*. Cambridge: Cambridge University Press.

Slaughter, A. and J. Crisp, (2009) 'A surrogate state? The role of UNHCR in protracted refugee situations', *UNHCR New Issues in Refugee Research*, Paper 168.

Steiner, N., M. Gibney, and G. Loescher, (eds.) (2003) *Problems of Protection: The UNHCR, Refugees, and Human Rights*. New York: Routledge.

SCHR (Steering Committee for Humanitarian Response). (2010) 'Accountability to disaster-affected populations', *Forced Migration Review*, July 2010, 35: 50–52. Available online at www.fmreview.org/en/disability/FMR35/50-52.pdf (accessed 15 September 2015).

Tong, J. (2004) 'Questionable accountability: MSF and Sphere in 2003', *Disasters*, 28(2): 176–189.

Trinh, H. (2005) 'UNHCR and accountability: the non-reviewability of UNHCR decisions', *Forced Migration and the Contemporary World: Challenges to the International System*. Poland: Wydawnictwo I Drukarnia PPHU.

Türk, V. and E. Eyster, (2010) 'Strengthening accountability in UNHCR', *International Journal of Refugee Law*, 22(2): 159–172.

Türk, V. (2013) '64th Session of the Executive Committee of the High Commissioner's Programme'. Available online at www.unhcr.org/cgi-bin/texis/vtx/home/opendoc PDFViewer.html?docid=524d26059&query=rights based approaches (accessed 15 September 2015).

UNHCR. (1980) 'Addendum to the report of the United Nations High Commissioner for refugees', 3 November, A/35/12/Add.1. Available online at www.refworld.org/docid/3ae68c374.html (accessed 15 September 2015).

UNHCR. (1986) 'Report of the United Nations High Commissioner for refugees', 1 August, A/41/12. Available online at www.refworld.org/docid/3ae68c600.html (accessed 15 September 2015).

UNHCR. (1987) 'Note on international protection (submitted by the High Commissioner)', A/AC.96/694 EXCOM Reports, 3 August.

UNHCR. (1996). 'Project Delphi: plan of action (EC/46/SC/CRP.48)'. Available online at www.unhcr.org/3ae68d0924.html (accessed 15 September 2015).

UNHCR. (2003). 'Post management model', *Discussion paper*. Geneva: UNHCR.

UNHCR. (2006) 'Practical guide to the systematic use of standards and indicators in UNHCR operations'. Available online at www.unhcr.org/40eaa9804.pdf (accessed 15 September 2015).

UNHCR. (2010) 'Measure for measure: a field-based snapshot of the implementation of results based management in UNHCR', PDES/2010/13 November. Available online at www.unhcr.org/4cf3ad8f9.pdf (accessed 15 September 2015).

UNHCR. (2011) Executive Committee of the High Commissioner's Programme, Establishment of an independent audit and oversight committee. EC/62/SC/CRP.24. Rev.2, 5 July. Available online at www.unhcr.org/cgi-bin/texis/vtx/home/opendocPDF Viewer.html?docid=4d665dbd9&query=Audit (accessed 15 September 2015).

UNHCR. (2012) *The State of the World's Refugees: In Search of Solidarity; A Synthesis.* Geneva: UNHCR. Available online at www.unhcr.org/4fc5ceca9.pdf (accessed 15 September 2015).

UNHCR. (2013) 'Request for proposal: No. RFP/2012/507 – for the provision of a biometric identity management system', 31 December. United Nations High Commissioner for Refugees. Available online at www.unhcr.org/50c85dd69.pdf (accessed 15 September 2015).

UNHCR. (2014) 'Age, gender, diversity: accountability report 2013'. Division of International Protection, UNHCR, June. Available online at www.unhcr.org/548180b69.pdf (accessed 15 September 2015).

UNHCR. (2015a) 'Worldwide displacement hits all-time high as war and persecution increase', June 18. Available online at www.unhcr.org/558193896.html (accessed 15 September 2015).

UNHCR. (2015b) 'Populations of concern to UNHCR', in *UNHCR Global Appeal 2015 Update.* Available online at www.unhcr.org/5461e5ec3c.html (accessed 15 September 2015).

UNHCR. (2015c) 'Policy on the protection of personal data of persons of concern to UNHCR'. Available online at www.refworld.org/docid/55643c1d4.html (accessed 15 September 2015).

UNHCR. (n.d.a) 'Durable solutions'. Available online at www.unhcr.org/pages/49c3646cf8.html (accessed 15 September 2015).

UNHCR. (n.d.b) 'Staff figures'. Available online at www.unhcr.org/pages/49c3646c17.html (accessed 15 September 2015).

UNHCR. (n.d.c) 'What we do'. Available online at www.unhcr.org/pages/49c3646cbf.html (accessed 15 September 2015).

UN Secretary General (UNSG). (2003) 'Secretary-General's bulletin: special measures for protection from sexual exploitation and sexual abuse', 9 October. ST/SGB/2003/13. Available online at www.unhcr.org/refworld/docid/451bb6764.html (accessed 15 September 2015).

UNHCR and Save the Children. (2002) 'Note for implementing and operational partners by UNHCR and Save the Children-UK on sexual violence and exploitation: the experience of refugee children in Guinea, Liberia and Sierra Leone based on initial findings and recommendations from Assessment Mission 22 October–30 November 2001'. Geneva and London: UNHCR and Save the Children-UK. Available online at www.savethechildren.org.uk/sites/default/files/docs/sexual_violence_and_exploitation_1.pdf (accessed 15 September 2015).

Valticos, N. (1998) 'Contrôle', in R. J. Dupuy (ed.), *A Handbook on Organisations*, pp. 461–484. Dordrecht: Martinus Nijhoff.

Verdirame, G. (2011) *The UN and Human Rights: Who Guards the Guardians?* Cambridge: Cambridge University Press.

Verdirame, G. and B. Harrell-Bond, (2005) *Rights in Exile: Janus-Faced Humanitarianism.* New York and Oxford: Berghan Books.

Wigley, B. (2006) *The State of UNHCR's Organizational Culture: What Now?* UNHCR EPAU/2006/0.

Wigley, B. (2015) 'Constructing a culture of accountability: lessons from the Philippines', *Humanitarian Exchange Magazine*, 63: 13–16.

Wilde, R. (2005) 'Enhancing accountability at the international level: the tension between international organizations and member state responsibility and the underlying issues at stake', *ILSA Journal of International and Comparative Law*, 12(2): 395–415.

2 UNHCR and the complexity of accountability in the global space

Niamh Kinchin

The simple nobility of the core mandate of the United Nations High Commissioner for Refugees (UNHCR), to protect refugees worldwide, belies the complexities the organisation faces within an accountability framework. Although refugees and beneficiaries are, of course, of crucial importance to any accountability discussion involving UNHCR,[1] this chapter focuses on how the intricacies of UNHCR's various and diverse relationships impact more broadly its accountability *and* how its accountability should be defined in the first place. If UNHCR's accountability is based on the pluralism inherent in its context, its unique relationships will emerge as the true drivers of its accountability obligations and not preconceptions of what it *should* be accountable for.

This chapter, which draws its analytical framework from political science and legal scholarship, combines literature-based methodology with research on the impact of binding and non-binding international law and organisational practices on the relationships of 'global actors'.[2] Political science literature raises important questions about assumptions regarding the highly contested meaning of accountability within different contexts (Mashaw 2005; Mulgan 2000; Grant and Keohane 2005), whereas legal scholarship considers how accountability may be applied within what Kingsbury *et al.* (2005, p. 18) call a 'global administrative space'. This chapter aims to construct a bridge between these perspectives by suggesting that an analysis of the nature and application of accountability in the global space must begin with an appreciation of the pluralism of the context.

The chapter proceeds in the following manner. The first part of the chapter considers current perspectives on accountability as a normative value of the global space. Divergences in the theory support the theoretical framework of this chapter, i.e. the fluidity of accountability allows it to be contextually responsive to respond to the pluralism of the global space by using the relationships of diverse individual actors as the starting point for understanding their accountability obligations.

The second part of the chapter addresses how UNHCR's relationships shape its accountability obligations. In Part A, UNHCR's institutional relationships, which are those that exist either between or within institutions, are explored. UNHCR's accountability relationships with the UN General Assembly (UNGA) and Economic and Social Council (ECOSOC), the UN Secretary General (UNSG), the Executive Committee and external humanitarian bodies reveal that the accountability obligations created by UNHCR's legal obligations, on the one hand, and its organisational practices and culture, on the other hand, do not always cohesively exist. Part B addresses UNHCR's participatory relationships with refugees and 'others in need of international protection'. As this section reveals, UNHCR's accountability relationships with refugees and others in need of international protection have evolved beyond the limitations of its original protection mandate. Finally, Part C considers the accountability obligations created by UNHCR's relationships with the states, which are complicated by legal obligations that make the *states accountable to UNHCR* in its supervisory role, and organisational factors that make *UNHCR accountable to the states* as voluntary contributors to its funding.

Pluralism and accountability in the global space

'Complex and chameleon like' (Mulgan 2000, p. 555), 'a placeholder for multiple contemporary anxieties' (Mashaw 2005, p. 15), accountability has never been a static concept; however, it is mutable enough to expect significant divergence in its analysis. According to Jerry Mashaw (2005, p. 15), accountability needs to be 'unpacked' so that the repertoire of 'accountability regimes', which are the ways in which different people, groups and institutions in our lives call us to account, may be understood. Supporting 'being called to account' as the core meaning of accountability, Richard Mulgan (2000, p. 571) lamented over an extension of the meaning of accountability to include implications of individual responsibility, the public interest and institutional checks and balances.

Focusing on accountability at the international level, Ruth Grant and Robert Keohane (2005, p. 5) argued for a model-based approach to accountability. They defined 'participatory models' of accountability by relationships where 'the performance of power-wielders is evaluated by those who are affected by their actions', whereas 'delegation models' refer to relationships where the power-wielder is accountable to the power-delegator for the way it exercises the power that has been delegated to it.

In their seminal paper on Global Administrative Law (GAL),[3] Kingsbury *et al.* (2005) conceived accountability in the global space in reference to one of three normative concepts. First, the pragmatic 'intra-regime accountability' takes for granted a given order and seeks to ensure that the parties within that order perform their roles according to the internal law (Kingsbury *et al.* 2005, p. 44). Second, accountability may have the normative purpose of protecting the rights of those who are the subject of regulation. Third, accountability is observed to be a means of implementing democracy, which is implicitly challenged by Simon Chesterman's (2008, p. 43) view of GAL as distinct from the demands that globalization become more 'democratic', its true role being to 'help frame the questions of accountability and sketch out some appropriate responses'. In a piece sceptical of GAL's capacity to create consistent principles and values, Carol Harlow (2006) considered accountability as a part of the 'good governance' agenda that is just one of several potential principles for GAL's development. In contrast,

Nico Krisch (2006) identified accountability as the fundamental value of GAL, its primary concern being to whom accountability is owed in a pluralist order. David Dyzenhaus (2009, p. 11) argued that GAL is concerned with more than legal accountability understood as procedural law and must focus on the legitimacy of substantive and constitutive law.

Despite the differences in approach, scholars who consider accountability in the global space, for the most part, recognise the potential for variance in its definition and normative values (Kingsbury *et al.* 2005; Harlow 2006; Krisch 2006; Grant and Keohane 2005). There is, however, little appreciation that the pluralism inherent in the global space may require a different approach to accountability altogether. If accountability is to be contextually responsive in the global space, a global actor's relationships, structure and purpose must be at the forefront to the accountability enquiry.

The relationships of UNHCR reveal the way that the 'push and pull' of organisational and legal factors determine the way its accountability obligations evolve. Being an organisation, UNHCR's relationships are identified by its structure and purpose. UNHCR's structure, the 'formal system of dividing up work tasks, coordinating the resultant activities of employees, and specifying reporting relationships to enable the achievement of organizational goals' (Smith 2012, p. 132), is also defined by its place within the institutional system of the UN. UNHCR's purpose is articulated by its constitution and subject matter, which determine with whom and how it maintains relationships.

How UNHCR's relationships generate accountability obligations depends on the sources of its accountability, which are determined by its functions. International law and institutional practice create obligations and responsibilities that are transformed into *accountability obligations* when contextualised within UNHCR's relationships because UNHCR will be 'held to account' to fulfil those obligations and responsibilities to a certain standard. A relationship-based approach to accountability reveals the diversity, complexity and potential inconsistencies in UNHCR's accountability.

'To whom and for what?' How UNHCR'S relationships define what it is accountable for

The second part of this chapter examines UNHCR's institutional, participatory and State-based relationships to identify how these relationships create accountability obligations that are unique to UNHCR.

UNHCR's institutional relationships

UN General assembly and ECOSOC: legal accountability v. functional autonomy

UNHCR has an institutional relationship with the UNGA, which is created by its statute and its position as a UN subsidiary organ. Paragraph 1 of UNHCR's statute[4] declares that UNHCR assumes the function of international protection 'under the auspices of the United Nations' and that it acts 'under the authority of the General Assembly'. The first part of this provision indicates that UNHCR is a subsidiary organ of the UN, which has been created pursuant to Articles 7 and 22 of the UN Charter. The second part indicates that UNHCR acts at the direction of the UNGA and not the UNSG (Goodwin-Gill and McAdam 2007, p. 429) or any other principal organ of the UN.

UNHCR has a similar relationship with ECOSOC, which is a body internal to the UN that was established to coordinate the work of the UN's 14 specialised agencies. This relationship, derived from paragraphs 3 and 11, require the High Commissioner to follow policy directives and report to the UNGA through ECOSOC.

UNHCR's relationship with UNGA/ECOSOC is shaped hierarchically by UNHCR's position as a subsidiary organ and is dictated by the express words of UNHCR's statute. The relevant provisions of UNHCR's statute that create legal obligations become *accountability obligations* because UNHCR is accountable to the UNGA for complying with them.

Paragraph 3 requires the High Commissioner 'to follow policy directives given him by the General Assembly or the Economic and Social Council'. Paragraph 9 gives UNGA the authority to determine additional activities in which the High Commissioner may engage. In practice, paragraphs 3 and 9 translate to the annual adoption of 'omnibus' resolutions, which clarify the UNGA's concerns and priorities regarding global displacement and 'situational' resolutions that refer to specific countries (Türk 2007, p. 481). Although paragraph 11 declares that UNHCR is to report to the UNGA through ECOSOC, in practice UNHCR submits its annual reports to the UNGA directly (Lewis 2012, p. 13), removing ECOSOC as a 'buffer' and diminishing any authority that may have once been inherent in this role. Furthermore, although UNHCR is responsible for following policy advice provided by ECOSOC, its resolutions do not tend to dictate policy that exclusively relates to refugees but addresses matters that may more generally affect refugees, such as violence against women.[5]

Although much of UNHCR's relationship with the UNGA/ECOSOC is dictated by its statute, when the limitations of a principal's authority over a subsidiary body and the reality of UNHCR's independence are understood, the relationship becomes defined in such a way as to limit the practical control that the UNGA exercises over UNHCR. For a subsidiary organ of the UN to be lawfully established by a principal organ, it must be under its authority and control.[6] Regardless of how 'authority and control' are defined, it does not extend to dictating the way that the subsidiary organ conducts its functions or makes its decisions, the lawfulness of which depends on whether the subsidiary is acting within the power of its own mandate (Sarooshi 2000, p. 86). Placed within the language of accountability, the accountability obligations created by the relationship between UNHCR and UNGA/ECOSOC can be determined by the ordinary meaning of the terms of UNHCR's statute combined with subsequent UNGA resolutions (i.e. UNHCR's mandate), as well as its *functional autonomy*.[7]

In international law, functional autonomy means the 'distinction, in terms of legal powers and purposes, between an organisation and its member states' (Brownlie 2008, p. 677). In its 2002 report on the accountability of International Organisations (IO), the International Law Association (ILA) extended the term to describe the duties of 'parent organs', which 'have a duty to exercise a degree of control and supervision over subsidiary organs which corresponds to the functional autonomy granted'.[8] UNHCR's functional autonomy is based on a combination of its legal and institutional autonomy (Barnett and Finnemore 2004). UNHCR's legal autonomy comes from its international legal personality, which is compatible with objectives and functions that it derives from the UN (Verdirame 2011, p. 62) and its ability to act and speak independently (d'Aspremont 2001, p. 63). UNHCR's institutional autonomy means that it is a 'purposive actor in its own right with independent interests and capabilities' (Loescher 2001, p. 34) and is demonstrated by that fact that it exercises a separate or 'corporate will' (White 2011, p. 301) to the UN rather than the 'aggregate opinion' of member states (Klabbers 2002, p. 12). The fact that UNHCR has been delegated a specific field of 'technical expertise' (*ibid.*) over which it has complete responsibility also indicates its institutional autonomy. Other factors pointing to UNHCR's institutional autonomy are its bureaucratic independence (White 2011, p. 302) in the form of a self-sufficient, decision-making secretariat, its differently constituted membership to the UN (de Wet 2008, p. 1995) and the fact that states do not have the direct power to appoint its executive heads (Martini 2006, p. 24).

These observations are not intended to suggest that UNHCR is a completely autonomous organisation. The fact that it is a subsidiary organ is enough to counter such a suggestion. However, UNHCR has developed significant autonomous features, which ensure that its relationship with UNGA/ECOSOC is conducted according to a 'limited control model'. 'Limited control' means that neither UNGA nor ECOSOC generally acts beyond the terms of UNHCR's statute, leaving UNHCR with significant but not unlimited independence in decision-making, policy development and advice.

However, where a relationship is inter-institutional and the subordinate party is a subsidiary of the principal, accountability must be reciprocal. The ILA recommendations that an organ of an IO that has delegated the exercise of any of its powers or functions remains fully accountable for the way in which those powers or functions are exercised[9] reflect a strong compulsion against tyrannical, unbridled authority and arbitrary decision-making. Applied to UNHCR, the UNGA as supervisor is also accountable to UNHCR for not abusing its position of power and for meeting standards of behaviour expected of it in its supervisory role.

In conclusion, the accountability obligations created by the relationship between UNHCR and UNGA/ECOSOC are, for the most part, confined to those specifically created by UNHCR's statute and, more generally, to account for the way it executes its competence. Despite the statutory references to UNHCR being 'under the authority of the General Assembly', neither the UNGA nor ECOSOC exercises unbridled power over UNHCR in a way that creates accountability for UNHCR to follow its directions without question.

Although UNHCR's statute foresees a limited role for the UNSG in UNHCR's day-to-day operations and policy development, the 'intangible authority' inherent in the role makes the relationship hierarchical.

Paragraph 13 of UNHCR's statute provides that the election and re-election of the High Commissioner for Refugees is made by the UNGA on the proposal of the Secretary-General, which is given formality and transparency in the form of an UNGA decision. However, although the appointment of senior officials within the UN may be a transparent process, the removal of those officials from office is more opaque.

In 1989, High Commissioner Jean-Pierre Hocké resigned because of an accusation that he had used Danish contributions for a refugee education fund to pay for entertainment and first-class air travel for himself and his wife.[10] In 2005, High Commissioner Ruud Lubbers resigned after being accused of sexually harassing a female employee. Although both Commissioners *resigned*, the extent to which their decisions were free from political pressure, particularly from the Secretary-General, merits questioning. Although presented as freely made decisions, it seems that both Hocké and Lubbers were placed in positions where they were left with little choice. At the news conference announcing his resignation, Hocké stated that his resignation did 'not reflect any sentiment of culpability on my part concerning any of my doings' and mentioned the 'destructive intentions of some people here and elsewhere.'[11] Lubbers spoke directly regarding the pressure to resign placed on him by Secretary-General Kofi Annan. In his resignation letter, he stated that Annan had given him two choices: resign or face suspension and charges of breaking UN rules. Maintaining his innocence, Lubbers said: '[t]o be frank, and despite all my loyalty, insult has now been added to injury and therefore I resign as High Commissioner'.[12]

Resignation is a useful way to maximise damage control in difficult circumstances. Whether transparent or 'unspoken', the authority inherent in the ability of the Secretary-General to influence the resignation of a High Commissioner without the need for more formal removal procedures suggests that UNHCR is more subordinate to the Secretary-General than it would initially appear.

Although paragraph 17 of UNHCR's statute states that '[t]he High Commissioner and the Secretary-General shall make appropriate arrangements for liaison and consultation on matters of mutual interest', the authority implicit in the role of Secretary-General, the 'chief administrative officer of the organization',[13] gives rise to the likelihood that he or she will make decisions that have no basis in UNHCR's statute or its legal position as a subsidiary organ of the UN. A clear example of this situation is the reprimand of High Commissioner Sadako Ogata by Boutros Boutros-Ghali in February of 1993. After High Commissioner Ogata ordered the cessation of aid to several parts of Yugoslavia because militants were impeding its delivery, Secretary-General Boutros-Ghali publicly rebuked her and overturned her decision by ordering UNHCR to resume humanitarian assistance to the area.[14] The Secretary-General is given no specific authority to make such an order outside of the authority of the UNGA and ECOSOC to issue policy directives or for the UNGA to determine additional activities.[15] Boutros-Ghali's actions went well beyond those expected of a principal organ, which the ILA considers only to extend to the overruling of a decision of a subsidiary body in circumstances where that decision was *contrary to applicable legal rules*.[16] It is difficult to see how a decision regarding humanitarian aid delivery could be so defined. The actions of the Secretary-General were extraordinary not only because they exposed political conflicts over UN programme management[17] but also because they were a clear indication that the authority of the UN over its subsidiary organs, *albeit* in the guise of the Secretary-General, has the potential to extend beyond legal rules into 'interference' with *policy* decisions made at the most senior levels, which may constitute a partial breach of UNHCR's mandate (Gilbert 1998, p. 356).

As illustrated through UNHCR's relationship with the UNSG, organisational factors, such as inherent authority, can have the effect of expanding the accountability obligations owed by a subordinate body to a principal. In UNHCR's case, the accountability obligations created by paragraph 17 of its statute to liaise and consult with the Secretary-General on matters of mutual interest are expanded by the inherent and perhaps unpredictable nature of the authority of the UNSG.

External humanitarian bodies: accountability to ensure cooperation and participation

From the time that UNHCR was created and the Convention Relating to the Status of Refugees ('Refugee Convention')[18] became the primary instrument for the protection of refugees, a shift from UNHCR's traditional protection role to increased humanitarian intervention and 'pragmatism' has occurred (Loescher 2001a, p. 28). Although UNHCR still undertakes activities associated with its original mandate, it now manages the physical protection of refugees, community development and the provision of aid. This shift has meant increased collaboration with other bodies involved in humanitarianism and new accountability obligations for all involved.

UNHCR creates partnerships with external humanitarian bodies, which are classified as either operational or implementing partners. Operational partners work with UNHCR to protect and assist refugees, with the aim of achieving durable solutions.[19] Implementing partners are operational partners that have signed an implementing agreement for UNHCR to delegate responsibility for the implementation of humanitarian assistance and for which it provides funds through a standard Sub-Project Agreement.[20]

Internal UNHCR policy guides outline expectations for the partnerships that all parties are accountable for meeting.[21] External humanitarian bodies are accountable to UNHCR for adhering to its rules and procedures as well as its established policies and complying with the laws and policies of the country in which they operate.[22] The partners are accountable to each other for adhering to 'Best Practice' principles,[23] being effective collaboration, transparency, competence and professionalism.

UNHCR also works collaboratively with external humanitarian bodies through its involvement in the Inter-Agency Standing Committee (IASC) Initiatives. Predicated by the humanitarian crisis in Darfur and a lack of coordination in humanitarian situations generally, the aim of the Initiatives was to strengthen preparedness and technical capacity, provide predictable leadership and accountability to affected populations and clarify the division of labour between agencies by creating subject-specific 'clusters'.[24]

IASC's initial disregard for the importance of *inter-agency accountability*[25] was a failure to acknowledge that a collaborative approach to humanitarian response requires organisational practices, such as participative decision-making, communication, negotiation and team building[26] that generate accountability for members to collaborate with each other in an inclusive way. As cluster leader over 'camp control and management', 'protection' and 'emergency shelter', UNHCR is accountable to other humanitarian organisations for ensuring their effective inclusion in the cluster process. More recently, IASC has acknowledged 'informal accountability of humanitarian organisations to their peers for meeting their responsibilities and adhering to relevant national and international standards' (Kauffmann and Krüger 2010, p. 37) and 'accountability of humanitarian organizations to cluster leads and to their peers' (Steets and Grünewald 2010, p. 34).

UNHCR's relationship with humanitarian agencies extends to an accountability obligation to ensure their participation in its processes. UNHCR allows for the attendance of 'non-member observers',[27] other UN bodies, intergovernmental organisations and NGOs (Corkery 2006, p. 111) in its annual ExCom sessions and invites UN bodies to attend one of its four annual sessions of the Standing Committee, which is the body that drafts ExCom Conclusions. Participation by NGOs takes a more active form as participants in UNHCR's Annual Consultation, which aims to raise issues and give NGOs the ability to network and exchange views.[28]

The first source of UNHCR's accountability obligation to ensure participation of external humanitarian bodies is internal regulation. Rules of procedure require the annual sessions of the ExCom to be public and create an obligation to invite UN bodies to attend Standing Committee sessions.[29] The consultative role of NGOs in Standing Committee meetings was established by ECOSOC resolutions, which, based on Article 71 of the UN Charter, state that ECOSOC is given the authority to 'make suitable arrangement for consultation with non-governmental organizations which are concerned with matters within its competence'.[30]

Arrangements for participation in Standing Committee meetings were formalised by ExCom decisions in 1997[31] and in 2004 for contributions to the drafting of ExCom Conclusions by NGOs.[32]

The second source of UNHCR's accountability obligations regarding participation is more normative. Although NGOs and other humanitarian organisations may *at best* exert 'moral authority' in their advocacy and advisory roles (Bentz and Hasenclever 2011, p. 203), and although the practical problems associated with ensuring their meaningful participation are acknowledged,[33] such bodies possess expertise that makes important contributions to the development of international refugee law and policy, which supports UNHCR's responsibilities to ensure the *effectiveness* of international refugee law (Lewis 2012, pp. 23, 37–38).[34]

UNHCR's relationships with external humanitarian bodies are increasingly defined by accountability. Although all of the parties participating in either UNHCR's partnerships or the IASC Initiatives are accountable to each other for effective collaboration, UNHCR has specific accountability obligations to humanitarian organisations to ensure their participation in its processes.

The Executive Committee: accountability to follow advice

Paragraph 4 of UNHCR's statute confers the power to establish an advisory committee on refugees, which 'is to consist of representatives of States Members and States non-members of the United Nations' and which are to be 'selected by the Council on the basis of their demonstrated interest in and devotion to the solution of the refugee problem'. After various iterations, the ExCom was formed in 1957. The ExCom's terms of reference were defined in the UNGA resolution that established it, which among other duties regarding funding and project approval, required it 'to advise the High Commissioner, at his request, in the exercise of his function under the Statute of his Office'.[35]

A relationship between UNHCR and the ExCom is created by the statutory requirement that the High Commissioner request the opinion of the advisory committee 'in the exercise of his functions'.[36] The High Commissioner is to seek the opinion of the ExCom when difficulties arise, such as those regarding 'any controversy concerning the international status of ... persons'.[37] Opinions come in the form of Conclusions on International Protection, which are adopted annually by the UNGA. The ExCom Conclusions are drafted by the Standing Committee and represent international consensus on protection issues that stem from the Refugee Convention and the Protocol Relating to the Status of Refugees.[38]

Although seeking opinions may be interpreted as limiting the ExCom to giving *advice* to UNHCR (Holborn 1975, p. 92), it is arguable that the relationship between UNHCR and the ExCom creates accountability obligations for UNHCR to *follow* ExCom's advice because of the way that ExCom Conclusions are given weight by the resolutions of the UNGA. In Resolution 1673 (XVI), the UNGA requested that the High Commissioner 'abide by directions that the Committee might give him in regard to situations concerning refugees'.[39] Additionally, Resolution 1166 (XII) requires the ExCom to *approve* any projects related to its advice regarding the appropriateness of international assistance 'to help to solve specific refugee problems remaining unresolved after 31 December 1958 or arising after that date'. Furthermore, the terminology used in Resolution 1166 (XII) to define other aspects of the relationship between UNHCR and the ExCom reflects principal/subordinate roles. For example, the role of ExCom is to *authorise* the High Commissioner to make appeals for funds and to *give directives* regarding the use of the emergency fund. Accordingly, UNHCR has an accountability obligation to follow ExCom Conclusions that derive from the hierarchical nature of their relationship.

UNHCR's participatory relationships

UNHCR has a relationship with refugees that is created by paragraph 1 of its statute, which states that the 'United Nations High Commissioner for Refugees … shall assume the function of providing international protection … to refugees who fall within the scope of the present Statute …' The High Commissioner's *rationae personae*,[40] however, is more complex than UNHCR's statute implies. Not only is UNHCR's relationship and therefore accountability obligations with refugees *not* limited to an understanding of the term as derived from its statute but it also has a relationship with 'others in need of international protection' who are not considered to be a part of its statutory mandate.

Refugees: an expanded accountability to protect

Paragraph 6A (ii) of UNHCR's statute declares a person to be a refugee if he or she has a well-founded fear of persecution, is not located within his or her country and is unable or, in some circumstances, unwilling to protect himself or herself. Accordingly, 'refugee' includes *stateless persons*, who do not have a nationality and are outside the country of former habitual residence. Although it may be argued that *returnees* also come within UNHCR's mandate by virtue of being former refugees who have voluntarily agreed to return to their country of origin (Türk 2007, p. 485), its statute expressly places returnees within the competence of the High Commissioner by stipulating that his or her functions include facilitation of 'the voluntary repatriation of such refugees, or their assimilations within new national communities'[41] and 'assisting governmental and private efforts to promote voluntary repatriation or assimilation within new national communities'.[42]

UNHCR's *rationae personae* is not, however, limited to refugees, including returnees and stateless persons, as defined by its statute alone. UNHCR's supervisory mandate, which is established by paragraph 8(a), extends its mandate to refugees who are protected by international conventions. The primary international convention for the protection of refugees is the Refugee Convention, which is to be read with the 1967 Protocol. Although the definition of a refugee under the Refugee Convention is similar to that provided by UNHCR's statute, it is wider in scope because 'membership of a particular social group' is a criterion for a well-founded fear of persecution,[43] meaning that such refugees fall within the competence of UNHCR.

The Convention Governing the Specific Aspects of Refugees Problems in Africa ('OAU Convention') includes, in its definition of refugee, those people in Africa who have been displaced by external aggression, among other things.[44] Similarly, the Cartagena Declaration on Refugees[45] recommends that the definition of a refugee within Central America, Mexico and Panama include 'persons who have fled their country because their lives, safety or freedom have been threatened by generalized violence, foreign aggression, internal conflicts, massive violation of human rights or other circumstances which have seriously disturbed public order'. UNHCR's *rationae personae* is expanded to incorporate these definitions of refugees.

As UNGA and ECOSOC policy directives contribute to UNHCR's mandate, they also have the capacity to expand the scope of its *ratione personae*. For example, early UNGA resolutions extended protection to Hungarian refugees who had been displaced due to events *after* 1951[46] and later requested the High Commissioner to go beyond its mandate and 'use his *good offices*' to assist Chinese refugees in Hong Kong[47] and other groups.[48] In 1961, the UNGA issued a resolution that requested the High Commissioner to 'pursue his activities on behalf of the refugees within his mandate, *or those for whom he extends his good offices*,[49] meaning that UNHCR's mandate is no longer limited to 'old' (i.e. pre 1951) refugees as specified in the Refugee Convention and Statute.[50]

Asylum seekers, who may or may not be refugees, may also be considered refugees. Refugee status is declaratory, meaning that where an asylum seeker has made a claim for refugee status, he or she may be entitled to international protection on the basis that he or she *could* be a refugee (Türk 2007, p. 483). Furthermore, to attempt to separate 'asylum seekers' from 'refugees' would be impractical in large group influx situations where individual Refugee Status Determination (RSD) is difficult.

Several provisions of UNHCR's statute *expressly* create accountability obligations relating to refugees. Paragraph 1 defines UNHCR's role as assisting governments in the facilitation of refugees' assimilation within new national communities. Paragraph 10 gives the High Commissioner the power to administer and distribute funds for the purpose of assistance to refugees. Fundamentally, paragraph 1 defines the function of UNHCR as 'providing international protection'. To be fully understood, paragraph 1 must be contextualised by paragraph 8. Paragraph 8 specifies a number of the High Commissioner's functions that constitute international protection, which includes the promotion of the conclusion and ratification of international refugee conventions and the supervision of their application.[51]

Other provisions of UNHCR's statute require UNGA resolutions and UNGA or ECOSOC policy directives to clarify UNHCR's accountability obligations to refugees.[52] As an early example, UNGA determined that 'additional activities' included requests to participate in 'humanitarian endeavours'.[53] Although 'humanitarian endeavours' were simply defined as those 'for which the Office has particular expertise and experience' and, indeed, appeared to be linked to UNHCR's core mandate,[54] a clearer relationship between UNHCR's role and humanitarian activities soon began to emerge. In 1984, the UNGA urged UNHCR to pursue its efforts in 'development-orientated assistance',[55] which is a concept developed at the Second International Conference on Assistance to Refugees in Africa in 1984, based on the 'need to integrate refugee projects into the development process'[56] and included emergency relief and support for returnees and technical and capital assistance for the countries to which they returned.[57] In later years, UNHCR was asked to effectively address, through emergency preparedness and response mechanisms, situations that cause or threaten to cause mass exoduses.[58]

Although the express obligations are framed as a way for UNHCR to assist governments to achieve specific outcomes, they are accountability obligations that UNHCR owes *to refugees* because their pre-existing accountability relationship is 'participatory'. A participatory relationship means that theoretically if not practically, a party who is subject to or is affected by another party's actions should be entitled to hold it accountable (Grant and Keohane 2005). Decisions regarding voluntary repatriation, the administration of funds for refugee assistance and international protection are matters that directly affect refugees' interests. Although the obligation to undertake additional activities and follow policy directives are directly linked to UNHCR's legal accountability obligations to UNGA and ECOSOC, they are also accountability obligations that UNHCR owes to refugees. Activities have invariably been of a humanitarian character and, therefore, affect the rights and interests of refugees at the most fundamental level. Both the express provisions of UNHCR's statute and the 'additional activities' discussed above create accountability obligations that UNHCR owes to refugees because they arise within the context of their relationship.

Others in need of international protection: a limited accountability to provide
assistance, transparency and participation

'Others in need of international protection', for the most part, refers to internally displaced persons (IDPs) (see Bradley in this volume), who have been displaced from their homes but have not crossed an international border and, therefore, have become persons *of concern* to international law as part of human rights law (Gilbert 1998, p. 362). Although IDPs do not come under UNHCR's mandate because they have not crossed an international border, UNGA resolutions since the 1970s have increasingly expanded UNHCR's assistance to people who fall within this category.[59] The UNGA expressly acknowledged UNHCR's continuing role in IDP assistance in 1992,[60] which it subsequently confirmed in numerous resolutions.[61] Despite ongoing controversy regarding whether and to what extent UNHCR should be involved with IDPs,[62] UNHCR can be described as having a participatory relationship with IDPs that is restricted but has the potential to evolve.

Like its relationship with refugees, UNHCR is accountable to IDPs for adhering to UNGA's resolutions that request it to provide assistance to them. For example, in 2011, the UNGA requested UNHCR to 'take concrete action to meet the protection and assistance needs of … displaced persons' in Africa.[63] However, because the provisions are usually general in nature (e.g. 'protection and assistance needs'), the precise accountability obligations created by the relationship are better understood through 'non-legal', policy-based or 'operational' means.

In 2011, IASC undertook a review of the IASC Initiatives and found significant weaknesses in leadership and coordination. IASC's response was to develop the Transformative Agenda ('TA') that established TA Protocols, which 'set the parameters for improved collective action in humanitarian emergencies'.[64] The three key areas of the TA are better leadership, improved *accountability* to all of the stakeholders and improved coordination. 'Accountability' meant 'Accountability to Affected People', and a sub-working group endorsed an operational framework that provided guidance to improve participation, information provision and the handling of feedback and complaints from the affected people.[65] The TA protocols become accountability obligations that UNHCR, as a cluster leader within the IASC Initiatives framework, owed to IDPS, or the 'affected people'.

There are, however, several important caveats on UNHCR's role as cluster leader and, therefore, limitations for which it is accountable to IDPs. UNHCR insisted that its role be limited to sector leader over 'camp control and management', 'protection' and 'emergency shelter' and that it does not coordinate clusters where the cause of the humanitarian crisis is 'human made calamities' (e.g. nuclear accident) or natural disasters.[66] The reasons for UNHCR's reluctance to fully extend its assistance to IDPs include lack of donor interest, operational constraints, the presence of other UN agencies in the field and the institution's risk of asylum.[67] In 2011, however, UNHCR appeared to shift its policy regarding IDPs and natural disasters when it attempted to gain a mandate for natural disasters and climate change. States did not generally support UNHCR's initiative, appearing reluctant to relinquish control over developments in protection.[68]

As cluster leader, UNHCR is accountable to IDPs for coordinating humanitarian responses, *albeit* in limited circumstances, in a way that allows for their participation, provides them with adequate information and allows for their feedback and complaints. UNHCR's accountability relationship with IDPs has the potential to evolve, particularly considering emerging questions regarding how potential 'climate change refugees' are to be treated in regard to assistance and protection (Koser 2008, p. 17). These accountability obligations are 'organisational' rather than 'legal' because they are based on non-mandated or 'non-binding' programmes and are complementary to the accountability obligations regarding IDPs that originate in UNGA resolutions.

UNHCR's relationships with states

UNHCR's 'Mandate Relationship' with states: states' accountability obligations to cooperate with UNHCR

UNHCR's mandated role of providing international protection implicitly requires it to form relationships with states to execute that function. Paragraph 1 of UNHCR's statute requires the High Commissioner to seek 'permanent solutions for the problem of refugees *by assisting Governments …*' (*emphasis added*). Paragraph 8(a) requires the High Commissioner to provide for the protection of refugees in the following manner:

> (a) Promoting the conclusion and ratification of international conventions for the protection of refugees, *supervising their application* and proposing amendments thereto;

Although the term 'supervising their application' is not defined in UNHCR's statute, it is clarified in corresponding State duties in the Refugee Convention and other 'international conventions for the protection of refugees' that make it clear that the accountability obligations in this relationship are those owed by states to UNHCR, and not the reverse. Article 35 of the Refugee Convention requires the states to cooperate with UNHCR to exercise its functions and facilitate its duty of supervising the provisions of the Refugee Convention. Article 36 requires the states to provide statistical data and information on the condition of refugees, the implementation of the Refugee Convention and on laws, regulations and decrees that may relate to the refugees. Express duties of State cooperation are also found in Article II of the 1967 Protocol[69] and Article VIII of the OAU Convention. Other instruments for the protection of refugees express broad support for UNHCR's supervisory function[70] or generally for UNHCR's functions,[71] which can be interpreted as an implied acceptance of UNHCR's supervisory mandate (Türk 2001, p. 140). UNHCR's supervisory mandate may also supplement the supervision of international law instruments administered by other IOs, where those instruments expressly refer to refugees[72] (Türk 2001, p. 145). It has been argued that where states are not signatories to the Refugee Convention and Protocol or other relevant refugee instruments, their actions regarding refugees may still be 'supervised' by UNHCR because its capabilities extend to 'those norms and principles of international law applicable to refugees that apply to all states, regardless of accession to international instruments' (Türk 2001, p. 145). In addition to international instruments, the states' obligations to cooperate with UNHCR have been confirmed by various UNGA resolutions.[73]

When paragraph 8(a) of UNHCR's statute is read with the relevant parts of the Refugee Convention, the Protocol and other refugee instruments, it is clear that UNHCR's supervisory mandate creates legal accountability obligations for the *states* to cooperate with UNHCR and assist it in its supervisory role.

UNHCR's 'organisational' relationship with the states: impact of the State interests on UNHCR accountability obligations

The organisational factors reveal the accountability relationship between UNHCR and the states to be more opaque than 'legal' or 'mandate' elements alone would convey.

UNHCR's budget is funded by two sources. The first source comes from the UN regular budget, which in 2013 allocated UNHCR USD 46, 323, 700.[74] The second source of UNHCR's funding is from voluntary contributions, which are provided by governmental donors (including the European Union), UN funds and intergovernmental and private donors (corporate and individual). In 2013, UNHCR received USD 2,965,412,397 in voluntary funding and the top three donors, which were the United States, Japan and the European Union,[75] consisted of approximately 52 per cent of UNHCR's voluntary contributions.

Because the majority of voluntary contributors to UNHCR's funding are the states, financial and funding concerns have become intertwined with political factors, and the nature of accountability has shifted according to diplomacy, domestic policy and State self-interest. UNHCR has a history of making policy decisions that reflect the interests of its largest donors. During the Cold War, UNHCR's decision to award refugee status to individuals fleeing from Communist regimes was influenced by the anti-Communism policies of the West, notably the United States (Loescher 2001b, p. 202). In a 1994 interview,

High Commissioner Ogata conceded that 'Government funds in the general programs are not earmarked, but the funds spent on special programs reflect strongly the interests of the donors ... So, if you ask me if foreign policy is reflected in funding priorities, then yes' (Berrie *et al.* 1994, p. 422). The election and actions of individual High Commissioners have not escaped the State influence. High Commissioner Poul Hartling has been accused of 'toeing the line' on highly politicised issues, such as Indo-China and Central America, 'fearful that he would upset either his biggest donor, the United States, or the host states' (Berrie *et al.* 1994, p. 422). Gil Loescher (2001b, p. 248) also claimed that the United States was highly influential in the election process of several of the High Commissioners, citing the example of Jean-Pierre Hocké in whom they were 'clearly enamoured of' and who 'almost single-handedly won him the post of High Commissioner'.

Importantly, the power of UNHCR's voluntary contributors to earmark their funding means several displacement situations will receive more attention and thus more funding than others. The displacement that has been caused by war, violence or natural disaster receives the most concentrated media focus, which encourages public interest and, in turn, governmental action. The negative effects of earmarking practices have long been a recognised concern (Väyrynen 2001) and are a matter that Lindskov Jacobsen addresses in this volume in relation to UNHCR's biometric refugee registration. Other reasons that a State may choose to fund displacement situations are its physical location in relation to refugee movements (Smillie and Minear 2003, p. 7), its foreign policy and its historical linkages. Conversely, several states have shown reluctance to deploy troops to emergency situations where their strategic interests are limited (Smillie and Minear 2003, p. 7).[76] Although UNHCR's policy and practice 'have been driven both by state interests and by the Office acting independently or evolving in ways not expected nor necessarily sanctioned by states' (Loescher 2001a, p. 34), the State influence in UNHCR's funding programmes has precipitated a shift in its accountability obligations from performing its mandate and objectives efficiently, effectively and transparently[77] to adhering to State interests.

Although UNHCR's mandate creates binding legal accountability obligations that the states owe to it, UNHCR owes accountability obligations to the states that are created by organisational factors that introduce the potentially volatile elements of politics and ethics into the relationship.

Conclusion

Contextually responsive accountability is hardly revolutionary. There are few scholars of accountability theory who would suggest that it is a static concept to which subject and context are but irrelevant detail. In the global space, however, contextually responsive accountability means responding to pluralism, not the development of a universal definition of accountability that is the 'best fit' for the context. The dynamism, complexity and diversity of the actors within the global space mean that accountability depends on the individual character, functions and relationships of the actors who operate within it, and to whom and for what an individual actor is accountable is key.

Although accountability to refugees and beneficiaries remain central to UNHCR's accountability, this study of UNHCR's institutional, participatory and State-based relationships reveals that UNHCR's accountability obligations are also varied, intersecting and occasionally conflicting. Although UNHCR has legal accountability obligations that are created by its statute and mandate, other accountability obligations that arise from 'organisational factors', such as policy and operational issues can expand, conflict with and clarify those obligations. The way that binding legal standards, organisational practices, moral and ethical issues, State interests and the realities of power impact UNHCR's relationships are the ultimate determinants of UNHCR's accountability obligations, not an externally imposed understanding of what it should be accountable for. Once this perspective is fundamentally understood, the design and implementation of *effective* accountability mechanisms can commence.

Notes

1 Beneficiaries and 'downward accountability' are explored in other chapters in this volume.
2 Bodies that conduct decision-making and regulation in the global space, including international organisations (IOs), transnational agreements or networks made between State executives, hybrid public/private organisations, non-governmental organisations (NGOs) and multinational corporations.
3 An area of scholarship that suggests that traditional principles of public law can be utilized to provide accountability in the global context or 'global administrative space'.
4 The Statute of the Office of the United Nations High Commissioner for Refugees, contained in the Annex to *Resolution on Statute of the High Commissioner for Refugees*, GA Res 428(V) UN GAOR, 5th sess, 325th plen mtg, Doc/A/Res/428 (v) (1950) ('UNHCR Statute').
5 *Strengthening Crime Prevention and Criminal Justice Responses to Violence Against Women*, ESC Res 2010/15, UN ESCOR, 45th plen mtg, UN Doc E/2010/15, 22 July 2010.
6 *General Assembly Official Records*, 9th Session, Annexes, Agenda Item 67, at p. 13, A/C 1/758, paras. 1 and 2; *Repertory of practice of United Nations organs*, p. 228.
7 International Law Association – *Committee on Accountability of International Organizations, Third Report Consolidated, Revised and Enlarged Version of Recommended Rules and Practices* (RRP's), New Delhi Conference ('ILA Report'), 2002, p. 6.
8 *ILA Report*, p. 6.
9 *ILA Report*, p. 1.
10 Lewis, P. 'U.N. refugee chief quits over his use of funds', *The New York Times* (New York), 27 October 1989.
11 'Hocke says resignation was his decision', *Associated Press*, 27 October 1989.
12 'U.N. refugee chief Lubbers resigns over sex allegations', *Associated Press*, 20 February 2005.
13 UN Charter, Article 97.
14 'U.N Chief rebukes Aid Chief, restores relief', *The Times* (New York), 20 February 1993, 14A.
15 UNHCR Statute, paras. 3 and 9.
16 *ILA Report*, p. 6.
17 Above n 13. Boutros-Ghali is quoted as saying: 'I am supposed to direct this operation'.

18 Opened for signature 28 July 1951, 189 UNTS 150 (entered into force 22 April 1954) Article 1A(2) ('Refugee Convention').

19 *Partnership: an operations management handbook for UNHCR's partners* (February 2003), *Partnerships handbook*, p. 30.

20 Ibid., glossary.

21 See *Framework agreement for operational partnership (UNHCR and NGO)* (26 July 2003) and *Partnerships handbook*.

22 *Partnerships handbook*, p. 31.

23 Ibid., p. 33.

24 *Inter-agency standing committee guidance note on using the cluster approach to strengthen humanitarian response* (24 November 2006).

25 '[t]he cluster approach itself does not require that humanitarian actors be held accountable to sector leads'. Ibid, p. 2.

26 Ibid.

27 States that are not members of the ExCom.

28 'Annual consultations with NGOs'. Available online at www.unhcr.org/pages/49f9b49f6.html (accessed 5 May 2015).

29 UNHCR Ex Comm. 55th sess, UN Doc A/AC.96/187?Rev.6 (2005), rules 33 and 38.

30 See *Arrangements for consultation with non-governmental organizations* ESC Res 1296 (XLIV), UN ESCOR, 43rd sess, 1520th plen mtg, UN Doc E/RES/1296 (XLIV) (23 May 1968); *Consultative relationship between the United Nations and non-governmental organizations*, ESC Res 1996/31, sess, 49th plen mtg, UN Doc E/RES/1996/31, 25 July 1996.

31 *Decision on Non-Governmental Organization (NGO) observer participation in the work of the Executive Committee of the High Commissioner's programme and its standing committee*, UNHCR Ex. Comm. 48th sess, 8th stand. Comm. Mtg, [Annex: Decision III] UN Doc A/AC.96/888, 1997.

32 *Decision on working methods of the Executive Committee of the High Commissioner's programme and its standing committee, including NGO observer participation in the work of the committee*, UNHCR Ex. Comm. 55th sess, [Decision E] UN Doc A/AC.96/1003, 2004.

33 *Note on review of the process for drafting Executive Committee Conclusions on international protection*, 18 November 2005, pp. 13–14.

34 Lewis describes UNHCR's statutory obligations to promote the ratification of treaties and to supervise states' application of those treaties as a responsibility to ensure the effectiveness of international refugee law.

35 GA Res 1166(XII), UN GOAR, 12th sess, 723rd plen mtg, UN Doc A/Res/1166(XII), 26 November 1957, p. 5.

36 UNHCR Statute, para. 1.

37 Ibid.

38 Opened for signature 31 January 1967, 606 UNTS 267 (entered into force 4 October 1967), Article II.

39 GA Res 1673 (XVI), UN GAOR, 16th sess, 1081st plen mtg, UN Doc A/RES/1673(XVI), 18 December 1961, p. 1.

40 To whom its mandate extends.

41 UNHCR Statute, para. 1.

42 Ibid., para. 8©.

43 *Statements of Mr. Petren of Sweden*, UN Doc A/CONF.2/SR.3 at 14, 19 November 1951. UN Doc A/CONF.2/SR.19, 26 November 1951, p. 14.

44 Signed 10 September 1969 1001 UNTS 45 (entered into force 20 June 1974), Article 1(2).

45 22 November 1984, Annual Report of the Inter-American Commission on Human Rights, OAS Doc. OEA/Ser.L/V/II.66/doc.10, rev. 1, at 190-93 (1984–85) ('Cartagena Declaration').

46 GA Res 1006 (ES-II), UN GAOR, 2nd emergency special sess, 573rd plen mtg, UN Doc A/RES/1006(ES-II), 10 November 1956, p. II.1.

47 GA Res 1167 (XII), UN GAOR, 12th sess, 727th plen mtg, UN Doc A/RES/1167 (XII), 11 December 1957.

48 GA Res 1499 (XV), UN GAOR, 15th sess, 935th plen mtg, UN Doc A/RES/1499 (XV), 5 December 1960, p. d.
49 GA Res 1673 (XVI), p. 1.
50 Refugee Convention 19, Article 1A(2); UNHCR Statute, para. 6A (ii).
51 UNHCR Statute, para. 8(a).
52 See paras. 9 and 3, discussed under 'UN General Assembly and ECOSOC: legal accountability v functional autonomy'.
53 GA Res 2956 (XXVII) UN GAOR, 27th sess, 2107th plen mtg, UN Doc A/RES/2956 (XXVII), 12 December 1972, p. 7.
54 'Commending the results obtained by the High Commissioner in the accomplishment of his *humanitarian task of providing international protection to refugees* within his mandate and promoting permanent solutions to their problems' (*emphasis added*).
55 GA Res 39/140 UN GAOR, 39th sess, 101st plen mtg, UN Doc A/RES/39/140, 14 December 1984, p. 7.
56 *Second International Conference on assistance to refugees in Africa (ICARA II): report of the Secretary-General*, 22 August 1984, A/39/402.
57 Ibid., p. 60.
58 GA Res 50/182 UN GAOR, 50th sess, 99th plen mtg, UN Doc A/RES/50/182, 22 December 1995, p. 9.
59 *Assistance to Sudanese refugees returning from abroad*, GA Res 2958 (XXVII) UN GAOR, 27th sess, 2107th plen mtg, UN Doc/A/Res/2958 (XXVII), 1972.
60 GA Res 47/105 UN GAOR, 47th sess, 89th plen mtg, Doc/A/Res/47/105, 1992.
61 GA Res 66/135, 65th sess, 89th plen mtg, Agenda Item 62 UN Doc A/RES/66/135, 19 December 2011, p. 6.
62 *Internally displaced persons: the role of the United Nations High Commissioner for refugees*, 6 March 2000, p. 3.
63 GA Res 66/135, p. 14.
64 *IASC principals transformative agenda*, Inter-Agency Standing Committee. Available online at www.humanitarianinfo.org/iasc/pageloader.aspx?page=content-template-default&bd=87 (accessed 16 September 2015).
65 Ibid.
66 *UNHCR's role in IASC humanitarian reform initiatives and the strengthening of the inter-agency collaborative response to internally displaced persons situations*, 20 September 2005, p. 6.
67 *UNHCR's operational experience with internally displaced persons*, Division of International Protection, September 1994, pp. 75–76.
68 McAdam, J. 'Creating new norms? The Nansen initiative on disaster-induced cross-border displacement', *APMEN* 2013. Available online at http://www.brookings.edu/research/opinions/2013/04/01-nansen-displacement-mcadam (accessed 23 October 2015).
69 Article II of the Protocol mirrors the text of Articles 35 and 36 of the Refugee Convention.
70 Cartagena Declaration, preamble.
71 Convention implementing the Schengen Agreement of 14 June 1985 between the governments of the states of the Benelux Economic Union, the Federal Republic of Germany and the French Republic, on the gradual abolition of checks at their common borders, 19 June 1990 (entered into force 1 September 1993), Article 28.
72 Convention on the rights of the child, opened for signature 20 November 1989, 1577 UNTS 3 (entered into force 2 September 1990), Article 22.
73 GA Res 428 (V).
74 *UNHCR Global Report* 2013, p. 117.
75 Ibid., p. 109.
76 Consider the reluctance of the United States to become operationally involved in the refugee crisis in the African Great Lakes in the 1990s.
77 *ILA Report*, p. 11.

References

Barnett, M. and M. Finnemore. (2004) *Rules for the World: International Organizations in Global Politics.* Ithaca, NY: Cornell University Press.

Bentz, S. and A. Hasenclever. (2011) '"Global" governance of forced migration', in A. Betts and G. Loescher (eds.), *Refugees in International Relations*, pp. 185–212. Oxford, UK: Oxford University Press.

Berrie, S. D., G. E. Trimarco and S. Weerackody. (1994) 'The evolution of UNHCR: Mrs. Sadako Ogata, U.N. High Commissioner for refugees. (Refugees and International Population Flows) (Interview)', *Journal of International Affairs*, 47(2): 419–428.

Brownlie, I. (2008) *Principles of International Law*, 7th ed. Oxford, UK: Oxford University Press.

Chesterman, S. (2008) 'Globalization rules: accountability, power and the prospects for global administrative law', *Global Governance*, 14(1): 39–52.

Corkery, A. (2006) 'The contribution of the UNHCR Executive Committee to the development of international refugee law', *Australian International Law Journal*, 13(1): 97–127.

d'Aspremont, J. (2011) 'The multifaceted concept of autonomy of international organizations and international legal discourse', in R. Collins and N. D. White (eds), *International Organizations and the Idea of Autonomy*, p. 63. New York: Routledge.

de Wet, E. (2008) 'Holding international institutions accountable: the complementary role of non-judicial oversight and judicial review', *German Law Journal*, 9(11): 1987–2012.

Dyzenhaus, D. (2009) 'Accountability and the concept of (global) administrative law', *Acta Juridica* 1: 3–31.

Gilbert, G. (1998) 'Rights, legitimate expectations, needs and responsibilities: UNHCR and the new world order', *International Journal of Refugee Law*, 10(3): 350–388.

Goodwin-Gill, G. and J. McAdam. (2007) *The Refugee in International Law*, 3rd ed. Oxford, UK: Oxford University Press.

Grant, R. W. and R. O. Keohane. (2005) 'Accountability and abuses of power in world politics', *American Political Science Review*, 99(1): 29–43.

Harlow, C. (2006) 'Global administrative law: the quest for principles and values', *European Journal of International Law*, 17(1): 187–214.

Holborn, L. W. (1975) *Refugees; A Problem of Our Time: The Work of the United Nations Commissioner for Refugees 1951–1972.* Lanham, MD: Scarecrow Press.

Kauffmann, D. and S. Krüger. (2010) '*Myanmar' IASC Cluster Approach Evaluation, 2nd Phase Country Study*, London, UK: Global Public Policy Institute.

Kingsbury, B., N. Krisch and R. B. Stewart. (2005) 'The Emergence of Global Administrative Law', *Law and Contemporary Problems*, 68 (3&4): 15–61.

Klabbers, J. (2002) *An Introduction to International Institutional Law*, 2nd ed. Cambridge: Cambridge University Press.

Koser, K. (2008) 'Gaps in IDP protection', *Forced Migration Review*, 31: 17.

Krisch, N. (2006) 'The pluralism of global administrative law', *European Journal of International Law*, 17(1): 247–78.

Lewis, C. (2012) *UNHCR and International Refugee Law: From Treaty to Innovation.* New York: Routledge.

Loescher, G. (2001) 'The UNHCR and world politics: state interests vs institutional autonomy', *International Migration Review*, 35(1): 33–56.

Loescher, G. (2001a) 'UNHCR and the erosion of refugee protection', *Forced Migration Review*, 10: 28–30.

Loescher, G. (2001b) *The UNHCR and World Politics: A Perilous Path.* Oxford, UK: Oxford University Press.

Martini, C. (2006) 'States' control over new international organization', *Global Jurist Advances*, 6(3): 1–25.

Mashaw, J. (2005) 'Structuring a "dense complexity"; accountability and the project of administrative law,' *Issues in Legal Scholarship*, 5(1): 1–38.

Mulgan, R. (2000) 'Accountability: an ever-expanding concept?', *Public Administration*, 78: 555–573.

Sarooshi, D. (2000) *The United Nations and the Development of Collective Security: The Delegation by the UN Security Council of its Chapter VII Powers*. Gloucestershire, UK: Clarendon Press.

Smillie, I. and L. Minear. (2003) 'The quality of money: donor behavior in humanitarian financing', Paper presented at the Conference on Good Donor Behaviour, Stockholm, June 2003.

Smith, P. E., W. Yellowley and M. Farmer. (2012) *Organizational Behaviour*. London: Hodder Education. Publishing information: Global Public Policy Institute.

Steets, J. and F. Grünewald. (2010) '"Uganda" IASC cluster approach evaluation, 2nd phase country study'. Global Public Policy Institute.

Türk, V. (2007) 'Freedom from fear: refugees, the broader forced displacement context and the underlying international protection regime', in V. Chetail (ed.), *Globalization, Migration and Human Rights: International Law Under Review*, Volume II, pp. 475–522. Brussels: Bruylant.

Türk, V. (2001) 'UNHCR's supervisory responsibility', *Revue Quebecoise de Droit International*, 14(1): 135–158.

Väyrynen, R. (2001) 'Funding dilemmas in refugee assistance: political interests and institutional reforms in UNHCR', *International Migration Review*, 35(1): 143–167.

Verdirame, G. (2011) *The UN and Human Rights: Who Guards the Guardians?* New York: Cambridge University Press.

White, N. D. (2011) 'Layers of autonomy in the UN system', in R. Collins and N. D. White (eds), *International Organizations and the Idea of Autonomy*, p. 298. New York: Routledge.

3 Advancing UNHCR accountability through the Law of International Responsibility

Maja Janmyr

Introduction

As this volume illustrates, United Nations High Commissioner for Refugees (UNHCR) engages in numerous activities that impact the lives and human rights of individuals worldwide. It is today more clear than ever that UNHCR occupies a challenging place in the international arena when it is both entrusted with an ambitious mandate and is frequently caught in a vice between the preferences of actors, such as donor governments, and host states. It is to be a norm entrepreneur, supervisor and enforcement agency of refugee rights simultaneously as it is expected to be a cooperative partner to the states and NGOs as well as the ultimate provider of material assistance. In several cases, perhaps most notably in refugee status determination procedures or in the management of refugee camps, UNHCR may function as a surrogate or *de facto* state, often sub-contracting important tasks to its so-called implementing partners (Janmyr 2014a; Slaughter and Crisp 2009). The global refugee figures being the highest since World War II, UNHCR is also involved in more, and increasingly complex, situations. This unprecedented scale of displacement has put a strain on UNHCR's organizational and economic resources and has, thus, important implications for the way UNHCR operates on the ground.

In the majority of these situations, UNHCR performs its functions with excellence. It has nevertheless proven extremely difficult to judicially address instances of misconduct or situations where UNHCR fails to fulfil its mandate. The extensive privileges and immunities of international organizations have traditionally meant that international organizations, such as UNHCR, have been largely protected from judicial processes. Based on the provisions in the UN Charter and the Convention on Privileges and Immunities of the UN, national courts have long understood that the UN has absolute immunity from their jurisdiction. The recent work by the International Law Commission (ILC) aiming to elaborate a framework for holding international organizations responsible for wrongful conduct, nevertheless, signals an important shift in the thinking concerning these issues and is, as such, indicative of a chipping away of the privileges and immunities of international organizations. Among the many legal approaches to accountability for international organizations, the responsibility of international organizations under international law is, furthermore, often considered to be a more clearly defined and developed legal approach to address the internationally wrongful conduct of international organizations (Reinisch 2005, pp. 121–122). Considering accountability through the prism of international law, this chapter takes a framework approach to exploring accountability.

Starting from the notion that there is a normative gap in accountability with respect to the acts of UNHCR under its international protection mandate, this chapter explores the potential of the ILC's 2011 Articles on the Responsibility of International Organizations (ARIO) to become a framework for holding the organization responsible under international law. It begins with an introduction to the law of international responsibility and the ARIO, and then considers UNHCR's obligations in regard to the ARIO's concepts of wrongful act and breach of an international obligation. It continues with an exploration of the question of attribution, focusing on the conduct of UNHCR organs and agents, and highlights the issues of implementing partnerships and multiple attribution of conduct, that is, holding several actors responsible for a certain misconduct or omission. Before concluding, this chapter discusses the practical limitations—not the least being the lack of a judicial forum for individuals to sue international organizations—of applying the ARIO to an international organization, such as UNHCR.

Generally on the Articles on the Responsibility of International Organizations

The law of international responsibility plays a fundamental role in the modern system of international law and is generally understood to comprise the body of principles that determine when and how the states and international organizations may be liable to another for breach of an international obligation (Crawford *et al.* 2010). As such, the rules of international responsibility do not set forth any particular obligations but rather determine when an obligation has been breached and the legal consequences of that violation. The rules are, as such, 'secondary' that address the basic issues of responsibility and the remedies that are available for breach of 'primary' or substantive rules of international law. They establish the conditions for an act to qualify as internationally wrongful, the circumstances under which actions of officials and other actors may be attributed to the state or the international organization, general defences to liability and the consequences of liability.

Due to the historical primacy of states in the international legal system, the law of state responsibility is the most evolved structure of international responsibility. The Articles on the Responsibility of States of Internationally Wrongful Acts (ARSIWA) were adopted by the International Law Commission in 2001 (ILC Report 2001). However, after a ten-year process, the ILC adopted its long-awaited Articles on the Responsibility of International Organizations in the summer of 2011 (ILC Report 2011). As with the law of state responsibility, the ARIO is premised on the idea that '[e]very internationally wrongful act…entails…international responsibility' (ARIO, Article 3). The elements of an internationally wrongful act of an international organization are consistent with those of a state, i.e. attribution to an international organization under international law, and a breach of an international obligation of that international organization (ARIO, Article 4).

The ILC's efforts to develop the ARIO have been far from straightforward. Many important international organizations, UNHCR included, appear to have disassociated themselves completely from the ILC's work on the responsibility of international organizations by failing to seize the opportunity to respond to the ILC's invitation for comments on the ARIO during the process. The ARIO have been the subject of critical commentary by states, international organizations and scholars alike (Boon 2011; d'Aspremont and Ahlborn 2011; von Bogdandy and Platise 2012). The primary criticisms have concerned the general lack of practice to support the contents of the ARIO rules and the ARIO's resemblance to the ILC's ARSIWA. In contrast to the ARSIWA, which referred to existing rules and largely codified customary international law, the ARIO were drafted without extensive practice from which to draw. This situation is, in large part, due to the previously mentioned privileges and immunities, where international organizations enjoy generous grants of immunity both as institutions and for their individual agents. There are consequently few cases where principles of responsibility have been invoked before any national or international courts (Reinisch 2008). As a result, whereas the ARIO codify several principles of responsibility that are considered customary international law (ILA 2004, p. 254), the Articles propose a number of more novel principles. The ILC also recognizes the following in its Commentary: '...[t]he fact that several of the present draft articles are based on limited practice moves the border between codification and progressive development in the direction of the latter' (ILC 2011, para. 5).

In December 2011, the UN General Assembly annexed the ARIO to Resolution 66/100, in which it welcomed the conclusion of the ILC's work in this regard and its adoption of the ARIO and a detailed commentary on the subject. The final form that the ARIO might be given was scheduled to be examined by the General Assembly in 2014; however, it was considered to be premature and was, therefore, *de facto* postponed to the 72nd Session of the General Assembly in 2017.[1] As I will highlight in this chapter, several critical aspects of the ARIO's application to UNHCR merit a strengthened engagement on the part of UNHCR in this process.

Applying the Articles on the Responsibility of International Organizations to UNHCR

International responsibility is generally triggered following the decision that a breach of international law has occurred (Crawford and Watkins 2010, p. 284). Under the ARIO, an international organization is responsible for an internationally wrongful act when conduct consisting of an action or omission is *attributable* to the organization and constitutes a *breach of an international obligation* (ARIO, Article 4).

Before discussing attribution of conduct, I will consider what constitutes a breach of an international obligation in the specific case of UNHCR.

Breach of an international obligation

UNHCR as a bearer of international obligations

One of two elements of an internationally wrongful act of an international organization is that it constitutes a breach of an international obligation of that international organization. Under the ARIO, such a breach occurs 'when an act of that international organization is not in conformity with what is required of it by that obligation, regardless of the origin or character of the obligation concerned' (ARIO, Article 10 (1)). An international obligation, then, may arise under the rules of the international organization, and under treaties, customary international law or general principles of international law (ILC 2011, p. 31). This understanding is also reflected in the view of the ICJ in its advisory opinion in the *Interpretation of Agreement of March 1951 between the WHO and Egypt* (1980) case, in which it explains the following: '[i]nternational organizations are subjects of international law, and, *as such*, are bound by any obligations incumbent upon them *under general rules of international law*, under their constitutions or under international agreements to which they are parties' (italics added). This perspective essentially means that the international obligations of UNHCR may derive from treaty or customary international law, as well as from the 'rules of the organization', and these obligations determine what a breach of international law is under the law of international responsibility.

Obligations under customary and treaty law

The most basic norms of international humanitarian and international human rights law are today considered part of international customary law (Clapham 2006, pp. 85–87), and there has been an increasing recognition that such law binds not only states but also, by virtue of their legal personality, international organizations (Akande 2010; Klabbers 2009, pp. 39–44; McBeth 2009, p. 1105). Additional provisions may be found in the specific legal conventions pertaining to human rights and refugees; however, the majority of these treaties contain no provision for the accession of international organizations. UNHCR, as part of the UN, is furthermore bound to the UN Charter, which lays the basis for the obligation of the UN to respect human rights. This general obligation arises under a combination of Article 1 of the UN Charter, which *inter alia* obliges the UN to promote and encourage 'respect for human rights and for fundamental freedoms', and Article 2, which obliges the UN to act in accordance with certain principles 'in pursuit of the purposes stated in Article 1'. Although it is undisputed that a legal obligation to observe human rights on the part of the UN, and through this, also on UNHCR, exists, it is less clear exactly what human rights are encompassed within the obligation (Janmyr 2014a, p. 237f). The UN Charter does not readily provide a definition of what is meant by 'human rights and fundamental freedoms'.

Obligations under the 'rules of the international organization'

One of the thorniest issues arising from the ARIO's understanding of international obligations is the concept of the 'rules of the international organization', which include the 'constituent instruments, decisions, resolutions and other acts of the international organization adopted in accordance with those instruments, and established practice of the organization' (ARIO, Article 2 (b)). The ILC's commentary sheds light on the debate in relation to the nature of the rules of an international organization, in which several argue that all of the rules form part of the international law, whereas others hold the contrary view, meaning that they merely form the internal law of the organization (ILC 2011, pp. 32–33). A convincing argument is, nevertheless, that certain rules of an international organization fall within international law, whereas others, predominately those of an administrative character, are excluded from forming part of international law. This argument appears to correspond well with the view of the ICJ in the *Reparation for Injuries* case, where it found that the '...rights and duties [of the organization] will depend upon its purposes and functions as specified or implied in its constituent documents and functions in practice'. While deciding on the nature of the rules of an international organization is decisive in determining which obligations the organization is bound by with regard to international responsibility, the ILC concedes that the nature of the rules of an international organization should be decided on a case-by-case basis (ILC 2009, p. 15).

The rules of the organization are nevertheless an important source of human rights obligations for UNHCR. Consistent with the ARIO, the rules of UNHCR may thus be the UNHCR Statute, which sets out the objectives and functions of UNHCR; several decisions and resolutions of the UNHCR, UN General Assembly and the UN Security Council and other acts of UNHCR as adopted in accordance with its instruments; and the established practice of UNHCR (Janmyr 2014a, p. 244ff; see also Kinchin in this volume). Constituent instruments, such as the UNHCR Statute, are generally considered to be of a dual nature; on the one hand, they are international treaties or contracts between the states, governed by the law of treaties, whereas, on the other hand, they are of a constitutional character and are, as such, best governed by institutional law (Ahlborn 2011; Chinkin 1993, pp. 94–96). There is today a general acceptance that an international organization is bound by obligations arising under its constituent instrument. That said, with regard to UNHCR, it appears reasonable to generally regard the complete set of rules pertaining to UNHCR's commitments in relation to the protection of individuals under its mandate as obligations under international law.

UNHCR's mandate, found in the UNHCR Statute, provides it with broader human rights obligations than the obligation to respect customary human rights law. It evidences that UNHCR has been granted a unique role by the international community; it is specifically mandated to provide 'international protection' to refugees and seek 'permanent solutions for the problem of refugees'. Paragraph 1 of the Statute stipulates the following:

> The United Nations High Commissioner for Refugees, acting under the authority of the General Assembly, shall assume the function of providing international protection, under the auspices of the United Nations, to refugees who fall within the scope of the present Statute and of seeking permanent solutions for the problem of refugees by assisting Governments and, subject to the approval of the Governments concerned, private organizations to facilitate the voluntary repatriation of such refugees, or their assimilation within new national communities.

UNHCR's mandate of international protection

The function of international protection lies at the heart of UNHCR's mandate and its content should be regarded as *sui generis* (Schnyder 1965, p. 423) The Statute arguably binds UNHCR to provide international protection not only in a passive sense but also actively, for instance, by intervening vis-à-vis governments. As former High Commissioner Schnyder explained in 1965: '...international protection may be defined as the power, conferred by the international community to an international body, to take all necessary measures to replace the national protection of which refugees are deprived, because of their very condition' (Schnyder 1965, p. 423). As such, international protection, to a large extent, seems to be based on the notion of *surrogacy* in which UNHCR steps in to provide the protection that a refugee's own state cannot or will not provide (Goodwin-Gill and McAdam 2007, p. 10). Importantly, a link seems to exist between UNHCR's international protection mandate and human rights. The Preamble to the 1951 Refugee Convention aptly summarizes the grand objective of international protection as follows: '...to assure refugees the widest possible exercise of...fundamental rights and freedoms', which all 'human beings [should] enjoy...without discrimination'.

Paragraph 8 of the Statute details the mandatory functions of UNHCR with regard to its international protection mandate as follows:

> 8. The High Commissioner shall provide for the protection of refugees falling under the competence of his Office by:
> a Promoting the conclusion and ratification of international conventions for the protection of refugees, supervising their application and proposing amendments thereto;
> b Promoting through special agreements with Governments the execution of any measures calculated to improve the situation of refugees and to reduce the number requiring protection;
> c Assisting governmental and private efforts to promote voluntary repatriation or assimilation within new national communities;

d Promoting the admission of refugees, not excluding those in the most destitute categories, to the territories of states;

e Endeavouring to obtain permission for refugees to transfer their assets and especially those necessary for their resettlement;

f Obtaining from Governments information concerning the number and conditions of refugees in their territories and the laws and regulations concerning them;

g Keeping in close touch with the Governments and inter-governmental organizations concerned;

h Establishing contact in such manner as he may think best with private organizations dealing with refugee questions;

i Facilitating the co-ordination of the efforts of private organizations concerned with the welfare of refugees.

Although it has never been clear whether this list was meant to be exhaustive or simply exemplary of what UNHCR might do to provide protection, the consistent interpretation of UNHCR has been that it is not meant to be exhaustive (Holborn 1975, p. 98; Weis 1968, p. 248).

UNHCR, rather than having a straightforward statement of its responsibilities, in addition to these express obligations, is also bound by a number of implied duties (Türk 2007, pp. 479–480; Klabbers 2009, p. 74; ILC 2003, para. 11). UNHCR's institutional practice illuminates the extent of these implied terms and is, therefore, imperative for any interpretation of UNHCR's Statute and the extent of UNHCR's rules (Janmyr 2014a, p. 248ff). This established practice is, thus, to be considered as 'rules of the organization' as understood in the ARIO. UNHCR's practice suggests that the power it *de facto* exercises often goes beyond the terms of its mandate, as explicitly specified in the Statute. The basis for this practice exists in UNHCR's informal normative framework, i.e. its policy statements, internal guidelines and operational codes. More explicitly, its institutional practice can be based on three different levels: the first level concerns the practice of the organization's political organ, that is, statements, conclusions and other material stemming from the Executive Committee; the second level concerns the practice of upper bureaucratic levels, such as statements made by the division heads or country representatives, UNHCR press releases and public statements; and, finally, the third level concerns UNHCR's actual conduct.

Attribution

Basic principle of organs and agents

The other element of an internationally wrongful act of an international organization is attribution to the international organization under international law. Although institutional and judicial practices seem far from consolidated in the area of attribution, there appears to be general agreement that third parties dealing with international organizations should be protected from harm in their relationship with international organizations. The ARIO predominantly envisions that international organizations be held responsible for unlawful conduct against other international organizations or states. As I will explain later in this chapter, the ARIO does not create a judicial forum for individuals to sue international organizations although it is UNHCR's beneficiaries, refugees and internally displaced persons who are at the heart of UNHCR's international law mandate.

In the *Cumaraswamy* advisory opinion, the ICJ notably stated that the UN 'may be required to bear responsibility for the damage…incurred as a result of acts performed by the United Nations or by its agents acting in their official capacity'. Article 6 (1) of the ARIO, therefore, reflects the basic principle of the attribution to an international organization of acts of its *organs* and *agents* in the following:

> The conduct of an organ or agent of an international organization in the performance of functions of that organ or agent shall be considered an act of that organization under international law, whatever position the organ or agent holds in respect of the organization.

The term 'organ' is defined in Article 2 (c) of the ARIO as 'any person or entity which has that status in accordance with the rules of the organization', whereas 'agent' is defined in Article 2 (d) as '…an official or other person or entity, other than an organ, who is charged by the organization with carrying out, or helping to carry out, one of its functions, and thus through whom the organization acts'. In both cases, the '[r]ules of the organization apply in the determination of the functions of its organs and agents' (ARIO, Article 6 (2)). These 'rules of the organization' are understood in the ARIO as 'in particular, the constituent instruments, decisions, resolutions and other acts of the organisation adopted in accordance with those instruments and established practice of the organisation'. That UNHCR staff are to be considered 'agents' for the purposes of ARIO is, thus, hardly controversial; however, the question of whether UNHCR's NGO implementing partners should be considered UNHCR 'agents' is more intricate.

When subcontractors act wrongfully: implementing partners as UNHCR agents

In fulfilling its mandate, UNHCR relies, to a large extent, on 'partnerships' with a wide spectrum of actors (UNHCR 2007). In 2013, for example, UNHCR collaborated with 733 NGOs worldwide. Many of these NGOs are present in refugee camps where they are typically hired by UNHCR to manage the camp and provide for the necessary food, health facilities, water/sanitation, schools, security and other essential services (Olsen and Scharffscher 2004, p. 387). UNHCR, for its part, negotiates conditions with government authorities, approves the campsite and functions as a supervisor or performance evaluator. Although it is often referred to as a 'partnership', the relationship between UNHCR and the NGO implementing partners has been described as essentially an 'unequal, contractor and service-provider relationship' (Kamiya 2007, p. 5). The increasing delegation of authority often produces a number of human rights concerns—indeed, the behaviour of UNHCR personnel and implementing partners hit the headlines in the early 2000s when a widely publicized scandal, concerning a 'chronic and entrenched pattern' of abuse in refugee camps, unfolded in Guinea, Liberia and Sierra Leone (Janmyr 2014b). In these situations, would UNHCR be responsible for the conduct of these NGO implementing partners? Although the typical contract between UNHCR and the NGO proposes to the contrary, an application of ARIO suggests otherwise.

Deriving from its mandate as expressed in the UNHCR Statute (Articles 10 and 12), UNHCR possesses a competence to delegate certain functions to its non-governmental implementing partners (Janmyr 2014b). UNHCR's relationship with its implementing partners is more concretely outlined in specific project agreements, such as a 'tripartite agreement' between UNHCR, the refugee-hosting government and an implementing partner, or a very similar 'bipartite agreement' between either UNHCR and the implementing partner or UNHCR and the host government. Many of these agreements include clauses stipulating that the NGO will not be considered an agent or staff member of the organization. UNHCR's model 'Tripartite Sub-Project Agreement', for instance, specifically stipulates that the implementing Agency shall be fully responsible for all of the services performed by the Agency personnel and that such personnel '*shall not be considered in any respect*' UNHCR staff members or have any other contractual link with the Office.

It nevertheless appears as though such implementing partners lie at the very core of ARIO's understanding of the term 'agent'. In drafting its definition, the ILC relied on certain statements of the ICJ, including those made in the *Reparation for Injuries Suffered in the Service of the United Nations* Advisory Opinion (1949), where the ICJ stated that the term 'agent' must be understood as follows:

> in the most liberal sense, that is to say, any person who, whether a paid official or not, and whether permanently employed or not, has been charged by an organ of the organisation with carrying out, or helping to carry out, one of its functions – in short, any person through whom it acts.

As later stated by the ICJ in its Advisory Opinion on the *Applicability of Article VI of the Convention on the Privileges and Immunities of the United Nations* (1989), the essence of the matter lies not in the agent's administrative position 'but in the nature of their mission'. The Special Rapporteur subsequently asserted the following:

> In order to establish attribution when an international organization acts through a person or entity that is not an organ…the decisive factor appears to be whether or not the person or entity has been charged by an organ of the international organization with carrying out, or helping to carry out, one of the functions of that organization. (ILC 2009)

The functions of interest here are those of the UNHCR, and these are *inter alia* set out in UNHCR Statute and were described earlier in this chapter. What is important is that through the specific sub-contracting agreements, NGOs are *charged* by

UNHCR to perform specific *functions*. It seems that these NGOs execute one or more functions of UNHCR, especially with regard to UNHCR's international protection mandate (Janmyr 2014b).

Regarding the common practice of including clauses in contracts between international organizations and private sub-contractors stipulating that the sub-contractor not be considered an agent or staff member of the organization, the Special Rapporteur has highlighted that this does not dispose of the question of attribution under international law (ILC 2009, para. 23). Specifically, 'this type of clause cannot exclude the possibility that, because of factual circumstances, the conduct of the private contractor would nevertheless be attributed to the organization under international law' (ILC 2009, para. 23). If one accepts this view, it would appear that under the ARIO, contractual clauses, such as those laid out in UNHCR's sub-contracting agreements, should not result in any legal effect in the international legal order.

State organs placed at the disposal of UNHCR

If, however, the persons or entities through whom the organization acts are organs of a state and are placed at the disposal of the international organization, then Article 7 applies. This would be the case when government agencies act as UNHCR implementing partners. Article 7 reads as follows:

> The conduct of an organ of a State or an organ or agent of an international organization that is placed at the disposal of another international organization shall be considered under international law an act of the latter organization if the organization exercises effective control over that conduct.

In this regard, the ARIO adopts the test of effective control to determine attribution of conduct (ILC 2004, para. 40). That said, effective control according to the ILC does not necessarily mean exclusive control, and the ARIO seem to provide for the likelihood of multiple attribution, which I will discuss later in this chapter.

Conduct exceeding or contravening instructions

Article 8 deals with the attribution to an international organization when the conduct of an agent of the international organization is *ultra vires*. The conduct of an agent of an international organization is *ultra vires* if it exceeds authority or contravenes instructions (ILC 2011, p. 26). Such conduct will only be attributed to the international organization if it occurs in an official capacity and within the overall functions of the international organizations. Article 8 specifies the following:

> The conduct of an organ or agent of an international organization shall be considered an act of that organization under international law if the organ or *agent acts in an official capacity and within the overall functions of that organization, even if the conduct exceeds the authority of that organ or agent or contravenes instructions.* (italics added)

The likelihood of attributing to an international organization acts that an organ takes *ultra vires* has, perhaps most famously, been acknowledged by the ICJ in its 1962 advisory opinion on *Certain Expenses of the United Nations*.[2] The 'rules of the organization' furthermore determine whether an act is in an official capacity and within the overall functions of the international organization. If a staff member of UNHCR or a UNHCR implementing partner, for instance, exploits refugees by demanding sexual favours in return for material assistance (UN Secretary-General 2002), this situation would seemingly be covered by Article 8 because the individual is acting in an official capacity and within the overall functions of UNHCR, although exceeding authority or contravening instructions. If, however, the staff member uses a vehicle owned by the organization to drive to a private party and gets into an accident on the way, then this situation would not be covered by Article 8 because the staff member is not acting in an official capacity or within the overall functions of UNHCR.

Whenever a conduct breaches both a rule of the organization that possesses an international law character and another rule of international law, Verdirame (2011, p. 125) has argued, *ultra vires* conduct can result in two separate internationally wrongful acts. Human rights violations would typically include a breach of both of these types of rules. This point is well illustrated by Verdirame's critique of encampment. He argues that this policy constituted a systematic breach of human rights law, primarily since it arbitrarily deprived individuals of their freedom of movement. Such a breach can hardly be considered to fall within the legal powers of UNHCR and would thus, in itself, constitute a violation of both the rules of the organization and of UNHCR's human rights obligations (Verdirame 2011, p. 232).

Attributing conduct to several actors

Several independent actors may have been involved occasionally in a certain wrongful conduct and it would, therefore, appear commonsensical to attribute this conduct to more than one of these actors. Traditionally, however, the international law of responsibility has been dominated by an approach based on the idea of the 'independent' responsibility of states, where the state alone is responsible for its own conduct and its own wrongdoings. In this approach, such responsibility is exclusive in that an act is generally only attributed to one actor at a time (Nollkaemper and Jacobs 2011, p. 10). The likelihood of international responsibilities being shared among multiple actors who contribute to injury has nevertheless increasingly been discussed in various international law forums (Dominicé 2010, p. 281). Although the ARIO and the ARSIWA both emphasize the exceptional nature of questions of sharing (ARSIWA, Articles 1 and 2; ARIO Article 19), the ILC has notably recognized that two separate acts, attributable to different actors, can result in a single injury (ILC 2009, commentary to Article 6). Indeed, the responsibility of one state or international organization does not preclude the responsibility of another state or organization with regard to a particular instance where damage is caused to a third actor. This situation is specifically recognized in Article 47 of the ARSIWA, which provides that if two states are responsible for the same wrongful act, each state can be held responsible. In relation to the ARIO, the UN Special Rapporteur has similarly explained the matter as follows:

> Although it may not frequently occur in practice, dual or even multiple attribution of conduct cannot be excluded. Thus, attribution of a certain conduct to an international organization does not imply that the same conduct cannot be attributed to a state, nor does vice versa attribution of conduct to a state rule out attribution of the same conduct to an international organization. One could also envisage conduct being simultaneously attributed to two or more international organizations, for instance when they establish a joint organ and act through that organ. (ILC 2004, p. 101)

Although a plurality of responsible actors has not been regularly demonstrated in practice, the recent *Nuhanovic* case (2011) in the Netherlands, nevertheless, demonstrated that situations producing multiple attribution of conduct are conceivable.

With regard to UNHCR operations, the most likely scenarios would involve attribution to UNHCR and the host state. However, it is not inconceivable that attribution of conduct also would be apportioned to UNHCR and the UN at large and UN (HCR) member states. The fact that UNHCR can be considered to be an independent international organization, autonomous from the UN and in control of its own operations, does not necessarily mean that the UN is absolved of its responsibility in the event of a wrongful act (Janmyr 2014a, p. 300f). Rather, the nature of the UN's relationship with the operational programmes would normally entail that the UN bear at least some responsibility for any UNHCR activity (Verdirame 2011, p. 17).

Due to UNHCR's legal personality, UNHCR's member states cannot generally be held accountable for its conduct (cf. ARIO, Article 62; Lauterpacht 1976, p. 407). There are, however, exceptions to this general rule. The ARIO seems to accept that the responsibility of an organization neither excludes responsibility of one or more member states nor does it exclude the responsibility of any international organization in which the international organization might be a member. Article 62 of the ARIO, for example, indicates the following:

> A State member of an international organization is responsible for an internationally wrongful act of that organization if:
> a it has accepted responsibility for that act towards the injured party; or
> b it has led the injured party to rely on its responsibility.

Member states may also incur responsibility through the other instances of *derivative responsibility* mentioned in the ARIO (complicity, direction and control, coercion and responsibility to seek to avoid compliance). Although the majority of the acts addressed by international organizations to states are non-binding, derivative responsibility may be engaged in cases where, for instance, UNHCR rejects a well-founded claim for refugee status followed by the applicant's deportation in breach of the principle of *non-refoulement* (Verdirame 2011, p. 128). The member state, in particular, incurs responsibility if it has accepted responsibility for a particular act or when the member state has 'led the injured party to rely on its responsibility' (ARIO, Article 62 (1) (a) and (b)). Such a situation may occur, for example in *D v. Turkey* (2006), where the European Court of Human Rights criticized UNHCR's rejection of an Iranian couple's refugee application in a case against Turkey, where the Turkish government had relied on UNHCR.

Defences for violations of international law: several examples

Attribution of conduct does not always entail an engagement of responsibility. The international law of responsibility has developed a system of 'defences' for violations of the law, known as circumstances precluding wrongfulness. Accordingly, if a defence is successfully relied on by UNHCR, the conduct in question is no longer wrongful in character. Articles 20–27 of the ARIO, containing defences of consent, self-defence, *force majeure*, distress, necessity and compliance with peremptory norms, draw largely on the corresponding articles on state responsibility. Perhaps the most frequently invoked defence with regard to international organizations is *force majeure*, which relates to the 'occurrence of an irresistible force or an unforeseeable event, beyond the control of the organization' (ARIO, Article 23). The Special Rapporteur has acknowledged that financial distress might, in certain circumstances, amount to *force majeure* in the following:

> Financial distress might constitute an instance of *force majeure* that the organization concerned could invoke in order to exclude wrongfulness of its failure to comply with an international obligation. The fact that the situation of *force majeure* may be due to the conduct of the organization's member states would not prevent the organization, as a separate entity, from availing itself of that situation. Noncompliance by the organization would raise the question... whether member states incur responsibility. (ILC 2006, para. 31)

It can generally be argued that the threshold for a successful invocation of *force majeure* with regard to an organization, such as UNHCR, should be higher due to the nature of UNHCR's work in emergencies and in the context of other unforeseen events.

Limitations and potentials of UNHCR accountability through the law of international responsibility

The previous sections have made it clear that one avenue for UNHCR accountability could be pursued under the ARIO framework. This finding essentially leaves us with two obvious questions: First, what are the practical limitations and potentials of applying the ARIO to UNHCR activities, i.e. how enforceable is this framework in reality? Second, is an application of the ARIO as a form for UNHCR accountability really desirable from the perspective of refugee protection? If so, under what circumstances?

Whatever form the ARIO eventually takes when it is examined by the UN General Assembly in 2017, it is conspicuously clear that there will be a number of practical hurdles when it comes to advancing UNHCR accountability through the law of international responsibility. Clearly most disturbing, the ARIO leave the victims of human rights violations largely overlooked in more ways than one. The ARIO do not create a judicial forum for individuals to sue international organizations; the scope of Part III of the ARIO, which deals with the content of international organizations' international responsibility, such as a duty of reparation for injury, is limited to obligations toward the states or other international organizations. Thus, only the states and international organizations have the right of invocation under ARIO, Article 43. In this regard, persons or other entities are not able to obtain remedies under this framework, i.e. the ARIO alone cannot be directly relied on when determining the remedies arising from breaches of human rights obligations owed by international organizations to individuals.

Under Article 33, individuals may nevertheless still be owed remedies by international organizations. Article 33 sets out a 'without prejudice' clause concerning any right, arising from the international responsibility of an international organization, which may accrue directly to a person or an entity other than a state or an international organization. This clause is identical to Article 33 of the ARSIWA. However, as von Bogdandy and Platise (2012) have indicated, the effects of this clause as played out in practice differ considerably between the states and international organizations. Numerous treaty regimes exist that provide special regimes of human rights protection and their enforcement and to which states are parties. Article 33 of the ARSIWA simply refers individuals to these regimes.

Regarding international organizations, no comparable protection exists, and Article 33 thus leaves individuals without any remedy for breaches of their rights by international organizations. This point is clearly aggravated by the fact that the ARIO do not consider the likelihood for individuals to seek remedies against international organizations before national courts, nor do they establish a scheme to work around the extensive privileges and immunities of international organizations. Recent cases and academic commentary demonstrated a 'nibbling away' at the edges of UN immunity (Freedman 2014), and this is indeed one of the most important issues to which the UN General Assembly will need to address in 2017.

Human rights violations by UNHCR may still be placed under the regime of diplomatic protection. In theory, individuals can generally bring their claims to international courts against international persons through their states (or other international organizations) representing them by way of diplomatic protection. In practice, however, the states (and international organizations) will generally have little incentive to become active. Such complaints come at a high political cost and have been considered to be one of the most drastic and confrontational legal measures (Leckie 1988, p. 259). In refugee situations, the individual concerned will generally not be a national of the state of residence and his/her home state will presumably not be interested in protection. These types of complaints also obligate the state or the international organization to do all the fact-finding itself to present a strong case, which will furthermore limit the usage of this regime.

From the perspective of refugee protection, an undesired outcome of applying the ARIO to UNHCR might be that UNHCR withdraws from several operations or chooses not to engage in situations with particularly challenging protection tasks. The ARIO may, as such, indirectly have the unintended consequence of limiting the capacity of UNHCR to discharge its mandate. One way to come to terms with such a situation may be, as I have proposed elsewhere, that any evaluation of UNHCR's international responsibility, at least in refugee camp situations, entails a concomitant evaluation of the host state's *willingness* and *ability* to provide refugee protection (Janmyr 2014a). Although this framework remains yet cursory, it might *de facto* limit the situations where UNHCR would be responsible, in addition to the earlier described circumstances precluding wrongfulness in the ARIO. Many of the ARIO's unintended consequences on the operations of UNHCR may be highlighted and discussed before the General Assembly's decision on what form the Articles shall take. The UN Secretary-General is currently compiling comments on the ARIO from both governments and international organizations, providing an ample opportunity for UNHCR to join the conversation on international responsibility and convey observations and opinions specific to UNHCR operations.

Concluding remarks

Notwithstanding severe constraints—of which the unlikelihood of individuals themselves to sue international organizations within the scope of the ARIO is surely the gravest—the development with regard to the responsibility of international organizations must be observed as a step in the right direction in the broader movement of accountability. As noted by Clarke (2014, p. 143), the ARIO 'are apt to become the leading source determining the responsibility of international organizations under international law'. The effects of the ARIO on the practice of UNHCR and other international organizations should therefore not be immediately dismissed. Indeed, early drafts of the ARIO were invoked by the European Court of Human Rights (ECtHR) in the controversial *Behrami* v. *France* case (2007), in which the ECtHR found that the acts of KFOR troops in Kosovo were attributable to the United Nations and not the troop-contributing states. More recently, the ARIO have also been explicitly drawn on in the *Nuhanovic* (2011) and *Mothers of Srebrenica* (2014) cases in the Netherlands.

One of the most welcome impacts of the ARIO on the practice of UNHCR may be with regard to UNHCR's management of its implementing partners. As I have previously explained, UNHCR has been repeatedly criticized for its failure to come to terms with flaws in the implementing arrangements (Janmyr 2014b). The solution provided by the ARIO highlights the importance of regulating the conduct of UNHCR's implementing partners more closely and establishing procedural guidelines for the follow-up of cases of misconduct and the repercussions to follow if the implementing partner commits or is alleged to have committed an act that constitutes an internationally wrongful act. It is expected that UNHCR improves procedures in the selection and administration of its NGO implementing partners.

In summary, this chapter has explored the rules of responsibility under international law in relation to international organizations as a framework to enhance UNHCR accountability. An application of the International Law Commission's Articles on the Responsibility of International Organizations would entail UNHCR being responsible for an internationally wrongful act when conduct consisting of an action or omission is attributable to the organization and which constitutes a breach of an international obligation. UNHCR's international obligations may derive from treaty or customary international law, as well as from the 'rules of the organization', meaning UNHCR's Statute; several decisions and resolutions of the UNHCR, UN General Assembly and the UN Security Council; other acts of UNHCR as adopted in accordance with its instruments; and the established practice of UNHCR. This chapter has also argued that the conduct of UNHCR's NGO implementing partners may be attributed to the organization and that a certain conduct may even be attributed to several actors at the same time. It considered the ARIO's circumstances precluding wrongfulness, which provide that attribution of conduct does not always entail an engagement of responsibility. Finally, this chapter presented several of the most obvious shortcomings of applying the ARIO to UNHCR, including the lack of remedies for victims of human rights violations, and suggested how several of these shortcomings might be overcome.

Notes

1 Without a vote, the General Assembly adopted Resolution 69/126 on the Responsibility of International Organizations, requesting the Secretary-General to prepare before the 72nd Session an initial compilation of decisions of international courts, tribunals and other bodies referring to the Articles and to invite governments and international organizations to submit information on their practice in this regard, as well as written comments on any future action regarding the articles.
2 As the ICJ noted in paragraph 168: 'If it is agreed that the action in question is within the scope of the functions of the Organization but it is alleged that it has been initiated or carried out in a manner not in conformity with the division of functions among the several organs which the Charter prescribes, one moves to the internal plane, to the internal structure of the Organization. If the action was taken by the wrong organ, it was irregular as a matter of that internal structure, but this would not necessarily mean that the expense incurred was not an expense of the Organization. Both national and international law contemplate cases in which the body corporate or politic may be bound, as to third parties, by an *ultra vires* act of an agent'.

References

Ahlborn, C. (2011) 'The rules of international organizations and the law of international responsibility', ACIL Research Paper No. 4.
Akande, D. (2010) 'International organizations', in M. Evans (ed.), *International Law*, pp. 252–283. Oxford: Oxford University Press.

Boon, K. (2011) 'New directions in responsibility: assessing the International Law Commission's Draft Articles on the Responsibility of International Organizations', *Yale Journal of International Law Online*, 37: 1–10.

Chinkin, C. (1993) *Third Parties in International Law*. Oxford: Clarendon Press.

Clapham, A. (2006) *Human Rights Obligations of Non–State Actors*. Oxford: Oxford University Press.

Clarke, L. (2014) *Public-Private Partnerships and Responsibility under International Law: A Global Health Perspective*. New York: Routledge.

Crawford, J. and J. Watkins. (2010) 'International responsibility', in S. Besson and J. Tasioulas, *The Philosophy of International Law*, pp. 283–298. Oxford: Oxford University Press.

Crawford, J., A. Pellet, S. Olleson and K. Palett (eds.). (2010) *The Law of International Responsibility*. Oxford: Oxford University Press.

d'Aspremont, J. and C. Ahlborn. (2011) 'The International Law Commission embarks on the second reading of Draft Articles on the Responsibility of International Organizations', *EJIL Talk*, May 16.

Dominicé, C. (2010) 'Attribution of conduct to multiple states and the implication of a state in the act of another state in the law of international responsibility', in J. Crawford, A. Pellet, S. Olleson and K. Palett (eds.), *The Law of International Responsibility*, pp. 281–291. Oxford: Oxford University Press.

Durieux, J.-F. (2000) 'Preserving the civilian character of refugee camps: lessons learned from the Kigoma programme in Tanzania', *Track Two*, 9(3): 25–35.

Freedman, R. (2014) 'UN immunity or impunity? A human rights based challenge', *European Journal of International Law*, 25(1): 239–254.

Goodwin-Gill, G. and J. McAdam. (2007) *The Refugee in International Law*. Oxford: Oxford University Press.

Holborn, L. (1975) *Refugees: A Problem of Our Time: The Work of the United Nations High Commissioner for Refugees 1951–1972*, Vol. 1. Metuchen, NJ: Scarecrow Press.

International Law Association. (2004) 'Berlin conference (2004): accountability of international organizations', *International Organizations Law Review*, 1: 221–293.

International Law Commission. (2001) 'Report on the work of its fifty-third session (23 April–1 June and 2 July–10 August 2001)', UN Doc. A/56/10.

International Law Commission. (2003) 'First report on responsibility of international organisations (prepared by G. Gaja, Special Rapporteur)', UN Doc. no. A/CN.4/532.

International Law Commission. (2004) 'Second report on responsibility of international organisations (prepared by G. Gaja, Special Rapporteur)', UN Doc. no. A/CN.4/541.

International Law Commission. (2006) 'Fourth report on responsibility of international organisations (prepared by G. Gaja, Special Rapporteur)', UN Doc. no. A/CN.4/564.

International Law Commission. (2009) 'Seventh report on responsibility of international organisations (prepared by G. Gaja, Special Rapporteur)', UN Doc. A/CN.4/610.

International Law Commission. (2011) 'Report on the work of its sixty-third session (26 April–3 June and 4 July–12 August 2011)', UN Doc. A/66/10.

Janmyr, M. (2014a) *Protecting Civilians in Refugee Camps: Unwilling and Unable States, UNHCR and International Responsibility*. Leiden: Brill.

Janmyr, M. (2014b) 'Attributing wrongful conduct of implementing partners to UNHCR: international responsibility and human rights violations in refugee camps', *Journal of International Humanitarian Legal Studies*, 5(1–2): 1–28.

Kamiya, M. (2007) 'A study of formal relationships between civil society and multilateral bodies: accreditation and other consultative modalities', Paper presented at the conference 'Building Bridges III: Engaging Civil Society from Muslim States and Communities with the Multilateral Sphere', Dhaka, October 27–28.

Klabbers, J. (2009) *An Introduction to International Institutional Law*. Cambridge: Cambridge University Press.

Lauterpacht, E. (1976) *The Development of the Law of International Decisions of International Tribunals*. Alphen aan den Rijn: Sijthoff & Noordhoff.

Leckie, S. (1988) 'The inter-state complaint procedure in international law: hopeful prospects of wishful thinking', *Human Rights Quarterly*, 10(2): 249–303.

McBeth, A. (2009) 'A right by any other name: the evasive engagement of international financial institutions with human rights', *George Washington International Law Review*, 40(4): 1101–1156.

Nollkaemper, A. and D. Jacobs. (2011) 'Shared responsibility in international law: a concept paper', Amsterdam Law School Legal Studies Research Paper No. 17.

Olsen, O. E. and K. Scharffscher. (2004) 'Rape in refugee camps as organisational failures', *International Journal of Human Rights*, 8(4): 377–397.

Reinisch, A. (2005) 'Accountability of international organizations according to national law', *Netherlands Yearbook of International Law*, 36(1): 119.

Reinisch, A. (2008) 'The immunity of international organizations and the jurisdiction of their administrative tribunals', *Chinese Journal of International Law*, 7(2): 285–306.

Schnyder, F. (1965) *Les Aspects Juridiques Actuels du Problem des Réfugiés*. Leiden: Académie de droit international.

Slaughter, A. and J. Crisp. (2009) 'A surrogate state? The role of UNHCR in protracted refugee situations', UNHCR New Issues in Refugee Research, no. 168.

Türk, V. (2007) 'Freedom from fear: refugees, the broader displacement context and the underlying international protection regime', in V. Chetail (ed.), *Globalization, Migration and Human Rights: International Law under Review*, Vol. 1, pp. 475–522. Brussels: Collection of the Geneva Academy of International Humanitarian Law and Human Rights.

UN Secretary-General. (2002) 'Investigation into sexual exploitation of refugees by aid workers in West Africa: note by the Secretary-General', UN Doc. A/57/465.

UNHCR. (1950) *Statute of the United Nations High Commissioner for Refugees*. Adopted by the UN General Assembly in Res. 428 (V), December 14.

UNHCR. (2007) 'NGO partnerships in refugee protection, questions & answers', Doc. No. UNHCR/ DERNGO/ Q&AA5 / ENG 3.

Verdirame, G. (2011) *The UN and Human Rights: Who Guards the Guardians?* Cambridge: Cambridge University Press.

von Bogdandy, A., and M. Platise. (2012) 'ARIO and human rights protection: leaving the individual in the cold', *International Organizations Law Review*, 9(1): 67–76.

Weis, P. (1968) 'The Office of the United Nations High Commissioner for refugees and human rights', *Les Droits de l'Homme: Revue de Droits de l'Homme*, 1(2): 243–254.

4 Narratives of accountability in UNHCR's refugee resettlement strategy

Adèle Garnier

Introduction

Adopting an institutionalist approach, this chapter investigates the narrative of accountability in the United Nations High Commissioner for Refugees (UNHCR) resettlement strategy and the diffusion of this narrative in Australia's humanitarian programme and the European Union's (EU) joint resettlement programme. It contrasts the diffusion of a narrative of policy reform by an international organization to an established and recent resettlement programme at the state and supranational levels, respectively. The UNHCR's reformist impetus is demonstrated to be uneven and change to the agency's accountability narrative in the sector of refugee resettlement is slow. Drawing on the nuanced understanding of institutional change described by Streeck and Thelen (2005), this unevenness is referred to as a *layered narrative of accountability* that not only results in institutional incoherence but also limits diffusion to the two resettlement programmes, whereby the modalities of diffusion remain distinct. The institutionalist approach, thus, allows for an in-depth and original analysis of the intricate nature of policy elaboration by a complex international organization, on the one hand, and of multi-levelled policy diffusion, on the other hand.

UNHCR has promoted the re-emergence of resettlement as a 'durable solution' for refugees from the late 1990s, resulting in significant internal reforms as well as global resettlement advocacy. However, as will be shown in the first section, the refugee agency's post-2006 commitment to accountability has not been fully embraced in the field of refugee resettlement. UNHCR's post-2006 accountability commitment has been described as a pledge 'to deliver results for populations of concern within a framework of respect, transparency, agreed feasibility, trust, delegated authority and available resources' (Türk and Eyster 2010, p. 159) so as to overcome decades-long criticism of the refugee agency's lack of accountability. In the field of refugee resettlement, however, explicit references to accountability focus primarily on clarity in the division of managerial responsibilities in resettlement operations. Still, other elements of UNHCR's resettlement strategy intersect with the agency's post-2006 understanding of accountability, especially rule-based, vulnerability-focused resettlement criteria. It is argued that the discrepancy between UNHCR's post-2006 understanding of accountability and its ambit in the sector of refugee resettlement results in a *layered narrative of accountability*. 'Layering' is one of five types of incremental institutional change discussed by Streeck and Thelen (2005).[1] It characterizes a process in which institutional reform goes forward yet is not all-encompassing. Limited reform creates a pattern of 'differential growth', as several parts of the institutions might change faster than others. Differential growth results in institutional incoherence (Ibid., p. 22ff). Whereas Streeck and Thelen's approach to institutional change includes an analysis of enforcement, this chapter only applies their concept to the level of policy elaboration.

The second section explores the diffusion of this layered narrative to Australia's long-standing humanitarian programme and to the EU's new joint resettlement programme. 'Accountability' is scarcely mentioned in either programme. Nevertheless, the EU joint resettlement programme aligns more closely with UNHCR's post-2006 definition of accountability than Australia's humanitarian programme. The timing and dynamics of policy elaboration contribute to explain the difference. The establishment of Australia's humanitarian programme long preceded the rise of UNHCR's post-2006 understanding of accountability. In contrast, the EU's joint resettlement programme was designed simultaneously as accountability was high on the agenda of the refugee agency, and UNHCR was closely associated with the design of the EU programme.

To explore this issue, the chapter analyzes policy documents on refugee resettlement released by UNHCR, Australian governments and community organizations and European institutions (European Commission, Council and Parliament). The implementation of UNHCR's narrative of accountability is not discussed. A significant body of literature has pointed at considerable discrepancies between policies and practices in the refugee agency's resettlement activities (e.g. Verdirame and Harrell-Bond 2003; Sandvik 2010a, 2010b, 2011; van Selm 2013); thus, it is highly likely that lack of implementation also affects accountability. This chapter, nevertheless, argues that it is critical to focus on the level of policy elaboration, or policy ideas. This is because ideas, including ideas that never become implemented policy, drive institutional continuity and change as well as institutional diffusion. The conclusion returns to this point.[2]

UNHCR, accountability and refugee resettlement

Refugee resettlement is 'the process by which some refugees are allowed to leave a country of asylum and start life anew in a third country that is willing to receive and protect them on a permanent basis' (Newland 2002). Resettlement was at the core of UNHCR's activities as the refugee agency was established in the aftermath of the Second World War (Loescher 2000). In contrast to the other 'durable solutions' for refugees, local integration and especially repatriation, resettlement found itself marginalized at the end of the Cold War in the context of a considerable increase of asylum claims in the Global North (Chimni 2004).

In 1994, an internal review suggested that UNHCR regained resettlement leadership (Frederiksson and Mougne 1994). To achieve this aim, Frederiksson and Mougne proposed a series of measures that became influential in the following decades (Sandvik 2010c; Garnier 2014a). The review emphasized both the humanitarian value of refugee resettlement as a protection instrument of last resort and its strategic value as an instrument allowing for 'burden-sharing' between countries of first asylum and resettling states. The humanitarian value of resettlement was intended to be enhanced with the establishment of rule-based, vulnerability-focused resettlement criteria. To increase the strategic value of resettlement, the review suggested organizational reforms, such as hosting regular multilateral forums to foster policy coordination with external partners, improving the standing of the Resettlement Section within UNHCR and increasing the responsibilities of field offices. Both the use of rule-based, vulnerability-focused resettlement criteria and an increase in responsibilities at the field office level would help address the 'widely acknowledged lack of accountability within UNHCR' (Frederiksson and Mougne 1994, p. 41), which caused a considerable degree of discretion in policy implementation.

UNHCR adopted the majority of these recommendations. For instance, a Resettlement Handbook aiming to guide resettlement practice was published in 1997 and has since been regularly updated. The Resettlement Handbook details rule-based, vulnerability-focused resettlement criteria. Resettled refugees should primarily be persons fearing persecution as defined in the 1951 Refugee Convention and the resettlement of vulnerable categories of refugees, such as women heading families and in acute danger of violence (women at risk) and refugees at immediate risk of persecution (emergency cases), should be prioritized. The 'strategic use of resettlement' was discussed at the Global Consultations on International Protection, which reframed the role of UNHCR in the xenophobia-laden context of the post-9/11 years and is promoted in the Agenda for Protection resulting from the Global Consultations (UNHR 2003).[3] The operational resettlement capacity has also expanded, and multilateral consultations with the states and NGOs aiming to foster policy coordination are organized each year.[4]

Explicit references to accountability remain, however, limited in resettlement documents attesting to the re-emergence of the protection instrument. 'Accountability' is absent or only mentioned in passing in UNHCR Executive Committee documents endorsing the resurgence of resettlement and presenting reforms following this endorsement (e.g. see UNHCR 1996, 2001, 2004a). Early editions of the Resettlement Handbook do not mention accountability (UNHCR 1998). In contrast, accountability is devoted some space in the 2004 edition of the Handbook (UNHCR 2004b).[5] Accountability is associated with the designation of a field officer accountable for resettlement practices and with the clear-cut division of responsibilities within UNHCR and between UNHCR and its partners involved in resettlement operations (Ibid., Section 6.2). The UNHCR Representative and Senior Protection staff in the field offices should establish an 'accountability framework' to ensure that resettlement activities, including recordkeeping, 'are carried out to the highest standards possible'.[6] Field-specific Standards Operating Procedures (SOPs) based on Resettlement Handbook guidelines should be designed to achieve this goal.[7] The 2004 Handbook details file maintenance and tracking procedures in the field offices. The PROFILE database is presented as a tool facilitating record keeping (Ibid., Sections 8.1 and 8.2) (see also Lindskov Jacobsen, Rochenback and Sandvik in this volume). Finally, resettlement training for the staff should introduce the concept of accountability (Ibid., Chapter 9). The first biennial Progress Report on Resettlement (UNHCR 2004c) explicitly mentions accountability, and the meaning of the term is similar to that expressed in the 2004 Resettlement Handbook.

In sum, these documents relate accountability to management practices aiming to ensure a proper division of labour within UNHCR and between the agency and its operational partners; refugee participation in such practices is not foreseen. Administrative technology (the PROFILE database) is presented as an asset to achieve this aim. In contrast, accountability is not explicitly put in relation to the upholding of refugees' human or legal rights. As mentioned above, the resettlement criteria presented in the Handbook are rule-based and vulnerability-focused (see UNHCR 2004b, Chapters 4 and 5); however, this presentation is dissociated from the notion of accountability.[8] Thus, the pre-2006 narrative of accountability in the field of resettlement is narrow because it focuses only on managerial practices. UNHCR itself, as well as its resettlement partners (only NGOs are explicitly mentioned), appear as the constituencies to be accountable to, whereas neither the states nor, more worryingly, the refugees are referred to when accountability is discussed.

This restrictive vision of accountability may reflect the above-mentioned 'widely acknowledged lack of accountability within UNHCR' deplored in the 1994 review. This lack of accountability remained a concern for the entire agency in the subsequent decade. The absence of a culture of accountability was denounced in an influential review of UNHCR's organizational practices conducted in the early 2000s (Wigley 2006). In reaction to the review, reforms were put in place to broaden and strengthen UNHCR's approach to accountability. These reforms included the adoption of a UNHCR-specific definition of accountability as a 'commitment to deliver results for populations of concern within a framework of respect, transparency, agreed feasibility, trust, delegated authority and available resources' (Türk and Eyster 2010, p. 159).[9] A Global Management Accountability Framework, clarifying chains of organizational responsibility within the entire agency as well as strengthening result-based management practices aimed to improve delivery, was also developed (Ibid.; see also Kinchin and Sandvik in this volume). The post-2006 definition of accountability makes no explicit reference to the human or legal rights of refugees; however, its primary constituency, 'populations of concern', is clear. It could be argued that a commitment to uphold the human and legal rights of populations of concern flows from the definition; yet, the absence of an explicit commitment is also a source of ambiguity.

How has UNHCR's post-2006 approach to accountability been integrated in the agency's refugee resettlement strategy? Notably, contrary to the inaugural biennial Progress Report on Resettlement, none of its followers mentions accountability (UNHCR 2006, 2008a, 2010a, 2012a, 2014b). Accountability is also not referred to in post-2006 documents focusing on the 'strategic use' of resettlement (for instance, see UNHCR 2009a). In contrast, the 2011 edition of the Resettlement Handbook, like the 2004 edition, entails several sections explicitly discussing accountability.[10] Although the chapter structure in the 2011 Handbook is different from the 2004 edition, the scope of accountability is largely similar in both.[11] The post-2006 definition of accountability is not mentioned in the 2011 Handbook. Again, accountability is explicitly referred to in relation to well-defined chains of responsibilities in the field offices (management and accountability framework) and between UNHCR and external partners. to record management and to training (UNHR 2011, sections 4.2.1, 4.2.2, and 5.6.2; 4.7.1; and 5.8.2, respectively). Accountability mechanisms still exclude the participation of refugees. Nonetheless, the content of accountability-focused sections in the 2011 Handbook is not entirely the same as in the 2004 edition. Compared to the 2004 version, the 2011 Handbook insists more strongly on the universality of standard operating procedures, which should be consistent with the headquarters' guidelines. Administrative tools are also given greater exposure. The registration database proGres, the resettlement tracking system CORTS (Consolidated Online Resettlement Tracking System), UNHCR-wide electronic record keeping system Livelink and biometric registration technology for refugee populations are presented, in addition to individual case files, as crucial contributions to proper record keeping (Ibid., Sections 4.7.2. to 4.7.4) (see also Lindskov Jacobsen in this volume). The importance of confidentiality is mentioned. However, the management benefits of these technologies (especially benefits regarding fraud reduction) are given more space than potential breaches of refugee privacy.[12]

As in the 2004 Resettlement Handbook, this understanding of accountability gives the impression that constituencies to be accountable to are primarily UNHCR staff and its operational partners rather than 'populations of concern', which are the main constituency of the post-2006 UNHCR definition of accountability. Even more so than in pre-2006 resettlement documents, resettlement selection criteria in the 2011 Resettlement Handbook emphasize the human and legal rights of refugees (UNHCR 2011, Chapters 3, 5 and 6).[13] These chapters do not refer to the concept of accountability. A similarly narrow and exclusive perspective on accountability is found in all of the editions of the self-study modules of the Resettlement Learning Programme (RLP) (UNHCR 2009b, 2010b, 2012b). Available since 2009, the RLP is designed to be used by UNHCR staff involved in resettlement activities, which ensures the dissemination of UNHCR's knowledge base on resettlement and, arguably, the reproduction of this knowledge. The training documents, thus, help to perpetuate a limited understanding of accountability in resettlement practice.

Using the concept of layering drawn from Streeck and Thelen (2005) and presented in the chapter's introduction, it is argued that the discrepancy between UNHCR's post-2006 definition of accountability and its understanding in the field of refugee resettlement results in *a layered narrative of accountability*. The findings of this section can be summarized as follows: Acknowledging widespread organizational dysfunction in the mid-2000s, UNHCR headquarters aimed to profoundly alter the refugee agency's understanding of accountability. However, an understanding of accountability had already been developed in the field of refugee resettlement in the context of the re-emergence of the protection instrument since the late 1990s. This understanding of accountability was not fundamentally altered by the headquarters' post-2006 reforms. Therefore, as a whole, UNHCR's approach to accountability appears to be a layered narrative and is increasingly lacking coherence.

The following sections investigate the impact of UNHCR's layered narrative of accountability in two distinct policy settings: Australia's long-established resettlement programme and the EU's new joint refugee resettlement programme.

Australia's humanitarian programme and UNHCR's layered narrative of accountability

Australia has been engaged in refugee resettlement since the end of the Second World War. The country has developed a formal humanitarian programme, including the planning of an annual resettlement intake, in the 1970s in the context of the Indo-Chinese refugee crisis (Viviani 1984).[14] Australia's resettlement policy has since involved close co-operation between the Department of Immigration,[15] community organizations and UNHCR (RCOA 2014). Additionally, the country has for decades been consistently the second or third most important resettling state, with an average of 13,000 to 14,000 places in the last decade (Philips 2015).[16] Contrary to asylum, which has been one of the most salient political issues in the country since the 1990s (Garnier and Cox 2012), refugee resettlement enjoys a high level of legitimacy among policymakers and in public opinion. It can, thus, be argued that Australia's resettlement policy has global relevance and constitutes a pertinent case in which to assess the influence of UNHCR's layered narrative of accountability.

'Accountability' is not explicitly mentioned in relation to refugee resettlement in documents describing Australia's current resettlement policy. For instance, the latest annual report from the Department of Immigration and Border Protection (DIBP) devotes a chapter to 'Management and Accountability' (DIBP 2014) focusing on administrative and legal oversight. The chapter mentions court cases in which the Department is in litigation with asylum seekers (Ibid., p. 257f) as well as investigations of the Australian Human Rights Commission into asylum-related matters[17]; however, there is no reference to oversight mechanisms in relation to refugee resettlement. 'Accountability' is mentioned once in the annual intake submission of the Refugee Council of Australia to the Minister of Immigration (RCOA 2014), but not in relation to resettlement.[18] RCOA's intake submission reflects national consultations with community organizations on Australia's refugee and asylum policy and is arguably the most important non-governmental report periodically evaluating and contributing to this policy.

On the surface, UNHCR's understanding of accountability does not appear to permeate Australia's resettlement policy. Still, there are intersections but also divergences between the agency's post-2006 accountability definition and core elements of Australian policy. The following paragraphs discuss the alignment of several elements of UNHCR's accountability definition: 'commitment to deliver results for populations of concern' and the framework of 'transparency', 'agreed feasibility' and 'available resources'[19] in the context of various editions of Australia's country chapter in UNHCR's Resettlement Handbook and other relevant policy documents.

Australia's 'commitment to deliver results for populations of concern' is ambivalent. On the one hand, annual resettlement intake planning allows for resettlement predictability and is a good predictor of effective result delivery. On the other hand, Australia only applies a narrow set of vulnerability-based resettlement criteria as defined by UNHCR. A major stream of Australia's humanitarian programme is dedicated to the resettlement of refugees according to the Refugee Convention criteria, and a proportion of this contingent is reserved for women at risk (UNHCR 2014c, p. 7). Yet, the country facilitates the resettlement neither of unaccompanied minors nor of the elderly nor of refugees with medical needs. Emergency cases are prioritized, and special consideration is given to survivors of torture; however, no particular contingent of places is foreseen for these categories (UNHCR 2014c, p. 6ff). Additionally, Australia's resettlement policy does not focus exclusively on refugees recognized on the basis of the Refugee Convention criteria. Another stream, the Special Humanitarian Programme (SHP), is dedicated to the resettlement of persons in danger of gross violations of human rights and whose application is supported by a member of the community in Australia. In 2013, the Community Proposal Pilot was introduced to allow for community organizations to sponsor Convention refugees or SHP cases (UNHCR 2014c, p. 2). Although these streams laudably expand the focus of resettlement, they are barely accessible to the most vulnerable refugees, who often have no links with the resettling states (RCOA 2014, p. 37). More concerning is the numerical link between the amount of allocated SHP places and the number of refugees recognized after an asylum claim in Australia. This link has existed since 1996 (Karlsen, Philips and Koleth 2011, p. 4). For every person granted a refugee visa in Australia, an allocated SHP place is deducted from the yearly intake. Australia is the only country in the world to do so. Community organizations and UNHCR have steadily criticized the link because it creates a controversial bind between asylum and resettlement, which are considered two separate humanitarian avenues (UNHCR 2012c, p. 7; RCOA 2014, p. 35).

As for 'transparency', not much detail is given in the 2014 Handbook country chapter on the processing of resettlement cases. The chapter only briefly mentions that Australia's resettlement procedure varies across the world and that Australia does not resettle on the basis of dossiers and does not offer recourse to refused resettlement candidates in the form of a merit review (UNHCR 2014c, pp. 5–6). In contrast, the 2009 edition of Australia's country chapter did mention that each resettlement candidate was interviewed (UNHCR 2004b, AUL, p.3.), and the 1998 edition implied that the applicants had access to judicial review (UNHCR 1998, AUL pages, Section 6.4). Worryingly, transparency thus appears to have decreased over time. Community organizations have complained about this lack of procedural information (RCOA 2014, pp. 37–38).

Alignment with UNHCR in regard to 'agreed feasibility' and 'available resources' is limited. First, it is well established that Australia has long devoted a larger proportion of its immigration budget to the deterrence of unwanted asylum seekers coming by boat rather than to refugee resettlement (Garnier and Cox 2012).[20] Resource diversion has meant that Australia's offering of resettlement places has remained stable or declined for many years. However, the country has recently demonstrated that it has the capacity to significantly and swiftly expand resettlement. In August 2012, the Gillard government decided without warning to increase Australia's humanitarian intake by 40% to 20,000 places.[21] The Refugee Council of Australia noted in its annual intake submission that thanks to excellent co-operation between the DIBP, the UNHCR Resettlement Service and the community sector, immediate implementation of the intake increase was a success (RCOA 2014, p. 25). Nevertheless, the Abbott government elected in 2013 did not maintain the increase, resulting in the waste of resources deployed by the community sector to deal with a larger contingent of refugees (Ibid.).

Overall, the diffusion of UNHCR's narrative of accountability in the Australian case is limited. First, it is striking that accountability is not explicitly referred to in relation to the refugee resettlement, whereas it is mentioned in relation to other aspects of Australia's migration policy. Second, alignment with UNHCR's post-2006 understanding of accountability is circumscribed. Although long-standing planned resettlement is a significant commitment to deliver results, Australia's understanding of 'populations of concern' is markedly distinct from that of UNHCR. Additionally, procedural aspects and resource allocations do not appear to be much influenced by UNHCR priorities; the discrepancies between Australia's and UNHCR's approach appears to have increased over time.

This limited diffusion of UNHCR accountability narrative is not surprising if one assumes that institutional change is primarily incremental, as Streeck and Thelen (2005) described. Australia's refugee resettlement policy, including modalities of co-operation between the immigration bureaucracy, community organizations and UNHCR, was established long before the re-emergence of resettlement on UNHCR's policy agenda as well as the agency's increased focus on accountability. Additionally, given the political legitimacy that refugee resettlement enjoys in Australia, it is not likely that domestic institutions have had incentives to promote externally driven organizational change in resettlement policy, especially as the layered nature of UNHCR's accountability narrative may have weakened the agency's reformist impetus. The following section assesses whether diffusion of UNHCR's accountability narrative is equally restricted in the EU case.

EU's joint refugee resettlement programme and UNHCR's layered narrative of accountability

Few EU member-states have a long experience with planned refugee resettlement.[22] Nonetheless, since 2000, the adoption of an EU joint resettlement scheme has been envisaged as part of the external dimension of the Common European Asylum System. The EU decision establishing the European Refugee Fund for the years 2008 to 2013 (ERF III), that is, the EU budget allocated for this period to the reception in the EU of persons in need of humanitarian protection, entailed an EU definition of refugee resettlement and provisions for financial support to EU member-states resettling refugees on the basis of this definition (OJEU 2007). The European Commission made a proposal for a joint resettlement scheme in 2009 (CEC 2009). Accordingly, the joint scheme would consist in the adoption of EU-wide annual resettlement priorities, in financial incentives for member-states to resettle according to these priorities, and in enhanced resettlement coopera-tion among member-states and between member-states, UNHCR and involved NGOs. Member-states' participation in the joint resettlement scheme would be voluntary. The scheme was eventually endorsed by the European Council and the European Parliament in 2012 (CEU 2012; EP 2012). The EU-endorsed definition of refugee resettlement for the purpose of EU funding was amended in the regulation establishing the Asylum, Migration and Integration Fund (AMIF), which sets rules for the allocation of the EU budget on migration and refugee matters for 2014 to 2020 (OJEU 2014). The joint scheme is the first ever designed supranational resettlement policy and, thus, an interesting case of institutional innovation in the field of humanitarian protection. Additionally, and in contrast to the Australian humanitarian programme, the scheme was developed as account-ability became increasingly significant for UNHCR. The EU joint resettlement scheme, thus, appears to be another pertinent case in which to investigate the dif-fusion of UNHCR's layered narrative of accountability.

'Accountability' is not explicitly referred to in any of the EU policy documents on refugee resettlement. UNHCR also does not mention the term in its 2008 background paper on the potential establishment of an EU resettlement scheme (UNHCR 2008b) nor in its comments to the 2009 Commission proposal for such scheme (UNHCR 2009c). However, several aspects of the scheme do align with UNHCR's post-2006 definition of accountability. The following paragraphs focus on similar elements of this definition as in the Australian case, analyzing EU policy documents as well as related UNHCR and NGO sources.[23]

Regarding the commitment to 'deliver results to populations of concern', both Article 13 of the ERF III decision and Article 17 of the AMIF regulation state that refugee resettlement, for the purpose of EU funding, must be based on a resettle-ment request from UNHCR. The refugee agency, thus, plays a central role in the administration of the joint resettlement scheme. Rule-based, vulnerability-focused resettlement criteria are also at the core of the scheme. According to Article 13 (3) of the ERF III decision, EU member-states receive a lump sum of 4000 € for each resettled refugee who meets the following UNHCR-endorsed vulnerability crite-ria: unaccompanied minors; children and women at risk; and persons with serious medical needs. Additionally, the ERF III lump sum is granted to member-states resettling refugees coming from countries in which the EU is involved in Regional Protection Programmes (RPPs), which promote the 'strategic use' of resettlement (Garnier 2014a, p. 946f). Article 17 (3) of the AMIF regulation amending the ERF III resettlement definition increased alignment with UNHCR resettlement criteria as follows. Each resettling EU member-state receives a lump sum of 6000 € per reset-tled refugee. The lump sum increases to 10,000 € if the resettled refugee meets the above-mentioned vulnerability criteria or requires emergency resettlement, belongs to another 'specific category falling within UNHCR resettlement criteria' or is identified by UNHCR as potentially benefiting from resettlement by the EU. There is, thus, a great deal of alignment regarding the understanding of 'populations of concern'. At the same time, the 10,000 € lump sum is allocated to refugees resettled from RPP countries and from regions identified as EU resettlement priorities according to the consultative procedure devised in the 2009 Commission proposal on the establishment of the joint resettlement scheme (CEC 2009, p. 8). The alignment between UNHCR and EU resettlement priorities is not a given, especially as the European Commission has highlighted the 'added value' of resettlement for EU's external relations (Ibid., p. 10).

UNHCR and the EU resettlement scheme seem to align regarding the 'framework of transparency' necessary to the accountable policy. The oversight mechanisms have been designed to ensure that resettlement criteria are respected by EU member-states. Each member-state must provide annual reports on resettlement efforts to the European Commission, which can request additional information. The Commission can also conduct 'unannounced spot-checks' to verify this information. Additionally, the European Asylum Support Office is tasked to monitor the effectiveness of resettlement practice (CEC 2009, p. 9; European Resettlement Network, n.d.).

Alignment over 'agreed feasibility' and 'available resources' is more problematic. On the one hand, UNHCR has steadily provided input for the design of the EU resettlement scheme both on its own and with the European NGOs (UNHCR 2008b, 2009c; UNHCR-ECRE 2008). The agency is involved in EU-funded, co-ordinated actions promoting resettlement alongside NGOs and the International Organization for Migration, for instance, within the European Resettlement Network.[24] Arguably, such policy co-ordination is favourable to the emergence of an 'epistemic community' (Haas 1992) sharing a common vision of resettlement. On the other hand, member-states' participation in the joint resettlement scheme is voluntary. Although joint resettlement actions involving several member-states have developed, the expansion of resettlement has so far remained modest. In 2012, EU resettlement places represented 8.3% of the globally available places (Bokshi, 2013, p. 49). Consequently, EU resources allocated to support the expansion resettlement (the above-mentioned 6,000 € or 10,000 € per resettled refugee) remain untapped.

In sum, although implementation is a critical issue for the EU joint resettlement scheme, alignment between the EU and UNHCR is significant. Whereas accountability is never explicitly referred to in the policy documents, the EU's and UNHCR's understanding of 'populations of concerns', for the most part, overlaps. Additionally, steps are taken to ensure procedural transparency in the definition of EU-wide policy priorities, and resources are foreseen to allow for the resettlement on the basis of rule-based, vulnerability-focused criteria. It can, thus, be argued that the diffusion of the UNHCR's narrative of accountability is greater in the EU case than in the Australian case. Policy elaboration in the EU case occurred as the UNHCR had already recast refugee resettlement and was in the process of transforming its accountability narrative. UNHCR efficiently promoted reforms through steady advocacy and within policy networks, and EU institutions (especially the Commission) proved to be receptive. Still, to return to this chapter's understanding of institutional change as incremental, the layered nature of UNHCR's accountability narrative may explain why EU policy elements aligning with the refugee agency's understanding of accountability are not referred to as belonging to the accountability narrative.

Conclusion

This chapter has highlighted how UNHCR's post-2006 understanding of accountability has been integrated in the refugee agency's refugee resettlement strategy. The chapter has also uncovered the influence of the resulting narrative in Australia's and the EU's refugee resettlement policy. It has been argued that unevenness in UNHCR reforms has resulted in a layered narrative of accountability. This layered narrative not only muddles UNHCR's approach to accountability because it lacks clarity but also weakens the influence of this approach on resettlement partners. This weakened influence is not homogeneous, and thus policy diffusion varies, because the conditions of reception of UNHCR's narrative of accountability can be more or less auspicious. In this respect, it has been shown that the EU's new joint resettlement scheme was a more auspicious terrain of diffusion than Australia's long-established refugee resettlement.

Conceptually, I hope to have shown that a focus on policy elaboration allows for a nuanced understanding of the layered nature of the concept of accountability within UNHCR and as reflected by other actors, thus contributing to the literature discussing the significance of ideas in international organizations' policymaking and policy diffusion (Finnemore and Sikkink 1998; Barnett and Finnemore 2004; Béland and Orenstein 2013). A more materialist investigation could build on this chapter's findings by assessing whether and how this protean concept of accountability actually impacts resettlement practice (for such a focus beyond the sector of refugee resettlement, see Linskov Jacobsen's discussion of refugee technology in this volume).

Normatively, the chapter has evidenced that, worryingly, the narrative of accountability in UNHCR refugee resettlement policy makes scant reference to the human and legal rights of refugees. Refugee rights do play a significant role in policy elaboration; however, they are not presented as a constitutive element of accountability. Perhaps even more concerning is the total lack of reference to refugees' participation. If the UNHCR addressed, in the future, the issue of incoherence it its accountability strategy that this chapter has identified, we hope that the voices and concern of refugee would be at the forefront and centre stage.

Notes

1 Whereas most institutionalist literature focuses on bursts of change and long periods of continuity (e.g. Pierson 2000; Capoccia and Kelemen 2007), Streeck and Thelen argued that institutional change is most often gradual and uneven. Significant reform occurs in small steps, which do not necessarily affect all parts of an institution at the same speed. In addition to layering, Streeck and Thelen's categories of institutional changes are displacement, conversion, drift and exhaustion (Streeck and Thelen 2005, p. 24ff).

2 The chapter is an original research project and reflects my interest in the dynamics and limits of institutional change in international organizations (see also Garnier 2014a, 2014b).

3 The Agenda for Protection does not consider that resettlement is the durable solution of last resort anymore. Local integration, repatriation and resettlement are put on an equal footing while the agency acknowledges that resettlement is only a durable solution for a small minority of refugees (UNHCR 2003, p. 78ff).

4 See Nakashiba (2013) and Garnier (2014a) for a more detailed overview of the influence of the 1994 review.

5 'Accountability' is referred to 26 times in the 2004 Resettlement Handbook.

6 On the significance of hierarchical control in the Resettlement Handbook's approach to accountability, see also Sandvik (2010b).

7 The Handbook mentions that '[g]iven the diversity of field contexts, specific resettlement procedures will differ from field office to field office. It is neither possible nor desirable to have a single, universal set of Standard Operating Procedures (SOPs) to be followed by all UNHCR field offices' (UNHCR 2004b, Section 6.2). This perspective reflects the 1994 review's commitment to decentralization in refugee resettlement operations. Such commitment is less pronounced in the 2011 edition of the Resettlement Handbook.

8 Importantly, the Handbook's focus on rules and vulnerabilities as central criteria of refugee selection for resettlement is no guarantee that the human rights of refugee candidates are respected in practice. As Sandvik (2010b, p. 299; see also Sandvik 2010a) has observed in the resettlement process of urban refugees in Uganda, these criteria can become a 'Weberian iron cage of rationally demarcated suffering' as resettlement candidates have to *perform* their suffering in a way that UNHCR resettlement officers consider to be consistent with the rules.

9 Interestingly, not many UNHCR executive documents or performance reports mention the post-2006 definition of accountability, as if it had quickly become self-explanatory (for a report explicitly referring to the definition, see the Age, Gender and Diversity Accountability Report 2013) (UNHCR 2014a).

10 'Accountability' is mentioned 37 times in the 2011 Resettlement Handbook.

11 There have been changes between 2004 and 2011, which can be observed as worrisome from the perspective of the UNHCR's post-2006 understanding of accountability. Sandvik (2008, p. 120) noted that although the resettlement form was freely available online in an appendix to the Resettlement Handbooks from 1997 and 2004, the 2007 edition does not contain this form, but instead operates with an annex 2 labelled 'internal'.

12 For instance, the default stance in regard to biometrics is to use them rather than exercise restraint: 'The use of biometrics in support of identity verification exercises among refugee populations is encouraged, *except* where no protection or operational benefit is expected to be gained from doing so' (UNHCR 2011, p. 157). The Handbook acknowledges the importance of 'safeguards' (Ibid.) without specifically mentioning what these safeguards would be.

13 As mentioned in footnote 8, a greater emphasis on the refugee rights in the Resettlement Handbook does not mean that the refugee rights are better protected in resettlement practice.

14 Australia's humanitarian programme also includes asylum policy.
15 Australia's Department of Immigration has changed names several times since it was established in 1947. It is currently called the Department of Immigration and Border Protection.
16 The United States is, by far, the largest resettling state, followed by Canada and Australia.
17 The Australian Human Rights Commission conducted one inquiry into the human rights of asylum seekers and refugees coming by boat to Australia and another into the human rights of children in immigration detention. The latter caused considerable political turmoil as it was released in February 2015 (Taylor and Mehdora 2015).
18 The report noted the 'lack of accountability' of the government and politicians 'for the impact of negative rhetoric' on asylum seekers and refugees in the community (RCOA 2014, p. 51).
19 The other elements of the definition, 'trust' and 'respect', are considered to be too subjective for the purpose of our analysis, whereas 'delegated authority' applies only to UNHCR as an international organization.
20 Since 2013, Australia also prohibited the resettlement in Australia of asylum seekers en route to Australia by boat and intercepted them at sea and sent them to 'transit processing centres' in Nauru and Papua New Guinea to have their asylum claims assessed. A bilateral agreement between the Australian and the Cambodian government foresees resettlement in this country. The deal has been denounced by community organizations (APRRN 2014).
21 The increase occurred as Australia was faced with a surge of 'boat arrivals' claiming asylum. Many potential claimants died at sea before being intercepted. The increase of resettlement places was observed as a disincentive for claimants to undertake a dangerous (and, from the perspective of the Australian government, unauthorized) boat journey to Australia (see Garnier 2014a, p. 950ff).
22 Only Denmark, Sweden, Finland and The Netherlands have had planned resettlement programmes in place for several decades. For an overview of EU member-states' involvement in refugee resettlement, see ICMC (2013).
23 There is no equivalent of a 'country chapter' on the EU (yet?) in the UNHCR Resettlement Handbook.
24 The European Resettlement Network (available at www.resettlement.eu/) aims to foster resettlement practice in the EU by connecting a variety of actors involved in refugee resettlement. It is coordinated by the UNHCR, the IOM and the International Catholic Migration Commission.

References

APRRN (Asia Pacific Refugees Right Network). (2014) *APRRN Statement on the Australia-Cambodia Deal*, 13 October 2014. Available online at www.aprrn.info/1/index.php/resources/publications-and-materials/aprrn-statements/292-aprrn-statement-on-the-australia-cambodia-refugee-resettlement-deal (accessed 18 September 2015).

Barnett, M. and M. Finnemore. (2004) *Rules for the World: International Organizations in Global Politics*. Ithaca: Cornell University Press.

Béland, D. and M. Orenstein. (2013) 'International organizations as policy actors: an ideational approach', *Global Social Policy*, 13(2): 125–143.

Bokshi, E. (2013) *Refugee Resettlement in the EU: The Capacity to Do it Better and to Do it More*, KNOW RESET research report 2013/04. Florence: European University Institute. Available online at www.know-reset.eu/files/texts/00013_20140108160733_knowresetrr-2013-04.pdf (accessed 18 September 2015).

Capoccia, G. and R. D. Kelemen. (2007) 'The study of critical junctures: theory, narrative, and counterfactuals in historical institutionalism', *World Politics*, 59(3): 341–369.

CEC (Commission of the European Communities). (2009) *On the Establishment of a Joint EU Resettlement Programme*. Brussels: EU, COM. 456 final. Available online at http://eur-lex. europa.eu/legal-content/EN/TXT/PDF/?uri=CELEX:52009DC0447&from=EN; www.refworld.org/docid/4aa51b632.html (accessed 18 September 2015).

CEU (Council of European Union). (2012) *Common EU Resettlement Priorities for 2013 and New Rules on EU Funding*, Press Release 6838/12 (Presse 62), March 8. Available online at www .consilium.europa.eu/uedocs/cms_data/docs/pressdata/en/jha/128823.pdf (accessed 18 September 2015).

Chimni, B. S. (2004) 'From resettlement to involuntary repatriation: towards a critical history of durable solutions to refugee problems', *Refugee Survey Quarterly*, 23(3): 55–73.

DIBP (Department of Immigration and Border Protection). (2014) *Annual Report 2013–2014, Part 4: Management and Accountability*. Canberra: DIBP. Available online at http://www.border.gov.au/ReportsandPublications/Documents/annual-reports/ DIBP_AR_2013-14.pdf (accessed 21 October 2015).

EP (European Parliament). (2012) *Financial Incentives for EU Countries to Take Up More Refugees*, Press Release, March 29. Available online at www.europarl.europa.eu/news/en/ pressroom/content/20120328IPR42048/html/Financial-incentives-for-EU-countries-to-take-up-morerefugees (accessed 18 September 2015).

European Resettlement Network (n.d.) *EU Funding for Resettlement (ERF/AMIF)*. Available online at www.resettlement.eu/page/eu-funding-resettlement-erfamif (accessed 18 September 2015).

Finnemore, M. and K. Sikkink. (1998) 'International norm dynamics and political change', *International Organization*, 52(4): 887–917.

Frederiksson, J. and C. Mougne. (1994) *Resettlement in the 1990s: A Review of Policy and Practices*. Geneva: UNHCR. Available online at www.unhcr.org/research/ RESEARCH/3ae6bcfd4.pdf (accessed 18 September 2015).

Garnier, A. (2014a) 'Migration management and humanitarian protection: the UNHCR's "resettlement expansionism" and its impact on policy-making in the EU and Australia', *Journal of Ethnic and Migration Studies*, 40(6): 942–959.

Garnier, A. (2014b) 'Arrested development? UNHCR, ILO and the refugees' right to work', *Refuge*, 30(2): 15–25.

Garnier, A. and L. Cox. (2012) 'Twenty years of mandatory detention: the anatomy of a failed policy', *Proceedings of the 60th annual conference of the Australian Political Studies Association*. Hobart: University of Tasmania.

Haas, P. (1992) 'Epistemic communities and international policy coordination', *International Organization*, 46(1): 1–35.

ICMC (International Catholic Migration Commission). (2013) *Welcome to Europe! A Guide to Resettlement*. Brussels: ICMC. Available online at www.resettlement.eu/sites/icmc.tttp.eu/ files/ICMC%20Europe-Welcome%20to%20Europe.pdf (accessed 18 September 2015).

Karlsen, E., J. Philips and E. Koleth. (2011) *Seeking Asylum: Australia's Humanitarian Program*, Parliamentary Library Background Note. Canberra: Parliament of Australia. Available online at www.aph.gov.au/binaries/library/pubs/bn/sp/seekingasylum.pdf (accessed 18 September 2015).

Loescher, G. (2000) *The UNHCR and World Politics: A Perilous Path*. Oxford: Oxford University Press.

Nakashiba, H. (2013) 'Postmillennial UNHCR refugee resettlement: new developments and old challenges', New Issues in Refugee Research, Research paper no. 265. Geneva: UNHCR.

Newland, K. (2002) *Refugee Resettlement in Transition*. Washington, DC: Migration Policy Institute. Available online at www.migrationpolicy.org/article/refugee-resettlement-transition (accessed 18 September 2015).

OJEU (Official Journal of the European Union). (2007) *Decision n° 573/2007 of the European Parliament and the Council of 23 May 2007 Establishing the European Refugee Fund for the Period 2008 to 2013*, 6 June. Brussels: EU. Available online at http://eur-lex.europa.eu/legal-content/EN/TXT/PDF/?uri=CELEX:32007D0573&from=EN (accessed 18 September 2015).

OJEU. (2014) *Regulation (EU) No 516/2014 of the European Parliament and the Council of 16 April 2014 establishing the Asylum, Migration and Integration Fund, amending Council Decision 2008/381/EC and repealing Decisions No 573/2007/EC and No 575/2007/EC of the European Parliament and of the Council and Council Decision 2007/435/EC*, 20 May. Brussels: EU. Available online at http://ec.europa.eu/dgs/home-affairs/financing/fundings/pdf/overview/regulation_eu_no_5162014_of_the_european_parliament_and_of_the_council_en.pdf (accessed 18 September 2015).

Philips, J. (2015) *Australia's Humanitarian Program: A Quick Guide to the Statistics since 1947*, Parliamentary Research Papers Series, 7 January 2015. Available online at www.aph.gov.au/~/media/05%20About%20Parliament/54%20Parliamentary%20Depts/544%20Parliamentary%20Library/Research%20Papers/2014-15/QuickGuides/QG-Humanitarian.pdf (accessed 18 September 2015).

Pierson, P. (2000) 'Path dependence, increasing returns and the study of politics', *American Political Science Review*, 94(2): 251–267.

RCOA (Refugee Council of Australia). (2014) *Australia's Refugee and Special Humanitarian Program: Community Views and Current Challenges and Future Directions*. Melbourne: RCOA. Available online at www.refugeecouncil.org.au/r/isub/2014-15_Intake%20sub.pdf (accessed 18 September 2015).

Sandvik, K. B. (2008) 'On the everyday life of international law: humanitarianism and refugee- resettlement in Kampala', PhD dissertation, Harvard Law School.

Sandvik, K. B. (2010a) 'Rapprochement and misrecognition: humanitarianism as human rights practice', in C. Eriksen and M. Emberland (eds.), *The New International Law*, pp. 139–157. Leiden, The Netherlands: Brill.

Sandvik, K. B. (2010b) 'Framing accountability in refugee resettlement', in J. Wouters *et al.* (eds.), *Accountability for Human Rights Violations by International Organisations*, pp. 287–310. Cambridge: Intersentia.

Sandvik, K. B. (2010c) 'A legal history: the emergence of the African resettlement candidate in international refugee management', *International Journal of Refugee Law*, 22(1): 21–47.

Sandvik, K. B. (2011) 'Blurring boundaries: refugee resettlement in Kampala – between the formal, the informal, and the illegal', *PoLAR: Political and Legal Anthropology Review*, 34(1): 11–32.

Streeck, W. and K. Thelen. (2005) 'Introduction: institutional change in advanced political economies', in W. Streeck and K. Thelen (eds.), *Beyond Continuity*, pp. 3–39. Oxford: Oxford University Press.

Taylor, L. and S. Mehdora. (2015) 'Brandis asked Gillian Triggs to resign before critical child detention report', *The Guardian*, 13 February. Available online at www.theguardian.com/australia-news/2015/feb/13/brandis-asked-gillian-triggs-to-resign-before-critical-child-detention-report (accessed 18 September 2015).

Türk, V. and E. Eyster. (2010) 'Strengthening accountability in UNHCR', *International Journal of Refugee Law*, 22(22): 159–172.

UNHCR (United Nations High Commissioner for Refugees). (1996) *Resettlement: An Instrument of Protection and a Durable Solution*, Executive Committee of the High Commissioner Programme, Standing Committee, 28 May. EC/46/SC/CRP.32. Available online at www.unhcr.org/3ae68cf618.html (accessed 18 September 2015).

UNHCR. (1998) *Resettlement Handbook*, Division of International Protection. Geneva: UNHCR.

UNHCR. (2001) *New Directions for Policies and Practice*. EC/51/SC/INF.2. Geneva: UNHCR. Available online at www.unhcr.org/3b3065f44.html (accessed 18 September 2015).

UNHCR. (2003) *Agenda for Protection*, third edition. Geneva: UNHCR. Available online at www.unhcr.org/3e637b194.html (accessed 18 September 2015).

UNHCR. (2004a) *Multilateral Framework of Understandings on Resettlement*, High Commissioner's Forum. FORUM/2004/6. Geneva: UNHCR. Available online at www.refworld.org/docid/41597d0a4.html (accessed 18 September 2015).

UNHCR. (2004b) *Resettlement Handbook*, Division of International Protection. Country chapters last updated September 2009. Geneva: UNHCR. Available online at www.refworld.org/docid/3ae6b35e0.html (accessed 18 September 2015).

UNHCR. (2004c) *Progress Report on Resettlement*, Executive Committee of the High Commissioner's Programme, EC/54/SC/CRP.10. Geneva: UNHCR. Available online at www.unhcr.org/40c70b964.html (accessed 18 September 2015).

UNHCR. (2006) *Progress Report on Resettlement*, Executive Committee of the High Commissioner's Programme, EC/57/SC/CRP.15. Geneva: UNHCR. Available online at www.unhcr.org/4486a22e2.html (accessed 18 September 2015).

UNHCR. (2008a) *Progress Report on Resettlement*, Executive Committee of the High Commissioner's Programme, EC/59/SC/CRP.11. Geneva: UNHCR. Available online at www.unhcr.org/484514632.html (accessed 18 September 2015).

UNHCR. (2008b) *Background Paper from UNHCR: EU Resettlement*, European Commission Consultation Meeting on the EU Resettlement Scheme, Brussels, 12 December. Available online at www.refworld.org/docid/496e19392.html (accessed 18 September 2015).

UNHCR. (2009a) *The Strategic Use of Resettlement*, Discussion Paper, Working Group on Resettlement, Geneva, 14 October. Available online at www.refworld.org/cgi-bin/texis/vtx/rwmain?docid=4b8cdcee2 (accessed 18 September 2015).

UNHCR. (2009b) *Resettlement In Context: International Protection and Durable Solutions*. Geneva: UNHCR. Available online at www.sheltercentre.org/sites/default/files/498700422.pdf (accessed 18 September 2015).

UNHCR. (2009c) *Comments on the Communication from the Commission on the Establishment of a Joint EU Resettlement Programme and the European Commission Proposal for the Amendment of Decision No 573/2007/EC Establishing the European Refugee Fund for the Period 2008 to 2013*. Geneva: UNHCR. Available online at www.unhcr.ch/fileadmin/rechtsinfos/Comments_on_Communication_from_the_Commission_on_the_Establishment_of_a_Joint_EU_Resettlement_Programme___Commission_Proposal_for__Amendment__of_Decision_establishing_Refugee_fund_-_2009.pdf (accessed 18 September 2015).

UNHCR. (2010a) *Progress Report on Resettlement*. Executive Committee of the High Commissioner's Programme, EC/61/SC/CRP.11. Geneva: UNHCR. Available online at www.unhcr.org/4c0526409.html (accessed 18 September 2015).

UNHCR. (2010b) *Resettlement Learning Programme*. Geneva: UNHCR. Available online at www.refworld.org/docid/4eba72d12.html (accessed 18 September 2015).

UNHCR. (2011) *UNHCR Resettlement Handbook*. Geneva: UNHCR. Available online at www.unhcr.org/cgi-bin/texis/vtx/search?page=search&docid=46f7c0ee2&query=resettlement%20handbook (accessed 18 September 2015).

UNHCR. (2012a) *Progress Report on Resettlement*. Executive Committee of the High Commissioner's Programme, EC/63/SC/CRP.12. Geneva: UNHCR. Available online at www.unhcr.org/5006a6aa9.html (accessed 18 September 2015).

UNHCR. (2012b) *Resettlement Learning Programme*. Geneva: UNHCR. Available online at www.refworld.org/docid/4ae6b9b92.html (accessed 18 September 2015).

UNHCR. (2012c) *UNHCR Submission to the Expert Panel on Asylum-Seekers*. Canberra: UNHCR. http://unhcr.org.au/unhcr/index.php?option=com_content&view=article&id=258&catid=37&Itemid=61 (accessed 21 October 2015).

UNHCR. (2014a) *Age, Gender and Diversity Accountability Report 2013*. Geneva: Division of International Protection, UNHCR. Available online at www.unhcr.org/548180b69.html (accessed 18 September 2015).

UNHCR. (2014b) *Progress Report on Resettlement*, Executive Committee of the High Commissioner's Programme, EC/65/SC/CRP.11. Geneva: UNHCR. Available online at www.unhcr.org/53aa90bf9.html (accessed 18 September 2015).

UNHCR. (2014c) *UNHCR Resettlement Handbook – Country Chapter Australia*. Geneva: UNHCR. Available online at www.unhcr.org/3c5e542d4.html (accessed 18 September 2015).

UNHCR-ECRE. (2008) UNHCR-NGO Joint European Advocacy Statement on Resettlement. Available online at www.ecre.org/topics/areas-of-work/resettlement/111.html (accessed 18 September 2015).

van Selm, J. (2013) *Great Expectations. A Review of the Strategic Use of Resettlement.* Policy Development and Evaluation Service, PDES/2013/13. Geneva: UNHCR.

Verdirame, G. and B. Harrell-Bond. (2003) *Rights in Exile. Janus-Faced Humanitarianism.* Oxford: Berghahn Books.

Viviani, N. (1984) *The Long Journey.* Melbourne: Melbourne University Press.

Wigley, B. (2006) *The State of UNHCR's Organisation Culture: What Now?*, Evaluation and Policy Analysis Unit EPAU/2006/01. Geneva: UNHCR.

5 UNHCR and accountability for IDP protection in Colombia[1]

Miriam Bradley

This chapter considers the role of the Office of the United Nations High Commissioner for Refugees (UNHCR), not in refugee protection, but in the protection of internally displaced persons (IDPs). Examining the work of UNHCR in Colombia between 1999 and 2010, it identifies several key challenges faced by UNHCR in developing strong and positive accountability relationships in IDP contexts. The chapter is equally concerned with the *accountability of UNHCR to different stakeholders*, as it is with *UNHCR efforts to hold other actors, namely, states, accountable*. In relation to these two dimensions of accountability, two main arguments are presented. First, the Colombian government set the terms of UNHCR's mandate and engagement in Colombia, and in allowing the state to prescribe objectives and proscribe activities, UNHCR effectively made itself accountable to the government. To the extent that the demands of the government conflicted with the protection needs and interests of IDPs, acquiescence to these demands came at the cost of downward accountability to the IDPs whom UNHCR is supposed to protect. Second, despite taking a highly legalistic approach to IDP protection, and consistently emphasising that the state bears responsibility for the protection of IDPs, UNHCR did not, for the most part, seek to hold the Colombian state accountable for this responsibility. Instead, UNHCR focused on supporting the state and, to some extent, helping other actors to hold the state accountable.

The analysis presented in this chapter has both practical and theoretical implications. On a practical level, a lack of downward accountability to beneficiaries (in this case, IDPs) and a failure to hold the state accountable can be expected to limit the effectiveness of UNHCR IDP protection efforts. In compliance with the demands of the government, UNHCR prioritised the objective of preventing displacement, which in some cases may conflict with the objective of protection. UNHCR similarly accepted a ban on interaction with non-state armed groups, despite the widespread acceptance among international humanitarian actors that such engagement is a necessary condition for improved protection outcomes. Furthermore, by supporting the state rather than holding it accountable, UNHCR worked to strengthen an institution that has itself posed a threat to IDPs. On a theoretical level, the chapter highlights some of the difficulties international organisations (IOs) face in holding accountable the states in which they are operational, and in making themselves accountable to the individuals they seek to help.

These difficulties seem to be particularly pertinent in operations for which the relevant IO lacks a clear mandate in international law (as is the case for UNHCR with IDP protection), and especially where the affected state is strong and assertive (as is the case in Colombia).

In the absence of an international legal mandate for IDP protection, UNHCR operates in IDP contexts at the invitation of the affected state, on what is effectively a contractual basis, with the terms of engagement agreed in a memorandum of understanding or other similar agreement between UNHCR and the state in question. Thus, UNHCR operates in Colombia at the invitation of the Colombian government, and staff members emphasised that this was a major factor in defining the limitations and scope of the organisation's activities.[2] This situation is by no means unique to the Colombian context. Indeed, a recent trend sees several governments of affected states becoming increasingly assertive in setting the terms of engagement for international humanitarian agencies working in their territory. There also exists a global trend towards increased institutionalisation (if not implementation) of IDP policy and legislation, characterised by the 1998 Guiding Principles on Internal Displacement (an international soft law framework), the African Union 'Kampala Convention'[3] (a regional hard law framework that came into force in 2012), and the development of national IDP legislation in several countries. Colombia was at the forefront of this trend, and the IDP law[4] in Colombia was developed during the latter stages of drafting the Guiding Principles, and was enacted before their publication. Colombia is at once characterised by a decades-long armed conflict that has produced one of the highest levels of internal displacement worldwide, and a strong administrative state with a long history of constitutional democracy and what is widely regarded as the most advanced institutional framework for IDPs in the world. The case of Colombia thus offers a good illustration of how these two trends affect the nature and scope of accountability relationships in UNHCR IDP protection work.

The analysis in this chapter builds on International Relations literature regarding the autonomy and behaviour of IOs. Much of this work deals with two related questions, concerning the extent to which IOs serve the interests of states, and the extent to which they (and the international regimes they oversee) can have an independent effect on state behaviour (Mearsheimer 1995; Keohane 1989; Hasenclever, Mayer, and Rittberger 1997; Hawkins, Lake, and Nielson 2006; Barnett and Finnemore 2004). However, this literature tends to focus on the question of IO autonomy in relation to member states, donor states and powerful states, rather than in relation to the (often much weaker) states in which IOs operate. In contrast, the analysis in this chapter is concerned with accountability relationships within a given country of operations, shedding light on the important relationship between an IO and the states in which it operates. Like other chapters in this volume, it draws attention to the plurality and complexity of UNHCR accountability relationships (see, in particular, the chapters by Kinchin and Lindskov Jacobsen).

The chapter is based on secondary literature regarding IDPs and UNHCR, publicly available UNHCR policy documents, and interviews with UNHCR staff in Colombia. Between July and September 2010, I interviewed twelve staff members (usually the head of office or, in some cases, a protection officer) in ten of the thirteen UNHCR offices in Colombia. Half of the interviewees were national staff, and half were expatriates. The interviews were conducted in English or Spanish, and followed a semi-structured format. The year 2010 can be seen as a critical juncture for two reasons. First, at the global level, UNHCR introduced a number of accountability mechanisms in the second half of the 2000's (see the introductory chapter in this volume), and by 2010 was considered to have improved significantly in this regard.[5] Second, Colombian IDP legislation has since been supplemented by the 2011 Victims' Law,[6] and the IDP issue has been largely supplanted by a focus on transitional justice (Lemaitre and Sandvik 2015). By focusing on 2010, therefore, we combine the peak institutionalisation of IDP law and policy in Colombia with an apparently strong system of accountability in UNHCR. In short, it is something of a 'least likely case' for accountability deficits (George and Bennett 2005, p. 121). The problems identified in this case are thus likely to be at least as bad in other IDP contexts with a strong and assertive state.

This chapter proceeds in six main parts. First, I offer a general discussion of accountability in the work of UNHCR. Second, I provide a brief outline of conflict, displacement and the work of UNHCR in Colombia. Third, I argue that accountability to the intended beneficiaries of UNHCR in Colombia (namely, the IDP population) is impeded because UNHCR has allowed the government to set the prevention of displacement as the primary objective for UNHCR. Fourth, I suggest that UNHCR has also allowed the government to restrict the activities that UNHCR can undertake – specifically in terms of contact with armed non-state actors – which limits the scope of UNHCR's IDP protection efforts. Fifth, I turn to the question of how far UNHCR holds the Colombian state accountable, showing how UNHCR sees itself as a partner to the state in a supportive, rather than a critical, role. Sixth, I argue that although UNHCR takes a highly legalistic approach to protection in which laws and norms are central, those laws and norms are not used primarily to hold the state accountable.

Accountability in UNHCR's IDP protection work

The existing literature on accountability and UNHCR has mainly focused on UNHCR's *refugee* protection mandate, and has highlighted two general deficits. First, it is argued that downward accountability from UNHCR to refugees has been lacking or insufficient (Verdirame and Harrell-Bond 2005; Verdirame 2011). As UNHCR became increasingly operational, in some cases operating as a 'surrogate state', making decisions that affect whether refugees receive protection and what type of protection they receive, the question of UNHCR accountability (or lack thereof) to refugees became of increasing concern (Farmer 2006; Hathaway 2005, pp. 991–1002; Loescher, Betts, and Milner 2008, pp. 84–85; Pallis 2004–2005). The deficit in downward accountability is not unique to UNHCR, and is, indeed, the central concern of the accountability movement in humanitarian action more broadly, exemplified by the establishment in 1997 of the Active Learning Network for Accountability and Performance in Humanitarian Action (ALNAP) and the

Sphere Project, and the establishment in 2003 of the Humanitarian Accountability Partnership (HAP).

Second, it is argued that UNHCR's ability to hold states accountable for their refugee protection obligations has been limited. When UNHCR was created in 1951, its mandate was for the protection of refugees, and a major part of that mandate was the supervision of the 1951 Convention Relating to the Status of Refugees (hereafter, the 1951 Convention). Article 35 of the 1951 Convention and Article 2 of its 1967 Protocol set out a supervisory role for UNHCR. In signing these treaties, states accept an obligation and responsibility for refugee protection, and mandate UNHCR to play a role in holding them accountable. However, the supervision system for the 1951 Convention and 1967 Protocol is considered by many to be weak or insufficient (Kälin 2003; Türk 2001). Critics have argued, for example, that this system does not amount to a transparent system to ensure accountability (Hathaway 2005, pp. 991–1002). There is no institutionalised public scrutiny or accountability, and neither is there any system of peer review (through which states would report to other states).

Both of these types of deficit have arguably been aggravated by UNHCR's upward accountability to the states that have mandated it. In all intergovernmental organisations, a line of accountability runs from the organisation to the states that created it, reflecting the authority delegated to the organisation by these different actors. In the case of UNHCR in particular, accountability runs via the UN General Assembly, the UN Economic and Social Council, and also to donor states. Yet, as many within the humanitarian accountability movement have indicated, such upward accountability can be in conflict with (downward) accountability to those that an organisation seeks to assist (Knox-Clarke and Mitchell 2011, p. 4). This upward accountability to states may also have compromised UNHCR's ability to hold the states accountable for their own refugee protection obligations. Specifically, it has been argued that the financial reliance of UNHCR on voluntary contributions from donor states makes the organisation vulnerable to political pressures in such a way as to compromise its supervisory function (Loescher 2001, p. 350; Loescher, Betts, and Milner 2008, p. 2; see also Niamh Kinchin's contribution to this volume).

Despite these insightful analyses, such literature does not address UNHCR accountability relationships with respect to IDP protection work, and lacks serious consideration of the role of the states in which UNHCR is operational. Where such states are weak and UNHCR takes on state functions (e.g. refugee status determination and refugee camp governance), the existing literature largely ignores *the accountability of the affected state*, and focuses instead on the (lack of) accountability of UNHCR to the refugees. The focus of this literature on downward accountability to beneficiaries is welcome, but it is important not to lose sight of the role that UNHCR is supposed to play in holding states accountable for their refugee obligations. In those contexts where UNHCR is operational, its supervisory function may be compromised not only by its financial reliance on voluntary contributions, but also by its need for invitation and acceptance by the affected state. This chapter therefore contributes to filling an important gap by specifically investigating accountability in UNHCR's IDP protection work, and by bringing to the fore the question of accountability between UNHCR and the states in which the organisation operates. It argues that where UNHCR is operational in the context of a strong and assertive state, there can be a line of accountability from UNHCR to that state. Just as it has been argued that upward accountability to member and donor states can compromise the ability of UNHCR to hold states accountable for their refugee protection obligations, this chapter shows how accountability to the states in which UNHCR undertakes IDP operations can compromise the accountability of UNHCR to IDPs, and the ability of UNHCR to hold those states accountable.

IDPs were designated as a distinct policy category in the 1990s, following a number of inter-related shifts at the international level. The end of the Cold War yielded the end of the bipolar structure that had constrained multilateral international action within sovereign states, providing the opportunity for the international community to become more involved in what had been considered the domestic affairs of states. Additionally, European and North American States were adopting increasingly restrictive asylum policies and practices in the 1980s and 1990s, and IDP protection came to be seen as both a humanitarian solution and a means to contain would-be refugees in their countries of origin (Dubernet 2001; Phuong 2004; Shacknove 1993). Thus, there existed not only the opportunity but also rational incentives for major states to support efforts to protect and assist IDPs in countries of origin. In addition, during the 1990s, a number of individuals presented ethical arguments in support of the same end. Most notably, the publications of Roberta Cohen, Francis Deng, Walter Kälin and Erin Mooney raised the profile of IDP needs and reconceptualised the international community's approach to sovereignty and intervention in situations in which national governments are unable or unwilling to protect their own citizens.

The international normative framework also took shape in the 1990s. In 1992, Francis Deng was appointed by Kofi Annan to be the first representative of the Secretary-General on IDPs, and six years later, he published the *Guiding Principles on Internal Displacement* (Deng 1998). Although the IDP issue was now firmly on the international agenda, and the Guiding Principles provided a soft law framework for the protection of IDPs, contestation persisted over what institutional arrangements should be adopted to address IDP needs. Some suggested that a new UN forced migration agency should be established to assume the responsibilities of UNHCR for refugees, and to protect and assist other – internally and externally – displaced persons (Martin 2004). Others, such as Richard Holbrooke, then US ambassador to the UN, proposed the creation of a new, IDP-specific agency (Turton 2011, p. 8). Yet others still suggested that an existing agency, most likely to be UNHCR, should assume responsibility for IDP protection.

However, the initial solution was neither to create a new agency nor to mandate an existing one to take responsibility for IDPs. Instead, IDP needs were to be addressed through inter-agency collaboration. Under the so-called collaborative approach, a non-operational Internal Displacement Unit was launched in January 2002 (and renamed the Inter-Agency Internal Displacement Division in 2004) to promote more effective inter-agency, operational responses to internal displacement. The aim was to ensure a greater focus on IDP needs across operational UN agencies; however, failings were identified in terms of gaps, overlaps and a lack of predictability. In an effort to address these shortcomings, the collaborative approach was replaced by the 'cluster approach' in 2005. The cluster approach refers to a coordination structure involving both UN and non-UN humanitarian organisations at both the global and country levels. Each cluster focuses on a particular aspect of emergency response,[7] and has a clearly defined lead agency and a provider of last resort. For conflict-induced IDPs, UNHCR is the Global Cluster Lead for the three clusters of protection, emergency shelter, and camp coordination and camp management. In situations where internal displacement is exclusively due to natural or man-made disasters, UNHCR has joint responsibility at the field level with UNICEF and the UN Office of the High Commissioner for Human Rights.

The cluster approach was designed to increase predictability and accountability for IDP protection. Although it has arguably generated greater predictability in response, it remains unclear just how accountability for IDP protection operates. Who is accountable for IDP protection? To whom are they accountable? And for what exactly are they accountable? The analysis in this chapter starts from the perspective that UNHCR is present and working to protect IDPs in any given context precisely because the state has failed in its responsibility, being either unwilling or unable to protect everyone in its territory. As UNHCR purports to be protecting IDPs, it should be held accountable for this work, and it should be accountable to the IDPs themselves for this work. Furthermore, because the state in question has primary responsibility for the protection of all those in its territory, UNHCR should seek to hold that state accountable for this responsibility. However, UNHCR does not have a legal mandate for IDP protection, and there is no international hard law framework specifically related to IDP protection. Thus, UNHCR does not have a mandated supervisory role akin to the supervisory function for refugee protection laid out in the 1951 Convention and 1967 Protocol. This situation puts UNHCR on a weaker footing – or, as one refugee law expert put it, in 'a legal and political minefield' – for its work with IDPs (Goodwin-Gill 2000). The remainder of this chapter examines how UNHCR navigated that minefield in Colombia.

Conflict, displacement and UNHCR in Colombia

In order to contextualise the work of UNHCR in Colombia, this section provides a brief outline of conflict and displacement in that context. The armed conflict in Colombia can be dated to the 1960s with the formation of two left-wing guerrilla groups, the Revolutionary Armed Forces of Colombia and the National Liberation Army (known by their Spanish initials FARC and ELN, respectively), both of which are still in operation today.[8,9] During the 1980s, wealthy landowners created paramilitary groups to protect themselves and their economic interests from guerrilla violence. In 1997, these paramilitary groups formed a national umbrella organisation, known as the United Self-Defence Forces of Colombia (AUC). In

2003, the AUC began to demobilise, and by the end of the demobilisation process in mid-2006, more than 30,000 paramilitary combatants had formally demobilised (Oficina Alto Comisionado para la Paz 2006, p. 8). However, in reality, some paramilitaries never demobilised and others rearmed after demobilising, resulting in the emergence of so-called new groups (also known as neo-paramilitaries, post-demobilisation groups, or emerging groups) using the same structures, controlling the same zones, and including some of the same individuals as the former AUC blocs (International Crisis Group 2007; US State Department 2010; Denissen 2010; Porch and Rasmussen 2008). All of these different non-state armed groups, as well as the armed forces of the state, have posed threats to the civilian population, and have contributed to the massive levels of internal displacement.

The figures on displacement are disputed; however, estimates for 2010 varied from 3.6 to 5.2 million, accounting for 8 to 11.6 per cent of the total population (IDMC 2011, p. 71). The causes of displacement in Colombia are complex and varied. Families, particularly those with teenage sons, often displaced to avoid recruitment into the FARC, ELN or other armed groups.[10] Individuals were often displaced because they were involved (or thought to be involved) in activism on issues that were sensitive for armed actors, including the public forces. For example, leaders of indigenous organisations and those who have spoken out on land issues or criticised authorities have often been targeted, particularly by the paramilitaries and neo-paramilitaries (Somos Defensores 2011, n.d.; Verdad Abierta 2011).[11] Entire communities were threatened and ordered to displace to clear land as part of the conflict strategy of different armed groups or to enable the implementation of megaprojects (Asociación de Cabildos Indígenas del Norte del Cauca 2014).[12] The aerial fumigation of coca crops has also been cited as a cause of displacement, due to the health impacts of the aerial spraying, the loss of licit and illicit livelihoods, or the military actions that often accompany such fumigation (Ceballos 2004).[13] Additionally, IDPs and other civilians face a number of threats to their security that do not necessarily result in displacement. Such threats include extrajudicial killings (US State Department 2010), disappearances (Defensoría del Pueblo 2011), kidnappings (Hanson 2009), landmine injuries (International Campaign to Ban Landmines 2009, p. 296), sexual violence (Oxfam 2009), bombings (Restrepo and Spagat 2004) and massacres (Restrepo and Spagat 2004; Verdad Abierta 2010).

UNHCR first became officially involved in Colombia in 1997,[14] providing advice to the Colombian government on the drafting of IDP legislation, which resulted in Law 387.[15] Subsequently, the Colombian government requested assistance on protection and the prevention of displacement, and in 1999 UNHCR signed a Memorandum of Intent with the government,[16] mandating UNHCR Colombia to strengthen national mechanisms for the prevention of displacement and the protection of IDPs (UNHCR 2008, p. 1). Since then, IDP law and policy have been further institutionalised, with such institutionalisation driven in no small part by the Constitutional Court. The Colombian Constitutional Court is independent, progressive and activist, often holding the government to account on human rights issues (Nunes 2010). The Court often issued decisions relating to

IDP issues, specifying how the legal framework must be implemented. A petition process, known as the *tutela*, permits an individual to file a claim against the violation of basic rights, and this process was used extensively by IDPs and IDP organisations (Lemaitre and Sandvik 2015, p. 18). In response, the Court issued decisions and follow-up orders that were decisive in the development of IDP policy in Colombia.

Against this background, this chapter argues that UNHCR had a specific mandate in Colombia, which was not primarily about protecting internally displaced populations directly, but rather about strengthening institutions and public administration (the top-down element), and about strengthening the organisations of the displaced population (the bottom-up element). Additionally, where communities were understood to be at risk of displacement, UNHCR sought to develop practical protection projects (examples include the building of schools, the canalisation of water and the restoration of health centres) with the aim of providing passive protection through UNHCR presence, bringing in the social agencies of the state and preventing displacement.[17]

The remainder of the chapter examines the accountability relationships implicit in the work of UNHCR in Colombia, and in the ways UNHCR goes about this work. The next two sections examine particular aspects of, respectively, the objectives and methods of UNHCR's IDP protection work in Colombia, to offer insights into the question to whom UNHCR is accountable. The following two sections explore the extent to which UNHCR holds the Colombian state to account.

Prevention of displacement

One of the primary objectives of UNHCR in Colombia is the prevention of displacement. Indeed, within the discourse and practice of UNHCR in Colombia, the protection of IDPs has been conflated with the prevention of displacement. However, displacement is very often a protective strategy, and focusing on preventing their displacement may be at odds with the protection needs of those at risk of displacement. Josep Zapater, a UNHCR official who formerly worked in Colombia, analysed the conceptual inconsistencies of the prevention of forced displacement, and the problematic practical implications of relying on this concept for the design of programming (Zapater 2010). He described participatory workshops undertaken by UNHCR in 2005 with indigenous communities deemed at risk of displacement. In those workshops, the affected communities questioned the construction by UNHCR of *forced displacement* as the central problem. Zapater highlighted two fundamental inconsistencies in this conceptualisation. First, displacement is often a protective strategy in itself. Second, even when conceptualised as a threat, forced displacement is one among many conflict-related threats (including assassination, kidnapping and land appropriation), and may not be the most serious. At worst, then, the objective of preventing displacement may be *in conflict with* the objective of protection, and at best, it may lead to a failure to prioritise the most severe threats or the most insecure civilians.

Despite the participants objecting to this conceptualisation in the 2005 workshops, when I conducted fieldwork in Colombia in 2010, it became clear that for UNHCR staff there, protection was still understood to be virtually synonymous with the prevention of displacement, and the two terms were often used interchangeably. In several of my interviews, it was only when pushed that interviewees separated the two concepts and recognised that they may be distinct, highlighting the fact that several of the risks of forced displacement fall outside the realm of UNHCR work, connected as they are to, for example, economic or infrastructure issues.[18] Even to the extent that a distinction was recognised, the prevention of displacement remained one of the primary functions of UNHCR work in Colombia, and is regarded by UNHCR officials as one of the most important parts of protection.[19] This institutional perspective is confirmed by an analysis of UNHCR Global Appeal documents, several of which highlight the prevention of displacement as one of UNHCR's 'main objectives' or 'strategic priorities' in Colombia (UNHCR 2002, p. 286; 2005, p. 353; 2006, p. 295; 2007a, p. 326; 2009, p. 10; 2011, p. 274; 2013a, p. 2).

In sum, emphasising the prevention of displacement is inherently problematic, and this conceptualisation of the protection problematique met with explicit objections from affected communities. However, the goal of preventing displacement did align with the objectives of the Colombian government. The 1999 Memorandum of Intent between UNHCR and the Colombian government specifically mandated UNHCR to work on the prevention of displacement.[20] Moreover, reducing the level of displacement in the country was a priority for the Colombian government,[21] because although significant successes had been achieved in reducing other conflict indicators, the level of displacement remained stubbornly high.[22] Thus the focus on the prevention of displacement by UNHCR can be understood as a direct response to the demands of the government.

Furthermore, as we shall see in the next section, it was not only UNHCR's objectives in Colombia but also the means with which UNHCR pursued those objectives, that were restricted by the terms of engagement set by the Colombian government, and ran counter to the best interests of the IDPs and others of concern to UNHCR.

Interaction with armed non-state actors

Both internationally and in the specific context of Colombia, armed non-state actors are a major cause of IDP insecurity, and of the threats that lead to displacement. Indeed, since the end of the Cold War, the proportion of one-sided violence (the use of lethal force, by governments or non-state armed groups, against civilians, that causes 25 or more deaths in a calendar year) perpetrated by non-state actors increased from 25 per cent in 1989 to 80 per cent in 2008 (Human Security Report Project 2011). In Colombia, non-state armed groups have been the primary perpetrators of many threats to civilians and the cause of much displacement. Kidnapping for ransom was once a major source of income for the FARC and, to a lesser degree, for the ELN (Hanson 2009). Landmines have primarily been used by the guerrillas in Colombia, and their use by the FARC, in particular, increased during the early 2000s (Human Rights Watch 2007, p. 15). From a sample of testimonies of incidents of sexual violence connected to the armed conflict collected by the Constitutional Court, 58 per cent were attributed to paramilitaries, 23 per cent to government forces and 8 per cent to guerrillas (Oxfam 2009, p. 14). Guerrilla bombings in large urban areas as well as in rural areas have been a significant cause of civilian injuries and of some deaths (Restrepo and Spagat 2004). Although massacres have also been committed by Colombian guerrilla groups, they were more commonly the tool of the former paramilitary organisations, and have also been perpetrated by neo-paramilitary groups (Restrepo and Spagat 2004; Verdad Abierta 2010). Assassination or the threat of assassination were frequently used by the former AUC paramilitary groups and the neo-paramilitaries to punish or prevent civilian behaviour that runs counter to paramilitary interests (Verdad Abierta 2011).

In light of their significant impact on protection outcomes, changing the behaviour of armed non-state actors should be a central focus of protection efforts. Better protection outcomes for IDPs and those at risk of displacement could be achieved if non-state armed groups abstained from threatening them, and such groups may also be able to play a more proactive protection role (Ruaudel 2013; South 2012). For these reasons, humanitarian policy analysts consistently argue that greater engagement with armed non-state actors is a necessary (if insufficient) condition for improved protection outcomes (Zeender 2005; ADH 2011; Jackson 2012; HPCR 2011). Similarly, within the UN, both the Office for the Coordination of Humanitarian Affairs and the UN Secretary-General have emphasised engagement with NSAGs as a necessary component of civilian protection efforts (UN OCHA 2006; UN Security Council 2009, para. 40). Ignoring armed non-state actors undoubtedly represents a dysfunctional approach to IDP protection in contemporary conflicts.

In Colombia, however, the government banned all organisations apart from the International Committee of the Red Cross (ICRC) and, at times, the Catholic Church from interacting with the non-state armed groups. In June 2005, President Uribe's High Commissioner for Peace issued to ambassadors, UN agencies and aid agencies active in Colombia 'Guidelines for the approach to be taken by international cooperation projects' (*El Tiempo* 15 June 2005). These guidelines stipulated that the language of armed conflict ('armed parties', 'conflict actors', 'non-state actors', etc.) should not be used in reference to Colombia, and prohibited activities that implied contact with the illegal armed groups. The then-head of UNHCR in Colombia, Roberto Meier, spoke out against these guidelines, specifically against the attempt to control the use of conflict-related language (*El Tiempo* 17 June 2005). However, UNHCR acquiesced to the ban on talking to illegal armed groups. As a consequence, at the time of interviews, UNHCR staff members did not engage with the FARC, ELN or other non-state armed groups, except when contact was required by the armed group in question, in which case UNHCR officials had little choice but to interact with them.[23] All staff received security training when they joined UNHCR, during which they were told to keep such contact to a minimum, and simply to explain the work of the organisation and the principle of neutrality.[24] UNHCR protocol strictly forbade giving or receiving information.[25] While broad acceptance of this prohibition conformed nicely to the demands of the Colombian government, it was unlikely to be in the best interests of the IDPs and others of concern to UNHCR.

By prioritising the prevention of displacement, and avoiding engagement with armed non-state actors, UNHCR set itself up to support the Colombian state, with the state determining the objectives that UNHCR pursued, and restricting the activities it could undertake. Where the prescriptions and proscriptions of the government conflict with the protection needs of IDPs and others of concern to UNHCR, the possibility of UNHCR accountability to those primary stakeholders is precluded. If anything, it puts UNHCR in a relationship in which it is account-able to the Colombian government rather than to the supposed beneficiaries of its work. What, then, of governmental accountability for IDP protection? The next sections explore how far UNHCR sought to hold the Colombian state to account.

Supporting the state

As can be seen in a number of documents and interviews, UNHCR generally conceives its role in relation to the affected states as that of a supportive part-ner. In 2007, UNHCR published four key documents relating to its IDP policy, all of which highlight the responsibility of the state (UNHCR 2007e, para. 19; 2007d, para. 27; 2007b, para. 6; 2007c, para. 19). Similarly, Excom conclusions[26] No. 75 (1993), No. 80 (1996), No. 105 (2006) and No. 108 (2008) all note that the primary responsibility for the welfare and protection of IDPs lies with the state concerned. However, UNHCR is mandated to work in IDP contexts precisely in cases where the state in question is failing to live up to that responsibility, either because of unwillingness or inability. Logically, where a state is unwilling, it needs to be pressured or persuaded, and where it is unable, it needs to be supported and assisted. In practice, a state is often some combination of unwilling and unable. In Colombia, for example, several branches of the state were arguably willing at the national level (the Constitutional Court, for example), but were unable to protect IDPs effectively due to a lack of will at the local level. Regardless, the approach taken by UNHCR was first and foremost about supporting and strengthening the state at both the national and local levels.

Providing support to a state that itself poses a threat can have enormously damaging consequences for IDPs (for a critique of how UN support for the state played out in Sri Lanka in 2009, for example, see Internal Review Panel 2012). In Colombia, UNHCR has taken a positive view of the will and ability of most institutions of the state to protect IDPs and those at risk of displacement, despite the fact that the state officials have themselves, through acts of commission and omission, been the source of threats. Links between the national military and the AUC paramilitary organisations have been well documented, and confirmed by the Supreme Court. Through these links, individuals at all levels of the national military facilitated some of the worst abuses of civilians in the Colombian conflict.

The military have also posed more direct threats. In the early 2000s, the 'falsos positivos' scandal emerged: in an effort to meet targets for combating the guerrillas, and to get rid of suspected guerrilla sympathisers without due process, Colombian soldiers murdered civilians and then dressed them in guerrilla uniforms to pass them off as guerrillas killed in combat (US State Department 2010). Despite all of this, UNHCR focused its efforts on strengthening the Colombian state.

In addition to the sometimes grave dangers of supporting an unwilling state, there can be a tension between strengthening and supporting the state, on the one hand, and holding the state to account on the other. Such a tension was evident in the work of UNHCR in Colombia. Although this dual role may be theoretically unproblematic, in practice when individual UNHCR staff members are working to support individual representatives of the state in various positions, they build a personal relationship that can make it difficult to criticise those same state representatives when they fail to fulfil their obligations. There was uncertainty among UNHCR staff members as to what the balance between these two parts of the UNHCR role should be. Some UNHCR officials suggested they would never criticise the state and would always take joint responsibility as a partner rather than as a supervisor.[27] Others suggested that part of their role was to criticise state institutions when UNHCR disagreed with their policies or practice. However, no evidence has suggested that such criticism occurred with any frequency. At both the national and local levels, for example, UNHCR was working with various institutions of the state, including Acción Social (the government aid agency). UNHCR staff noted many faults of Acción Social, but reported that UNHCR would not point out those faults and mistakes, but rather would try to help Acción Social improve.[28] UNHCR did so in a supportive role by providing technical and financial assistance to specific projects and channelling information from Bogotá to the departments and municipalities. In other words, it worked with them as a partner, not an independent critic, and most interviewees felt that UNHCR did not have a monitoring role.

In sum, UNHCR saw itself first and foremost as a partner to the Colombian state, and not as a critical voice. UNHCR supported the state through financial, technical and institutional assistance. It did not seek to draw attention to the shortcomings or weaknesses of the state, or to share evidence of the state's lack of will or capacity. However, this does not imply that UNHCR did nothing to hold the state to account. As we shall see in the next section, UNHCR sought to equip other actors with the information and tools to claim their rights and to hold the state accountable when it failed in its obligations. In this way, UNHCR may have indirectly contributed to holding the state accountable for its shortcomings.

Law, rights and accountability

In Colombia, as in an increasing number of IDP contexts, the domestic legal framework was absolutely central to the work of UNHCR. Reference to international law alone was understood to carry little weight in getting the social institutions of the Colombian state to respond at the local level, and the national legislation was so well advanced that there was understood to be little need for recourse to any other body of law. UNHCR identified the central problem to be that much of this legal framework was not applied in practice.[29] In an effort to improve the application of that framework, then, UNHCR undertook three main types of activity.

First, at the national level, UNHCR was permanently working with the Constitutional Court on IDP issues.[30] UNHCR saw the Court as the key driver of the IDP response of the Colombian state, and viewed support for the Court as a way to maximise leverage over national policy and practice (UNHCR 2008, para. 22). Thus, UNHCR was feeding the Court with information from the field offices on the (non-)implementation of official policy. Providing information to the Court was considered important because if the Court did not know what was going on at the local level, it could not devise an appropriate response. Such evidence contributed to the Court declaring an 'unconstitutional state of affairs' in 2004 because the government's obligations to IDPs were not being fulfilled,[31] and to two key follow-up orders in 2009, AUTO 004[32] and AUTO 005.[33] However, the decisions of the Constitutional Court were often not fully implemented at the local level (Carr 2009; Meertens 2010). UNHCR, therefore, also worked with local institutions with the aim of getting laws and decisions made in Bogotá understood and implemented at the departmental and municipal levels; often, the local government and Acción Social were not aware of new legislation and requirements, and UNHCR was the only organisation to receive information on new laws and decrees.[34] Communicating policy from Bogotá to the municipalities was considered important because if local officials had no knowledge of these laws and decisions, they were unable to apply them.

Second, UNHCR sought to support and strengthen control mechanisms that have a bearing on issues to do with displacement, such as the Procuraduría (Office of the Inspector-General) and the Defensoría del Pueblo (Office of the Human Rights Ombudsman). The Procuraduría is responsible for evaluating the compliance of state agencies with their obligations to the displaced population, and is empowered to impose sanctions in cases of non-compliance. The Defensoría only has the power to say what it sees is wrong, but can have an impact in conjunction with the Procuraduría.[35] In some regions, UNHCR was accompanying officials from both the Procuraduría and the Defensoría on field missions, as well as financing or subsidising posts in both.[36] In other words, although UNHCR would not have criticised those agencies tasked with responding to displacement, and nor would it have held them to account directly, it did support the state's own mechanisms for holding those agencies to account.

Third, UNHCR supported communities, groups and individuals in accessing their own rights. UNHCR undertook a number of projects throughout Colombia aimed at educating individuals, groups and communities in their rights, on the basis that if they did not understand the law, they would not have the necessary tools with which to claim their rights.[37] For example, a project funded by UNHCR and the Norwegian Refugee Council supported *consultorios jurídicos* (legal aid clinics) in universities throughout Colombia (UNHCR 2008, p. 11; 2013b, p. 2).

Through this project, UNHCR trained law students in IDP law so that the students could provide legal advice to individuals, thus helping those indidivuals to access rights and state programmes. Information regarding domestic law and the rights of individuals was also disseminated through the publication of various materials by UNHCR field offices. For example, pamphlets and calendars explaining key laws or decisions of the Constitutional Court relevant to the local community were widely distributed among the Afro-Colombian communities in the department of Chocó.[38] UNHCR also organised workshops for displaced organisations focused on particular aspects of the normative framework including, for example, land issues. Additionally, UNHCR worked to strengthen IDP organisations and, particularly, Afro-Colombian and indigenous organisations, with the aim of building the cohesiveness and skills they needed to represent themselves effectively.[39] Although UNHCR might support such organisations directly in their interlocution with local state agencies, it would not have directly supported legal action against the state. If IDPs wanted to take such action, they could do so, but UNHCR would not.[40]

Through various activities, then, UNHCR sought to provide a range of different actors with the information, knowledge and tools to be able to hold the state accountable, if they so chose. In this way, UNHCR aimed to improve the accountability of the Colombian state, albeit indirectly. However, the focus on domestic law imposes limits on such accountability mechanisms, in that the state can only be held accountable for the standards it has set in its own laws. Furthermore, the dangers often inherent in seeking legal redress in the context of violent conflict, and specifically the threats experienced by IDP organisations seeking to claim their rights in Colombia (Lemaitre and Sandvik 2015), may reduce the extent to which affected individuals and communities themselves are willing and able to hold the state to account.

Conclusion

There is a tension in the dual role in which UNHCR identifies both as a servant of the states in which it operates, and as a servant of displaced individuals and communities. UNHCR has multiple – and sometimes conflicting – accountability relationships. Thus, in service to the state, and potentially in conflict with the interests of IDPs themselves, UNHCR has prioritised the prevention of displacement in Colombia, and accepted a prohibition on engagement with non-state armed groups. Furthermore, UNHCR has conceptualised its own role as one of supportive partner rather than critic of the state. It has only sought to hold the state to account indirectly, through the provision of information and assistance to a range of domestic actors.

Of course, it could be argued that UNHCR has no choice but to conform to the desires and demands of the governments of the states on whose territory it engages in IDP operations. Agreements signed between UNHCR and the state in which it is operating set the terms of UNHCR engagement, and often specify the tasks UNHCR is entrusted to perform. As such, they imply that authority is delegated to UNHCR by the state. UNHCR is correspondingly accountable to the state for this engagement and these tasks. Moreover, the lack of an international legal mandate for IDP protection (as compared with the refugee protection function of UNHCR, or with the work of the ICRC, for example) make it difficult for UNHCR to insist on particular terms of engagement when it comes to IDP operations.

However, where the terms set by the state actually conflict with the protection of IDPs, it could equally be argued that UNHCR has a duty to reject those terms, even if in some contexts, such rejection may imply that UNHCR cannot work there. In fact, the likelihood is that in many contexts, UNHCR may be able to negotiate better terms without losing its invitation and acceptance. UNHCR wields a certain level of moral and expert authority (Barnett and Finnemore 2004). As such, it has some leverage it could use to set the terms of engagement more in line with the needs of the IDPs and others of concern to UNHCR than with the priorities of the government of the affected state. A more assertive UNHCR may be better able to represent the needs and interests of IDPs in relation to an assertive state. In contrast, in Colombia, there was a lack of clarity within UNHCR as to how far the organisation should state its own positions and hold the government accountable, and how far it should allow the government to dictate UNHCR mandate in that context. There is a risk that this uncertainty engenders a lack of confidence within UNHCR, which enables the government to set the terms of engagement more than would otherwise be the case.

The challenges of developing strong and positive accountability relationships are not unique to UNHCR. Operational international organisations work within the territory of nation-states, and they will usually do so only with the consent of the state concerned. Where they have a clear mandate in international law to fulfil particular functions or to undertake particular tasks – as does UNHCR for refugee protection, for example, or the ICRC for the protection of prisoners of war – that mandate may provide the confidence and leverage necessary to stipulate minimum conditions or terms of engagement. In the absence of such a mandate, however, and particularly in the context of a strong and assertive state, there is a risk that the organisation in question becomes first and foremost accountable to that state, rather than to the people it is intended to serve. As both strong and weak states become increasingly assertive in the face of international action that they consider to be neo-colonial, organisations must grapple with the extent to which they will compromise on the terms of their engagement, and the question of when and where red lines should be drawn.

Notes

1　The field research on which this chapter is based was undertaken as part of my doctoral research and was funded by travel grants from the Department of Politics and International Relations, St. Antony's College at Oxford University and a Santander Scholarship.

2 UNHCR interview, Apartadó.

3 African Union Convention for the Protection and Assistance of Internally Displaced Persons in Africa ('Kampala Convention'), 22 October 2009.

4 *Ley N° 387 por la cual se adoptan medidas para la prevención del desplazamiento forzado; la atención, protección, consolidación y estabilización socioeconómica de los desplazados internos por la violencia en la República de Colombia*, 18 July 1997.

5 See the introductory chapter of this volume.

6 *Ley N° 1448 Ley de Víctimas y Restitución de Tierras por la cual se dictan medidas de atención, asistencia y reparación integral a las víctimas del conflicto armado interno y se dictan otras disposiciones*, 10 June 2011.

7 The 11 clusters are: food security; camp coordination/management; early recovery; education; emergency shelter; emergency telecommunications; health; logistics; nutrition; protection; and water, sanitation and hygiene.

8 A formal peace process between the government and the FARC began in October 2012 and was ongoing at the time of writing this chapter (2015). However, the fieldwork for this chapter was undertaken between July and September 2010, when no such process was in place.

9 A number of other guerrilla groups have ceased to exist — for example, the EPL (1967–1991), the M-19 (1973–1990), Quintín Lame (1984–1991) and the ERP (1985–2007).

10 UNHCR interviews, Medellín, Mocoa.

11 UNHCR interviews, Apartadó, Barranquilla, Bogotá.

12 UNHCR interviews, Apartadó, Medellín, Mocoa, Villavicencio.

13 UNHCR interviews Pasto, Villavicencio.

14 UNHCR started working in several parts of the country before 1997, operating from what was then the UNHCR regional office in Venezuela.

15 *Ley N° 387.*

16 *Memorando de intención entre la Oficina del Alto Comisionado de las Naciones Unidas para los Refugiados (ACNUR) y el Gobierno de la República de Colombia, relativo al suministro de cooperación para el tratamiento del problema del desplazamiento forzado*, 28 January 1999.

17 UNHCR interviews, Apartadó, Barranquilla, Bogotá, Cúcuta, Mocoa, Neiva, Pasto.

18 UNHCR interviews, Apartadó, Cúcuta, Medellín, Quibdó.

19 UNHCR interviews, Apartadó, Barranquilla, Bogotá.

20 *Memorando de intención*, Artículo I; Artículo II; Artículo III.1.a.

21 Leaked cable, US Embassy, Bogotá, 20 April 2004, *PRM'S A/S Dewey's visit to Colombia*, para. 18. Available online at www.wikileaks.org/plusd/cables/04BOGOTA3943_a. html (accessed 20 May 2015).

22 UNHCR interview, Villavicencio.

23 UNHCR interviews, Bogotá, Quibdó.

24 UNHCR interview, Barranquilla.

25 UNHCR interviews, Barranquilla, Cúcuta.

26 The Executive Committee of the High Commissioner's Programme (Excom) is the governing body of UNHCR and meets annually in Geneva, with a Standing Committee that usually meets three times a year. Excom started in 1958 with 25 member states and has steadily expanded to 94 member states (at the end of 2014). Excom oversees the budget of UNHCR and is a forum for debate among member states on issues pertinent to the work of the organisation. Excom issues conclusions relating to particular policy issues, which are essentially guidelines both for UNHCR and for the states.

27 UNHCR interview, Villavicencio.

28 UNHCR interviews, Apartadó, Medellín, Villavicencio.

29 UNHCR interview, Quibdó.

30 UNHCR interview, Bogotá.

31 *Sentencia T-025/04, Abel Antonio Jaramillo y otros vs. Red de Solidaridad Social y otros*, T-025/04, Colombia: Corte Constitucional, 22 January 2004.

32 *Auto 004/09, Protección de derechos fundamentales de personas e indígenas desplazados por el conflicto armado en el marco de superación del estado de cosas inconstitucional declarado en sentencia T-025/04,* A004/09, Colombia: Corte Constitucional, 26 January 2009.

33 *Auto 004/09, Protección de derechos fundamentales de la población afrodescendiente víctima del desplazamiento forzado en el marco de superación del estado de cosas inconstitucional declarado en sentencia T-025/04,* Colombia: Corte Constitucional, 26 January 2009.

34 UNHCR interviews, Pasto, Quibdó, Villavicencio.

35 UNHCR interview, Pasto.

36 UNHCR interviews, Barranquilla, Cúcuta, Medellín, Neiva.

37 UNHCR interviews Apartadó, Barranquilla, Bogotá, Cúcuta.

38 UNHCR interview, Quibdó.

39 UNHCR interviews Apartadó, Barranquilla, Cúcuta, Medellín, Pasto.

40 UNHCR interviews, Apartadó, Quibdó.

References

ADH. (2011) *Rules of Engagement: Protecting Civilians Through Dialogue With Armed Non-State Actors.* Geneva: Geneva Academy of International Humanitarian Law and Human Rights.

Asociación de Cabildos Indígenas del Norte del Cauca. (2014) 'Colombia: desplazamiento forzado y proyectos de desarrollo'. Available online at www.nasaacin.org/informativo-nasaacin/contexto-colombiano/7198-colombia-desplazamiento-forzado-y-proyectos-de-desarrollo (accessed 20 May 2015).

Barnett, M. and M. Finnemore. (2004) *Rules for the World: International Organisations in Global Politics.* Ithaca: Cornell University Press.

Carr, S. (2009) 'From theory to practice: national and regional application of the guiding principles', *International Journal of Refugee Law,* 21(1): 34–47.

Ceballos, M. (2004) 'Fumigación de cultivos de uso ilícito y vulneración de derechos humanos en la frontera colombo-ecuatoriana', II Conferencia regional 'Migración, desplazamiento forzado y refugio', Universidad Andina Simón Bolívar, Quito, septiembre 1, 2 y 3 de 2004.

Defensoría del Pueblo (2011) 'Desaparición forzada 2011-08-29'. Available online at www.defensoria.org.co/red/?_item=0301&_secc=03&ts=2&n=1342 (accessed 16 February 2012).

Deng, F. (1998) 'Guiding principles on internal displacement', submitted by Francis Deng, Special Representative of the Secretary-General to the UN Commission on Human Rights, *International Journal of Refugee Law,* 10(3): 563–572.

Denissen, M. (2010) 'Reintegrating ex-combatants into civilian life: the case of the paramilitaries in Colombia'. *Peace & Change,* 35(2): 328–352.

Dubernet, C. (2001) *The International Containment of Displaced Persons: Humanitarian Spaces Without Exit.* Aldershot: Ashgate Publishing.

El Tiempo. (15 June 2005) 'Una iniciativa desafortunada'. Available online at http://www.eltiempo.com/archivo/documento/MAM-1695937 (accessed 28 April 2015).

El Tiempo. (17 June 2005) 'Circular del Comisionado podría causar la salida de ACNUR del país'. Available online at http://www.eltiempo.com/archivo/documento/MAM-1956035 (accessed 20 May 2015).

Farmer, A. (2006) 'Refugee responses, state-like behavior, and accountability for human rights violations: a case study of sexual violence in Guinea's refugee camps', *Yale Human Rights & Development Law Journal,* 9(1): 44–84.

George, A. L. and A. Bennett. (2005) *Case Studies and Theory Development in the Social Sciences.* London: MIT Press.

Goodwin-Gill, G. S. (2000) 'UNHCR and internal displacement: stepping into a legal and political minefield', in *World Refugee Survey 2000,* pp. 26–31. Washington, DC: US Committee for Refugees and Immigrants.

Hanson, S. (2009) 'FARC, ELN: Colombia's left-wing guerrillas'. Available online at www.cfr.org/publication/9272/farc_eln.html#p3 (accessed 15 December 2010).

Hasenclever, A., P. Mayer, and V. Rittberger. (1997) *Theories of International Regimes*. Cambridge: Cambridge University Press.

Hathaway, J. C. (2005) *The Rights of Refugees Under International Law*. Cambridge: Cambridge University Press.

Hawkins, D. G., D. A. Lake, and D. L. Nielson. (2006) *Delegation and Agency in International Organisations*. Cambridge: Cambridge University Press.

HPCR. (2011) *Humanitarian Action Under Scrutiny: Criminalizing Humanitarian Engagement*. Cambridge, MA: Harvard University Program on Humanitarian Policy and Conflict Research.

Human Rights Watch. (2007) *Maiming the People: Guerrilla Use of Antipersonnel Landmines and Other Indiscriminate Weapons in Colombia*. Washington, DC: Human Rights Watch.

Human Security Report Project. (2011) *Human Security Report 2009/2010: The Causes of Peace and the Shrinking Costs of War*. Oxford: Oxford University Press.

IDMC. (2011) *Internal Displacement: Global Overview of Trends and Developments in 2010*. Geneva: Internal Displacement Monitoring Centre.

Internal Review Panel. (2012) *Report of the Secretary-General's Internal Review Panel on United Nations Action in Sri Lanka*. New York: United Nations.

International Campaign to Ban Landmines. (2009) *Landmine Monitor Report 2009: Toward a Mine-Free World*. Ottawa, Canada: Mines Action.

International Crisis Group. (2007) 'Colombia's new armed groups', in *Latin America Report*. Brussels: International Crisis Group.

Jackson, Ashley. (2012) 'Talking to the other side: humanitarian engagement with armed non-state actors', in *HPG Policy Brief*. London: Humanitarian Policy Group.

Kälin, W. (2003) 'Supervising the 1951 convention relating to the status of refugees: Article 35 and beyond', in edited by E. Feller, V. Türk and F. Nicholson, *Refugee Protection in International Law: UNHCR's Global Consultations on International Protection*, pp. 613–666. Cambridge: Cambridge University Press.

Keohane, R. O. (1989) *International Institutions and State Power: Essays in International Relations Theory*. Boulder: Westview Press.

Knox-Clarke, P. and J. Mitchell. (2011) 'Reflections on the accountability revolution', *Humanitarian Exchange*, 52:3–5.

Lemaitre, J. and K. Bergtora Sandvik. (2015) 'Shifting frames, vanishing resources, and dangerous political opportunities: legal mobilization among displaced women in Colombia', *Law & Society Review*, 49(1): 5–38.

Loescher, G. (2001) *The UNHCR and World Politics: A Perilous Path*. Oxford: Oxford University Press.

Loescher, G., A. Betts and J. Milner. (2008) *UNHCR: The Politics and Practice of Refugee Protection into the Twenty-First Century*. Abingdon: Routledge.

Martin, S. (2004) 'Making the UN work: forced migration and institutional reform', *Journal of Refugee Studies*, 17(3): 301–318.

Mearsheimer, J. J. (1995) 'The false promise of international institutions', *International Security*, 19(3):5–49.

Meertens, D. (2010) 'Forced displacement and women's security in Colombia', *Disasters*, 34 (s2): S147–S164.

Nunes, R. M. (2010) 'Ideational origins of progressive judicial activism: the Colombian constitutional court and the right to health', *Latin American Politics and Society*, 52(3): 67–97.

Oficina Alto Comisionado para la Paz. (2006) *Proceso de paz con las autodefensas*. Bogotá: Presidencia de la República.

Oxfam. (2009) 'Sexual violence in Colombia: instrument of war'. *Oxfam Briefing Paper*, September 2009.

Pallis, M. (2004-05) 'The operation of UNHCR's accountability mechanisms', *New York University Journal of International Law and Politics*, 37: 869–918.

Phuong, C. (2004) *The International Protection of Internally Displaced Persons*. Cambridge: Cambridge University Press.

Porch, D. and M. J. Rasmussen. (2008) 'Demobilisation of paramilitaries in Colombia: transformation or transition?', *Studies in Conflict & Terrorism*, 31(6): 520–540.

Restrepo, J. and M. Spagat. (2004) *Civilian Casualties in the Colombian Conflict: A New Approach to Human Security*. Manuscript. London: Royal Holloway College.

Ruaudel, H. (2013) *Armed Non-State Actors and Displacement in Armed Conflict*. Geneva: Geneva Call.

Shacknove, A. (1993) 'From asylum to containment', *International Journal of Refugee Law*, 5(4): 516–533.

Somos Defensores. (2011) *Informe 2010: sistema de información sobre agresiones contra defensores y defensoras de derechos humanos en Colombia–SIADDHH*. Bogotá: Programa Somos Defensores.

Somos Defensores. n.d. *Sistema de información sobre agresiones a defensores(as) de derechos humanos: CIFRAS DE LA AGRESIÓN 2002-2008*. Bogotá: Programa Somos Defensores.

South, A. (2012) 'The politics of protection in Burma: beyond the humanitarian mainstream', *Critical Asian Studies*, 44(2): 175–204.

Türk, V. (2001) 'UNHCR's supervisory responsibility', *Revue Québécoise de Droit International*, 14(1): 135–158.

Turton, D. (2011) 'The politics of internal displacement and options for institutional reform', in *DEP n. 17: Deportate, esuli, profughe*.

UN OCHA. (2006) *Humanitarian Negotiations with Armed Groups. A Manual for Practitioners*. New York: UN OCHA.

UN Security Council. (2009) *Report of the Secretary-General on the protection of civilians in armed conflict*, 29 May 2009, S/2009/277.

UNHCR. (2002) *Global Appeal 2003*. Geneva: UNHCR.

UNHCR. (2005) *Global Appeal 2006*. Geneva: UNHCR.

UNHCR. (2006) *Global Appeal 2007*. Geneva: UNHCR.

UNHCR. (2007a) *Global Appeal 2008–2009*. Geneva: UNHCR.

UNHCR. (2007b) 'The protection of internally displaced persons and the role of UNHCR'. Informal consultative meeting, 27 February 2007. Available online at http://www.unhcr.org/excom/EXCOM/45dd5a712.pdf (accessed 5 September 2011).

UNHCR. (2007c) 'UNHCR's role in support of an enhanced humanitarian response to situations of internal displacement: policy framework and implementation strategy'. 4 June 2007, EC/58/SC/CRP.18. Available online at http://www.unhcr.org/refworld/docid/4693775c2.html (accessed 20 November 2011).

UNHCR. (2007d) 'UNHCR's role in support of an enhanced humanitarian response to situations of internal displacement: update on UNHCR's leadership role within the cluster approach and IDP operational workplans'. Informal consultative meeting between UNHCR and Excom, 25 May 2007. Available online at http://www.unhcr.org/464dd68f2.html (accessed 5 September 2011).

UNHCR. (2007e) 'UNHCR's role in support of an enhanced inter-agency response to the protection of internally displaced persons: policy framework and corporate strategy'. Informal consultative meeting between UNHCR and Excom, 30 January 2007. Available online at http://www.unhcr.org/45c1ab432.html. (accessed 24 February 2012).

UNHCR. (2008) 'UNHCR Colombia: best practices in a global context'. Available online at www.unhcr.org/refworld/docid/4d7a21dc2.html (accessed 7 November 2011).

UNHCR. (2009) 'Global appeal 2010–2011: Colombia'. Available online at www.unhcr.org/4b02ca0e9.html (accessed 20 May 2015).

UNHCR. (2011) *Global Appeal 2012–2013*. Geneva: UNHCR.

UNHCR. (2013a) 'Global appeal 2014–2015: Colombia'. Available online at www.unhcr.org/528a0a367.html (accessed on 27 October 2015).

UNHCR. (2013b) 'Global report 2012: Colombia'. Available online at www.unhcr.org/51b1d646b.pdf (accessed 20 May 2015).

US State Department. (2010) '2009 human rights reports: Colombia'. Available online at www.state.gov/g/drl/rls/hrrpt/2009/wha/136106.htm (accessed 15 December 2010).

Verdad Abierta. (2010) 'Bandas criminales, modelo 2010'. Last modified 17 December 2010. Available online at www.verdadabierta.com/component/content/article/202-conflicto-hoy/2898-bandas-criminales-modelo-2010 (accessed 19 September 2015).

Verdad Abierta. (2011) 'Amenazan a líderes de desplazados en Bolívar'. Available online at www.verdadabierta.com/rearmados/50-rearmados/3175-amenazas-contra-lideres-de-desplazados-en-bolivar (accessed 16 February 2012).

Verdirame, G. (2011) *The UN and Human Rights: Who Guards the Guardians?* Cambridge: Cambridge University Press.

Verdirame, G. and B. E. Harrell-Bond. (2005) *Rights in Exile: Janus-Faced Humanitarianism.* NewYork; Oxford: Berghahn Books.

Zapater, J. (2010) 'Prevention of forced displacement: the inconsistencies of a concept', in *New Issues in Refugee Research.* Geneva: UNHCR.

Zeender, G. (2005) 'Engaging armed non-state actors on internally displaced persons protection', *Refugee Survey Quarterly*, 24(3): 96–111.

6 Universalizing the refugee category and struggling for accountability: the everyday work of eligibility officers within UNHCR

Marion Fresia and Andreas von Känel

The distinction between refugees and migrants, far from being universal, appeared in the wake of the First World War and the fall of the last Empires. With the ascendancy of centralized nation-states in Europe, mobility across national borders became subject to increasing regulations. Conversely, the loss of legal protection from a state started to be framed as an "anomaly" (Malkki 1995). UNHCR was created in the early 1950s and the 1951 Convention relating to the Status of Refugees was drafted to resolve this "problem". To operationalize the distinction between refugees and migrants, Refugee Status Determination (RSD) was established, which became a key instrument of global and national refugee policies and an important device for the circulation of the individually based definition of the refugee inscribed in the 1951 Convention. Additionally, where the states were not signatory to the Convention or when they did not have their own national procedures, UNHCR was given the task to determine under its own mandate whether a person is eligible for refugee status. Presently, the UN agency conducts RSD in 67 countries, making it the second largest refugee status determination system in the world (UNHCR 2014).

"Mandate RSD" has been subjected to increasing scrutiny in the scholarship on UNHCR's Struggle for Accountability. A number of scholars have, in particular, highlighted the need to take more notice of "mandate" procedures because the UN agency is both judge and party to the Convention and is not subject to any external control mechanisms (Alexander 1999; Kagan 2002; Jones 2009). These approaches have contributed to a more critical appreciation of UNHCR's RSD procedure, generally examining it against the ideal of an exemplary procedure respectful of the principles of fairness, integrity, and due process. However, little attention has been given to how the Struggle for Accountability actually plays out in the everyday work of eligibility officers and in the actual decision-making process. Drawing on empirical studies of RSD, which have, so far, only focused on national asylum procedures in the Global North (D'Halluin 2008; Rousseau *et al.* 2002; Good 2007), this chapter aims to step back from an understanding of mandate RSD in terms of "accountability gaps". Rather than examining it for what it fails to do, we suggest looking at what *it does* and *how it is actually done* in the first place. In other words, we analyze the every-day politics, practice, and ethics of mandate RSD, and examine whether and how the latter are shaped by recent concerns for accountability within UNHCR. We show that if the Struggle for Accountability and the quest for fair, impartial, and objective decisions have become a central preoccupation in RSD bureaucratic work, the decision-making process itself remains, in practice, always situational and relational and informed by the states' interests and local political configurations. More specifically, we illustrate how UNHCR's endeavor to enrol states in the refugee cause and locally anchor the refugee label structures the practices and moralities of decision-makers, as much as concerns accountability. Conversely, we show how RSD itself becomes an instrument of the institutionalization, on a global scale, of an individualized definition of the refugee status, taking the appearance of a technical, legal, and objective endeavor. For our analysis, we mobilize a qualitative, ethnographic approach and draw on data collected in two UNHCR offices in Nouakchott and Ankara.[1] Both countries were perceived by the European Union since the early 2000s to be "transit countries", and in both countries, UNHCR was planning to transfer responsibility of RSD to the host states in the near future. As such, Mauritania and Turkey represent interesting starting points to study the entanglement of international refugee protection and state sovereignty and the ways in which the practice of mandate RSD is informed by the ultimate goal of having states develop or improve their own national procedures.

This chapter is structured as follows: in the first section, we provide a brief historical overview of UNHCR's engagement with RSD and explore, on a macro level, how mandate RSD has since the late 1990s been progressively incorporated into a wider regime of accountability with the development of procedural standards. In the second section, we turn to the Mauritanian case study and examine the every-day work of RSD. We look at how eligibility officers struggle to turn the localized, situational, and relational nature of their decision-making process into purely legal and objectified decisions, in a continual quest to balance the global principles of fairness, quality, and impartiality with the need to consider the network of actors and the local political context in which they operate. Finally, in the last section, we draw on the narratives of eligibility officers in Ankara to explore how they critically reflect and make sense of this struggle. With the majority recruited from among the young Turkish elite, we show how the daily work of classification (between refugees and migrants) and of account-making acts, for them, as a site of intense socialization to the refugee cause and to UNHCR's larger endeavor to universalize the refugee label. Altogether, these levels of analysis will shed light on several of the latent functions or effects of mandate RSD: In addition to attempting to protect refugees in countries where the refugee category has an often weak anchorage, what mandate RSD does, we will argue, is to steadily institutionalize—under the appearance of an objective, technical, and legal endeavor—an individualized definition of the refugee status and a specific, euro-centric, bureaucratic model of migration management on a global scale.

Worldwide institutionalization of a device of classification

UNHCR has started doing RSD nearly since its creation in the early 1950s. The first official mention of RSD dates back to a November 1951 memorandum by the High Commissioner. At that time, UNHCR had taken the responsibility to conduct RSD in two countries only; however, the High Commissioner already felt the need to assure governments that the sovereignty of states would be respected. The memorandum emphasized that RSD conducted by UNHCR should remain "exceptional" and "flexible" and should be done only when necessary and upon the request of governments (UNHCR 1951, p. 4). It further asserted that UNHCR did not intend to "set up special administrative machinery to determine eligibility" (op. cit., p. 2).

Despite these initial declarations, RSD operations turned into an administrative machinery as UNHCR expanded its activities worldwide, deriving its legitimacy from its supranational mandate, its "expertise" in refugee issues and its "neutrality" (Barnett and Finnemore 1999). On the operational level, UNHCR started taking complete or partial responsibility for individual RSD procedures, first in European countries that did not yet have a national procedure, and then, during the 1960s and 70s, mostly in Asia and Africa (UNHCR 2014, p. 15).[2] During the 1990s and 2000s, UNHCR's RSD procedures expanded at an unprecedented rate, as UNHCR became involved in an increasing number of countries after the end of the Cold War and as new states became party to the 1951 Convention. By 2001, more than 300 UNHCR staff were conducting RSD in 65 countries either under UNHCR's own authority or jointly with governments (UNHCR 2001).

In the course of its geographic expansion, UNHCR developed a strong "norm-setting" role for RSD. It became the only international actor to provide states with guidance on how to develop or improve their national procedures. Such guidance was formulated for the first time in 1977 in the Conclusion n° 8 of UNHCR Executive Committee (EXCOM)—consisting of UNHCR's member states—that defined the general basic principles of a procedure respectful of judicial rights in terms of access, fairness, and appeal. The Conclusion was followed by the first edition in 1979 of the UNHCR Handbook on RSD procedures and criteria, which provided detailed recommendations on how to interpret the refugee definition of the 1951 Convention. To this day, the Handbook remains a major reference in all of the refugee matters worldwide. In 1992, UNHCR re-edited the first Handbook on RSD procedures and during the 2000s, it produced a series of "guidelines on international protection".[3] This growing normalization of RSD must be understood in light of the wider standardization of all humanitarian activities during the 1990s and the need to develop new jurisprudence in face of the changing nature of asylum claims. It is also a response to the growing pressure from NGOs, lawyers, and human rights organization to make UNHCR and governments more accountable for the ways they distribute the refugee status (RSD Watch 2006, 2008).

Parallel to the rapid expansion of "mandate" RSD, UNHCR has encouraged governments to develop their own national procedures by employing long-lasting diplomatic negotiations to mobilize state administrations around the refugee cause and providing training on refugee law, legal expertise, direct funding to support national RSD systems and more indirectly financing and training NGOs on refugee matters. As of 2014, 117 states were running RSD procedures, whether alone or together with UNHCR, including 41 new procedures since the year 2000

(UNHCR 2014, p. 1). Among the reasons for the dramatic expansion of individual RSD procedures, UNHCR mentions the "increasing mixed population movements which complicate group-based responses" because of their heterogeneous nature, as well as deteriorating economic conditions, less receptive attitudes, and considerations of security in host societies (UNHCR 2014, p. 16). The advance of individualized approaches to RSD can also be observed as a direct consequence of EU pressure on so-called transit countries to develop migration and asylum systems to contain migration flows outside EU borders and "externalize" the burden of refugees and migrants (Audebert and Robin 2009; Valluy 2009).

Over time, UNHCR has established itself at once as a judge of individual cases, a norm-producer and a promotor of asylum procedures on a global scale. This unique concentration of power has provided the UN agency with significant leverage to diffuse and institutionalize a refugee definition based on individual persecution in countries where group-based responses and wider definitions had been dominant (yet often reserved to certain groups only, coming from border countries) or where the distinction between refugees and migrants was nonexistent (in non-Convention states, for instance). In the process, UNHCR has managed to make acceptable the idea that an international organization could distribute, in an area as sensitive as migration management, a legal status that to some extent escapes state control. Yet, this apparent success has relied on an on-going work of legitimization of UNHCR's engagement with RSD vis-à-vis state actors and increasingly human rights NGOs as well.

Struggling for legitimacy and accountability

UNHCR remains economically and politically dependent on state actors to be able to operate on their territories and enforce its mandate RSD decisions and, hence, cannot afford to ignore the states' interests and their political concerns regarding the impact that RSD may have on migration flows. The states have expressed concerns regarding mandate RSD as early as 1983: In EXCOM Conclusions n° 30 on "manifestly unfounded or abusive applications" a language of suspicion was, for the first time, institutionalized (EXCOM Conclusion n° 30, 1983). UNHCR's member states pointed at the "problem of high number of applications" and potential "abuses", depicted as "potential burden" for them. Today, in situations where UNHCR carries out RSD, local authorities are often defiant toward the asylum institution. Our case studies are illustrative in this regard: In Turkey and Mauritania, local authorities feared that individual RSD procedures might open the door to uncontrollable migration flows into their territories or be a way for European countries to shift the burden of migration management to them. In both countries, what appeared to be at stake in UNHCR's RSD procedure was not only to provide legal protection to the refugees but also to convince the states that the introduction of an individually based refugee definition in their territories did not constitute a threat to their sovereignty and was a legitimate enterprise.

UNHCR has simultaneously come under growing scrutiny from human rights NGOs. Far from contesting the legitimacy of the refugee category as certain states do, NGOs have called on UNHCR to uphold the standards it advocates for governments. A major criticism has been related to the lack of accountability, transparency, and the absence of external control mechanisms. Critics have identified gaps in UNHCR's procedures, such as the withholding of evidence from asylum-seekers, the tendency not to give written reasons to rejected asylum-seekers, the lack of an independent appeal procedure, the lack of access to legal advice, the length of the procedure, and finally, the fact that UNHCR relies primarily on junior staff or UN volunteers to conduct RSD assessments (Jones 2009; RSD Watch 2006, 2008; Alexander 1999). As Jones concluded, in a situation where the UN agency is both judge and party, "the independence of its interpretations of the Refugee Convention in its RSD decisions cannot be guaranteed" (2009, p. 54). UNHCR has responded to such criticism by further standardizing and normalizing its procedures, incorporating them in a wider regime of accountability. In 2005, it has released for the first time its *Procedural standards for RSD under UNHCR's mandate*, in an attempt to improve the "quality, fairness, and integrity" of UNHCR RSD (UNHCR 2005, pp. 1–2). Based on a rights-based approach, these standards included forms and checklists for registration, application, and assessments, aimed at reinforcing the consistency, objectivity, and impartiality of the decision-making process. Simultaneously, they were articulated to a results-based management approach, requiring from eligibility officers to reduce the backlogs of asylum claims by intensifying the number of interviews conducted per week.

"Accountability"—together with "efficiency"—have, therefore, been only a recent concern for UNHCR in the history of the development of its mandate procedures but have come to be observed as playing an important role in its quest for legitimacy vis-à-vis state actors, in terms of setting an example (UNHCR 2014, p. 17). These imperatives have added a new layer of norms and constraints on the UN agency, caught in a constant balancing between setting the example as an advocate for refugee rights by establishing fair and impartial procedures and simultaneously considering the states' concerns for their sovereignty. Shifting to an ethnographic approach, we now want to explore how this tension between being "accountable" and considering the states' interests plays out in the everyday work of RSD and is translated into practical rationalities that contribute to the decision-making process.

Every-day work of purification

At the time of our fieldwork in 2009, the UNHCR field office in Mauritania was in an ongoing process of enrolling national and local authorities in refugee protection. However, the attempt to institutionalize the refugee category stood on precarious footing in two ways: On the one hand, the discourse on illegal migration threatened to blur the boundary between refugees and migrants. On the other hand, the Mauritanian government saw little interest in investing in the nascent national RSD procedure. UNHCR had established its presence in Mauritania in 1989 (Lindstrom 2002, p. 25), in the aftermath of the conflict between Senegal and Mauritania. During the 1990s, UNHCR treated asylum claims sporadically during the missions of a Protection Officer, who flew in from Geneva "once or twice a year", until a permanent Protection Officer was installed in 2001 (op. cit., pp. 25–6). Following pressure from the European Union to play a more active role in migration control, Mauritania signed a readmission agreement with Spain in 2003. Starting in 2006, Spain provided technical and human assistance for surveillance and the systematic expulsion of migrants who had been returned by the Spanish government from the Canary Islands, interfered at high sea, or who were suspected to plan to irregularly cross over to Europe (Poutignat and Streiff-Fénart 2010). UNHCR Mauritania reacted to these developments by drawing attention to the link between migration and asylum on numerous occasions: In 2004, it conducted a three-month study on the migrant and refugee population residing in Mauritania, and in 2005, it helped to create a multi stakeholder *Study Group of Migration Flows* in the *Ministère de l'Intérieur*. In 2005, with financial and technical assistance from UNHCR, a national eligibility commission for RSD was constituted, drawing six members from different national ministries. In 2009, the national RSD procedure was still entirely dependent on UNHCR's funding and the office continued to conduct RSD under its own mandate.

Creating purified assessments

Similar to these attempts to create a favorable institutional environment for refugee protection, a gradual shift in the way RSD was conducted occurred in the mid-2000s because standardized written accounts for each individual case became a marker of good decision-making. Previously, the members of the protection unit had made decisions collectively during deliberative sessions, discussing cases in detail but spending little time on systematically writing up their assessments. This process became untenable following the UNHCR-wide normalization of the procedure outlined in the previous section of this chapter.[4] Even ahead of these changes initiated by the Geneva headquarters, the office had started to document its case files in more detail when it began submitting several cases to the national eligibility commission for review, meaning it had to justify its own decisions to an external actor. The increasingly well-documented case files drew on a positivist rhetoric. A finalized assessment form suggested a linear, neatly ordered and thoroughly argued process, leading logically and inevitably to the final decision through a chain of arguments held in systematic, neutral language. In her analysis of UNHCR's resettlement procedure, Sandvik accurately observed the following:

> [t]he underlying premise of UNHCR's reform and regularization agenda is that by adding a set of formal procedures, one can strip away layers of unofficial and illegitimate beliefs and values, thereby allowing accountability, global consistency, and transparency to be achieved. (2010, p. 42)

The changing standards of how RSD was conducted reflected an increasing emphasis on *account-ability* in the form of well-kept physical and electronic case files and detailed assessments.

Consistent with these developments, one of the central tasks for RSD workers was to create written assessments that corresponded to the norms of standard procedure. This process was especially visible in the final stage of the procedure when the supervisor would scrutinize the argument proposed by the eligibility officer in the written assessment form. The following excerpts illustrate how RSD workers negotiated a decision, often testing different registers of argumentation before returning to the institutionally sanctioned language of assessing. In the case under review, the asylum-seeker had explained during the RSD interview that he had suffered physical violence and death threats from family members and neighbors after disclosing his homosexual relationship. He told the RSD worker that he had been detained for several days by Mauritanian police on his way to the capital, after they had found pictures on him that showed him with his boyfriend. The supervisor (SV) challenged the negative assessment of the eligibility officer (EO1) in the following manner:

> SV: You wrote [reads from the written assessment]: "The conditions of the illegal detention he denounced is not a habitual practice of the police". In Mauritania? Are you kidding me? You say that this is not a practice in Mauritania? It is however completely a practice in Mauritania, they do whatever they want, even with our refugees.
> EO1: How are you going to cross two countries with pictures... well, I don't know. I don't believe him, in fact, that's it. I don't believe that if you're in a comparable situation...
> SV: [interrupts] But he can have the photographs nonetheless!

Drawing on experience of the context (past incidences of arbitrary arrests) and more abstract principles for assessing credibility (the fact that the asylum-seeker puts himself at risk does not diminish his credibility), the supervisor initially rejects the suggested assessment. After taking the defense of the asylum-seeker in this first instance, the supervisor gives another chance to the RSD worker (EO1) to re-frame his judgement, as indicated below:

> SV: I don't know... Don't we have another way to reject him? You're talking about a homosexual from Senegal. Is he really homosexual?
> EO1: But that's it, I don't even believe that he's homosexual! That is, if I go through to the analysis and I give him credibility on the fact that he is homosexual, I would have to accept him.
> SV: Yes, but you have to be able to say that [in the assessment]. You have to be able to say that you don't believe him, so...
> EO1: Well, that's something very subjective. If we can't reject him for absence of credibility, how can we reject him?

Against the idea that an assessment results from straightforward reasoning according to professional norms, this short exchange is indicative of the collusion of rationales in RSD: Giving the benefit of the doubt to the asylum-seeker (his story could be true) can be quickly neutralized by the need to reach a decision ("Don't we have another way to reject him?"). The importance given to proper form (being able to give an *account* that fits institutional requirements) creates additional constraints ("If we can't reject him for absence of credibility, how can we reject him?"); however, it does not magically erase the fact that the RSD worker's subjective conviction remains of crucial importance ("I don't believe him."). Indeed, adherence to formal standards and the writing up of decisions into coherent accounts articulates with, rather than nullifies, other rationales that structure decision-making. The argumentation presented in the final assessment form will be devoid of these complexities and ambiguities. Although interview forms now capture the entire dialogue held between the asylum-seeker and the RSD worker and can thus be re-examined and scrutinized for contradictions, the assessment itself is far from this degree of transparency and will ultimately be purified from arguments that do not fit the institutional language. Paradoxically, although the normalized procedure is meant to create transparency, it creates its own opacities (Thomson 2012; Sandvick 2011; von Känel 2010), revealing neither all nor necessarily the decisive processes and criteria that oriented the decision-making process.

The recurrence of suspicion and disbelief in the above excerpts provides a powerful starting point to further explore the tensions that are rendered invisible in purified assessment forms. In her ethnographic study on a UNHCR in Tunisia, Brunner (2010) showed how the politics of migration control the impact on RSD workers' interpretations of asylum-seekers' stories. She documented "implicit norms of suspicion" (op. cit.), according to which asylum-seekers were more likely to be identified as potential economic migrants when recounting motivations that did not correspond to the idealized figure of a victim of persecution and violence. Rather than reading such implicit norms of suspicion as a critique of individual decision-making, what interests us here is their inherently collective, political character.

Politics and localizing strategies

The production of assessments is not merely about the erasure of subjectivity but also about bracketing out the broader political context. The impression that RSD stands outside of politics requires constant negotiation. To be able to stabilize a universal refugee category, the protection office recurred to localizing strategies, constantly differentiating—in a more or less formalized manner—the treatment of different types of asylum-seekers and refugees according to the political context. For instance, the widespread discourse regarding Mauritania as a transit country in many ways complicated UNHCR's position toward state authorities. Under the regime of migration control, refugees and asylum-seekers ran the risk of being arbitrarily arrested and sometimes expelled. Several people arrested for being suspected of wanting to "illegally emigrate" to Europe were, therefore, simultaneously "persons of concerns" for UNHCR, so that advocating for the rights of refugees occasionally overlapped with advocating for the rights of "illegal migrants". In a context where the refugee category had weak legal and social anchorage and where many of the external resources were channelled into the control of migration, one protection officer was concerned that everything was "too mixed" and UNHCR's occasional interventions in favor of arrested refugees or asylum-seekers created "confusion" among authorities regarding UNHCR's mandate.

One of the *ad hoc* practices to stabilize the refugee category as distinct from that of the migrant was to channel only certain types of asylum seekers toward the national procedure. When one junior staff member suggested that the emerging national procedure should be open to all asylum-seekers to improve their status, a senior UNHCR staff contradicted resolutely as follows: "We don't *want* all [mandate] asylum seekers to be automatically registered [under the national procedure]! They are not all solid cases, and we want to protect our relationship with the ministry". According to this discourse, UNHCR needed to control which cases would become visible to Mauritanian authorities. Submitting only "solid cases" would help the broader goal of changing the authorities' perception of UNHCR's mandate and anchoring, in the long run, the refugee category in the local institutional and normative landscape. In this situation, UNHCR staff—in an act of anticipation—played its role as a gatekeeper to fulfil its role as an advocate.

Returning to the case of the homosexual asylum-seeker discussed earlier, we find a similar type of arrangement at work: The Mauritanian Ministry of Justice had previously notified the UNHCR that homosexuality was criminalized by Mauritanian law and had made it clear that if cases of homosexuals were to be submitted by UNHCR to the national eligibility committee, it would not accord refugee status to them and that Mauritania would likely expel the concerned asylum-seekers. UNHCR's ensuing practice was indicative of the permanent balancing acts that the organization performs between a rights-based approach and attention to host state concerns: The office still accorded refugee status to homosexuals. However, it did not refer these cases to the national commission, although several of them were among the best documented cases of persecution the protection unit had ever assessed. Because the refugees remained in conflict with national law, UNHCR would then try to resettle them, which is a lengthy, time-intensive process. The following informal discussion between three Eligibility Officers (EO1, EO2, and EO3) revolves around the case of the asylum-seeker in the above section and takes place ahead of the review with the supervisor:

EO2:   [Our supervisor] is not going to like your argumentation. You have to see if [the asylum seeker] is credible and if he is persecuted.

EO3:   Homosexuals are not persecuted [in Senegal] if they are discrete. If they chose to show it openly, yes.

EO1:   If we were very pure on international protection, maybe we'd have to recognize him. But then, there is also the question of the politics of the office and the management of cases. Not least because we will have to resettle them because we can't leave them in Mauritania. If we want to accept a homosexual, it should really be an extremely strong case. Otherwise we will end up giving protection to half of all homosexuals in Senegal!

The eligibility officer (EO1) argued that being "very pure on international protection" would result in straining the office's resources, especially because UNHCR had to resettle all of the homosexual asylum-seekers due to the stance of the Mauritanian Ministry of Justice. The likely "pull-factor" would threaten to overstretch the host government's willingness to cooperate on asylum matters in the future. Ultimately, it could thus erode UNHCR's capacity to live up to its protection mandate. The localizing strategy, while aiming to depoliticize RSD, in this case replaced one contentious issue (two contradictory bodies of law) with another one (having to spend more resources on these cases). Consequently, the incursion of politics into RSD here no longer appeared to be in opposition to UNHCR's protection mandate, but as its very premise.

In conclusion, these observations suggested that the emphasis on accountability and transparency displaces, rather than eliminates, politics from decision-making. Although such emphasis has undeniable effects on RSD practice (embodied in standard assessment forms and actualized by RSD workers in their attempts to make explicit their decisions according to institutionally accepted language), it does not override the inherently situational and relational character of the procedure. Localizing strategies serve to cushion political tensions and, as such, are a necessary supplement to the reproduction of the universal refugee category. In stark contrast to the assessment forms where all asylum-seekers are to be treated equally, localizing strategies differentiate asylum-seekers and refugees according to perceived political constraints. Simultaneously, a close-up view of RSD revealed that eligibility officers must navigate a range of—sometimes contradictory—practical rationalities: creating "transparent" written assessments, anticipating the supervisor's reaction, anticipating the state actors' objections to the large numbers of refugees (avoid a "pull factor") or to refugees who do not correspond to the image of the pure victim (render visible only "solid cases"), considering the scarce resources of the protection unit (build an imaginary limit of the number of cases who can be recognized without threatening UNHCR's mandate). Adding to the existing critical literature on RSD, addressing accountability in RSD could mean recognizing the deeply entrenched political complications that remain hidden behind the most recent attempts to create "transparency".

Production of refugee "experts": RSD and the making of accounts as a site of professional socialization

In this last section, we draw on the narratives of eligibility officers in Ankara to explore how they make sense of and critically reflect on the displacement of politics that the Struggle for Accountability supposes. More generally, we show how the daily work of classification and of account-making acts, for them, as a site of intense socialization and enrolment regarding the refugee cause.

With 20 staff entirely dedicated to RSD, the Ankara office had the reputation of being an "RSD industry". A large part of the staff consisted of young, newly recruited Turks, between the ages of 20 and 30 years, holding either temporary contracts or subaltern positions.[5] Valued and celebrated as being at the heart of UNHCR's activities, RSD work, just as emergency situations, was often described as the "front" of the institution, where staff members are "in close contact" with refugees and learn the "real and concrete work" of UNHCR (Fresia 2009). As such, it was considered as key experience to be gained, to prepare for full and legitimate membership in the organization with a permanent status. Paradoxically, the task described as the "heart" of UNHCR's protection mandate (the field, contact with refugees) was thus performed by those occupying the lowest, most precarious or most junior positions. All of the interviewees actually described this work as exhausting and emotionally intensive not only because they had to quickly acquire complex legal and technical expertise on refugee protection but also because every day they had to address the stories of suffering and desperate attempts by refugees to draw attention to their situation and to make decisions affecting people's futures. Additionally, they were asked to conduct at least eight interviews per week to respond to the imperative of efficiency in a context of heavy backlog, a context that could only make the work more challenging. Learning how to differentiate migrants from refugees and make their decisions accountable was, however, often described as the most interesting part of the job. For them, what was important and significant in RSD work was indeed to be able to find the "real" refugees in a fair and objective manner.

Embracing a new moral cause: finding the "real" refugees

The most important socializing effect of RSD work was in fact that RSD officers came to embrace the conviction that refugees should and could be sorted out from migrants. A majority of the interviewees mentioned that before joining UNHCR, they were unaware that refugees were "different" from other migrants and were entitled to specific rights because the majority of them did not have a background in refugee studies or refugee aid but rather in broader international studies. The interviewees expressed the following:

> Before, I was not aware of the importance of refugees. With UNHCR, I learned a lot about refugee law, and the situation of refugees in my country. I never realized before how harsh the Turkish police was with them, treating them like illegal migrants. So for me, my biggest satisfaction with the job is that we are trying to do something for those people, we are trying to soften the attitude of our government but also to sensitize people about the refugee problem. (Aleyna, national UNV)

By joining UNHCR, RSD workers made, therefore, their own the advocacy mission of UNHCR for refugee rights while embedding it in the specificity of the Turkish context. The need to differentiate refugees from other types of migrants through a specific legal status was uncontested and appeared to be a moral imperative, rather than an institutional or political one: It was observed as part of a broader struggle for human rights, one of the primary reasons why they joined a UN organization. In their narratives, the difference between both categories actually seemed to operate on an ontological level: Eligibility officers described their task as a quest for objective, pre-existing traits that define a person as a refugee.

With the dichotomy between refugees and migrants, RSD officers also embraced the underlying assumption that displacement is an "abnormality" that should be addressed through re-emplacement in a national order of things (Malkki 1995).

This assumption was at the heart of what can be described as an "ethics of conviction" (Weber 1995): Whatever the wider or immediate consequences of this complex task, finding the "real refugees" who were "out there" was what RSD workers had to do through the work of classification. This conviction was articulated to an ideal of objectivity, scientificity, and rationality, which was described as the only way to reduce uncertainty in the decision-making process and ensure its quality and fairness. Subjectivity and inconsistency in the process were acknowledged and occasionally harshly denounced; however, there was a belief that it could or should be reduced using a more rigorous formalistic and positivist approach. This belief was a pre-requisite to justify the relevance of the moral cause they had embraced and also a direct consequence of it. It also explained why objectivity, accountability and legal knowledge were the most valued qualities in RSD work and described as the most interesting part of the job: "*despite its repetitive dimension, what I prefer in the job is that we learn to be very precise in our legal arguments. We are forced to establish the facts and that helps to reduce subjectivity*" (Jeanne, intern).

Incorporating suspicion as part of the cause

The appropriation of UNHCR's moral cause and the quest for objectivity appeared to occur hand in hand with the acquisition of a culture of suspicion. RSD workers often presented objectivity and suspicion as two faces of the same coin, ultimately serving the purity of their cause. All mentioned that during the first year after their appointment, they experienced transitioning from a "liberal" to a more "cynical" stance vis-à-vis credibility. This transition occurred through peer-to-peer social control, especially exerted by supervisors who validate decisions. In Turkey, several RSD workers indicated making negative decisions in anticipation of their supervisor's reaction (whose reputation was that of a 'hard liner') and thus by fear of social sanction: '*There are some cases, I don't even try to convince him because I know his position, I know he won't believe the person, although I think the office could still make a case in her favor*' (Jeanne, intern). However, suspicion was also perceived as an effect of routine and 'fatigue' of hearing similar stories 'over and over again'.

Initially, new recruits found it hard to produce negative assessments and thought suspicion contradicted the principle of the "benefit of the doubt" and the "humanitarian spirit" of UNHCR. As time passed, they came to perceive suspicion as necessary. Asylum-seekers whose claims were rejected were, indeed, reframed as "abusers" who could potentially threaten and pollute UNHCR's cause and efforts to make of RSD a credible endeavor, as indicated below:

> if it is clearly an abusing case, those people waste our time because our time should be spent with the real refugees; and unfortunately there is not that many real cases as we are dealing with so many lies in our work (…), it is like a fight between the abusers of the asylum system and UNHCR's mission. (Kent, JPO)

As a result, RSD workers steadily built an imaginary limit to the distribution of the refugee status that they incorporated into their ethics of conviction: They perceived this limit as a prerequisite to preserve the purity of the refugee category and the very likelihood to reinforce its local anchorage and advocate for refugee rights. With little perspective to resolve the co-existence of a culture of advocacy and suspicion within UNHCR, the only viable alternative seemed to be exit: Certain young recruits insisted that they were still uncomfortable with the feeling of becoming increasingly suspicious and that they were thinking about quitting their job.

Contesting the politicization and shortcomings of the procedure

If they embraced UNHCR's moral cause and incorporated suspicion as part of it, RSD workers simultaneously critically reflected on the procedure. In their quest for objective and fair decisions, RSD workers were, indeed, extremely concerned by the intrusion of politics in the decision-making process. In Ankara, the politicization of the procedure and the differentiated treatments of refugees were particularly explicit as, in 2009, asylum-seekers coming from certain regions of Iraq benefitted from an accelerated procedure of recognition because they were eligible for an important US resettlement program, whereas asylum claims from Afghans were carefully and individually examined because Turkish authorities feared that granting them refugee status might create a pull factor. This politics of unequal treatment was often described as a factor of disappointment vis-à-vis UNHCR, that many RSD staff imagined as "neutral", "independent" or "above state interests" before joining it, as shown below:

> then I came to realize that the office deals with countries and so they have to be political… It was my biggest disappointment… Sometimes, I even feel I am working for the US government and not for UNHCR. (Aleyna, national UNV)

> I think the office could sometimes do more to recognize more refugees, but they are too cautious on certain cases like female adultery, they are too afraid of the pull factor effects (…) and even myself, I, now, I can see that I am taking my decisions not only in relation to the case itself, but first of all by anticipating the positions of others: my supervisor, the resettlement country, the Turkish authorities. (Jeanne, intern)

Despite the promise of standardized assessment forms, technologies and software, there was still a widespread feeling that the decision-making processes were not only politicized but also remained, to some extent, subjective and dependent on the reviewing officer (more or less liberal):

> It is very difficult, very difficult to take decisions (…) people saying they have converted to Christianity or that they are homosexual and how do you assess that in 3 hours (…). So that is my biggest concern, no matter how you do, I feel that my decision is based on my mind somehow and then on the mind of my supervisor, and I don't want to do that; certain types of people in the office just make up their mind, some are very positive with credibility and others

very negative, so you can actually choose the angle depending on your feeling towards the person. (Franz, JPO)

Finally, RSD staff felt that the demand for efficiency and the strong pressure to reach quantitative targets to reduce the length of the procedure contradicted with the will to improve the quality and fairness in the procedure, especially without additional human resources. The lack of resources of the office also led them to question in the following manner the wider humanitarian vocation of UNHCR, as they realized that once granted refugee status, those who were not eligible to resettlement programs did not benefit from significant advantages in Turkey:

> At the beginning, I really liked the job (…) but then I got very fed up with it, seeing that persons are stuck here whatever the results, if rejected or if recognized under UNHCR's extended mandate. In all cases, they are stuck here and we can't do much for them. (Aleyna, national UNV)

What characterized RSD as a site of socialization was, therefore, the experience of a number of tensions that run more widely throughout UNHCR: a tension between an ideal of positivism and neutrality, and the politically and socially situated nature of the refugee category; the tension between an exclusive logic of intervention based on the restrictiveness of refugee rights (which is based on national belonging) and UNHCR's more inclusive humanitarian aspirations based on human rights; and finally, the tension between an organization supposedly placed above the states' interests as the guardian of international refugee law, while being simultaneously highly dependent on the states to fulfil its mandate. Although the eligibility officers from the Ankara office were aware of these tensions, their critical engagement with the procedure did not produce significant change. First, their subaltern position within the institution and good working conditions—when compared to other jobs outside the UN—entailed a sense of loyalty toward the institution. As stated by Franz:

> it becomes this strange feeling that you don't know what you are doing and don't like what you are doing, but you can't complain because you should be grateful for working for the UN and have an overall higher salary than the average.

Most importantly, because their ways of making sense of the shortcomings of the procedure, for the most part, reproduced the moral and cognitive framework of UNHCR's mandate, they ended up accepting that the intrusion of politics in the decision-making process was inevitable and even necessary to the advancement of the refugee cause, as described below:

> I became less idealistic with time. I came to understand that denouncing and criticizing states or advocating for very liberal approaches like NGOs do not work. States will never open their borders to everyone anyway, so at least we are trying to ensure that those who need urgently some protection are not

expulsed. What we are doing is realpolitik. Without us, things would probably be worse I think. (Aleyna, national UNV)

In this context, "realpolitik" came to be valorized as a practical solution to the above-mentioned dilemmas. Others concluded that what was needed was even more standardization and formalization of the procedure to reduce subjectivity and make the system work even more efficiently, rather than differently. Strikingly, the critical awareness that the decision-making process was situational, contextual and sometimes politicized therefore did not lead RSD officers to question the idea that intrinsically "pure" and "genuine" refugees could be identified "out there" and could be differentiated from "false" refugees. Apart from one person in a supervisory role who mentioned that UNHCR should have a broader framework of action based on human rights rather than refugee rights, the RSD staff rarely questioned the need to differentiate refugees from migrants on the basis of individual persecution.

Overall, mandate RSD therefore acted as a strong site of recruitment and enrolment of Turkish local elites around the refugee cause. Local refugee experts were produced and socialized within UNHCR, and through them, the legitimacy of the refugee label could be anchored on the local level. Many of the RSD staff in Turkey were, indeed, trained by UNHCR with the hope that they would eventually be recruited as eligibility officers in national procedures and two of them, back in 2009, were already planning to do so. Producing and training legal experts in international refugee law, in which knowledge could potentially circulate within national administrations, was therefore an implicit function of the RSD device.

Conclusion

In this article, we examined UNHCR's RSD procedures not for what they fail to do (in terms of "accountability" gaps) but rather for what they do and how they are actually done. By inquiring into the every-day politics, practice and ethics of mandate RSD, we have shown how the Struggle for Accountability and the quest for fair, impartial and objective decisions have become a central preoccupation of eligibility officers. Yet, at the same time, the decision-making process remains primarily informed by the will to enrol states in the refugee cause, the need to sustain good diplomatic relationships with them and consider the specificities of local political configurations. If considering the states' interests and concerns has always been a condition for UNHCR to exert its mandate, it has become all the more important in a context where the UN agency is now trying to transfer the responsibility of RSD to a growing number of states (UNHCR 2014). As such, we have argued that mandate RSD should first be understood as part of a larger endeavor to universalize and locally anchor an individually based definition of the refugee status, in countries where the distinction between refugees and migrants is either not made or made according to more flexible definitions of the refugee (based on collective violence), yet often reserved to certain groups only. It does so by establishing worldwide standardized devices of classification entirely dedicated to sorting out refugees from migrants and by continuously working toward objectivation and purification of the refugee label and by producing and training "national" legal experts around the world who embrace the idea that refugees can and should be distinguished from migrants in an objective and "accountable" manner. All three processes—establishing transnational standardized procedures, naturalizing a bureaucratic label and producing legal experts—reinforce the illusion that distinguishing refugees from migrants is a neutral, objective and merely legal endeavor, when it is actually about achieving a moral and political goal through impersonal means. This depoliticization process continuously reinforces the regime of truth on which the refugee regime is based: a national order of things, a sedentarist view of categories of belonging and a Weberian model of the nation-state (Scalettaris 2013).

Our analysis demonstrated, however, that the process of universalizing the RSD device relies simultaneously on an on-going but implicit work of re-politicization, re-subjectivation and re-emplacement of the refugee-labelling process, which considers the specificities of the political and institutional configuration in which UNHCR operates to "obtain the political buy-in of states actors" (UNHCR 2014, p. 32). Considering the states' interests within the decision-making process is, indeed, perceived as necessary to reach the ultimate goal of having them adopt national procedures respectful of the 1951 Convention, thus making RSD less of a universal and more of a socially and historically situated practice, always embedded in specific national and political contexts. In other words, it makes of RSD a transnational device, yet constantly reinvested by the logics of national sovereignties. As Mary Douglas has indicated, "[a]ny structure of ideas is vulnerable at its margins" (2002 [1966], p. 121). The margins, here, constitute the political space where the distinction between refugees and migrants operates. Significant work goes into clarifying this distinction and into creating this political space. This work gives rise to suspicion of transgressors, which is compounded by UNHCR's limited political legitimacy, lack of resources and a widespread rhetoric against asylum abuse. Universalization and re-emplacement, advocacy and suspicion constitute intricately linked coordinates of UNHCR-RSD ethics and practice, reflecting the unique position of UNHCR as both a judge and a party to asylum procedures.

Understanding RSD procedures in terms of a larger endeavor to universalize the refugee category eventually implies a better understanding of how this category is not only constantly re-emplaced in specific national contexts but also articulated with other legal and normative frameworks. One can wonder, in particular, how the narrow definition of the refugee status based on individual persecution will articulate with wider, group-based approaches, once RSD procedures will be handed over by UNHCR to state actors. In a recent report, UNHCR itself noted that in situations where state actors take full responsibility for RSD, "RSD appear to be applied foremost to discourage asylum applicants so as to maintain the reputation of the country concerned as a transit country" (UNHCR 2014, p. 24). The report further outlined "the virtual non-recognition of refugees in a few countries (…) and the considerable challenges in the area of standards of proof and credibility assessment, the notion of persecution, applying exclusion and other issues" (op. cit., p. 30), and above all, highlights the risk that "individual RSD will be used to abolish group determination policies" (op. cit., p. 35). At a time of growing critique against the refugee definition of the 1951 Convention, perceived as too "euro-centric, inflexible and outdated" (Loescher, Betts and Milner 2008, p. 98), the renewed efforts of UNHCR, in the context of mixed migrations, to have the states develop national procedures based on this definition raise therefore numerous questions that must be closely monitored in future research.

Notes

1 In Nouakchott, one of the authors conducted ethnographic fieldwork in 2009 with a double hat of insider (as an intern within UNHCR) and outsider (as a researcher in the framework of a Master's thesis). With three protection staff working on RSD and 348 applications in 2011, the Mauritanian office was small. In Ankara, the primary methods of data collection consisted of in-depth formal interviews and informal conversations with nearly the entire RSD and protection staff of the office. At the time of research, Ankara was one of UNHCR's largest RSD operations in the world, both in terms of volume of applications (16,000 pending applications in 2011) and human resources (more than 20 staff members entirely dedicated to RSD). Our analysis has also been nourished by two other case studies on UNHCR-led procedures, conducted by two Master students from the University of Neuchâtel in Rabat (Rüfenacht 2010) and Tunis (Brunner 2010).

2 It did so upon the government's requests on the basis of a Memorandum of Understanding but also, in several cases, on its own initiative in non-Convention states.

3 Ten guidelines have been issued between 2002 and 2013. These guidelines are produced directly by UNHCR's Division of International Protection (DIP) to provide legal interpretative guidance on various types of claims to refugee status. Notably, although such recommendations were adopted by the EXCOM in the 1970s and 1980s, they were afterward primarily produced directly by DIP as a way to likely avoid negotiations that would otherwise be too political at the level of the EXCOM, which has grown in size over time and has become more politicized (Fresia 2014).

4 Collective deliberation of cases went against the principle of fair procedure, according to which appeals should be treated by an RSD worker who had not been previously involved in the case in the first instance decision.

5 This actually reflects the wider profile of eligibility officers in the majority of UNHCR offices, characterized by precarious contracts, junior positions and high turnovers (UNHCR 2011). In Ankara, eight were national Turkish UN volunteers (UNV, with a maximum five-year contract), whereas two were international, expatriated "junior professional officers" (JPO), with higher salaries but only a two- or three-year contract.

References

Audebert, C. and N. Robin. (2009) "L'externalisation des frontières des 'Nords' dans les eaux des 'Suds': l'exemple des dispositifs frontaliers américains et européens visant au contrôle de l'émigration caribéenne et subsaharienne", *Cultures et Conflits*, 73(1): 35–51.

Alexander, M. (1999) "Refugee status determination conducted by UNHCR", *International Journal of Refugee Law*, 11(2): 251–289.

Barnett, M. N. and M. Finnemore. (1999) "The politics, power, and pathologies of international organizations", *International Organization*, 53(4): 699–732.

Brunner, M. (2010) *La détermination du statut de réfugié (DSR). Etude de cas: les normes implicites de la crédibilité au HCR dans un pays d'Afrique du Nord*. Mémoire de Master, Université de Neuchâtel.

D'Halluin, E. (2008). *Les épreuves de l'asile: de la politique du soupçon à la reconnaissance des réfugiés*. Paris: École des hautes études en sciences sociales.

Douglas, M. (2002 [1966]) *Purity and Danger. An Analysis of Concepts of Pollution and Taboo*. London: Routledge and Keagan Paul.

Fresia, M. (2009) "Entre elitisme et communautarisme: la fabrique d'une identité collective chez les fonctionnaires internationaux du Haut Commissariat des Nations Unies aux réfugiés", *Revue européenne des migrations internationals*, 3(25): 167–190.

Fresia, M. (2014) "Building consensus within UNHCR's executive committee: global refugee norms in the making", *Journal of Refugee Studies*, 27(4): 514–533.

Good, A. (2007) *Anthropology and Expertise in the Asylum Courts*. Abingdon, New York: Routledge-Cavendish.

Jones, M. D. (2009) "Refugee status determination: three challenges", *Forced Migration Review*, 32(4): 455–477.

Kagan, M. (2002) "Assessment of refugee status determination procedure at UNHCR's Cairo office 2001-2002", *Scholarly Works 643*. Available online at http://scholars.law.unlv.edu/facpub/643 (accessed 25 May 2015).

Lindstrom, C. (2002) "Report on the situations of refugees in Mauritania". Available online at www.aucegypt.edu/fmrs/documents/ChanneNov.pdf (accessed 25 May 2015).

Loescher, G., A. Betts, and J. Milner. (2008) *The United Nations High Commissioner for Refugees (UNHCR): The Politics and Practice of Refugee Protection into the Twenty-First Century*. London: Routledge.

Malkki, L. H. (1995) "Refugees and exile: from 'refugees studies' to the national order of things", *Annual Review of Anthropology*, 24: 495–523.

Poutignat, P. and J. Streiff-Fénart. (2010) "Migration policy development in Mauritania: process, issues and actors", in M. Geiger and A. Pecoud (eds.), *The Politics of International Migration Management*, pp. 202–219. New York and London: Palgrave Macmillan.

Rousseau, C., F. Crépeau, P. Foxen, and H. France. (2002) "The complexity of determining refugeehood: a multidisciplinary analysis of the decision-making process of the Canadian Immigration and Refugee Board", *Journal of Refugee Studies*, 15(1): 43–70.

Rüfenacht, D. (2010) In search of legitimacy: an analysis on the application and use of expert knowledge. Master's thesis, University of Neuchâtel.

RSD Watch. (2006) *No margin for error. Implementation of UNHCR's procedural standards for refugee status determination at selected UNHCR field offices in 2006*. Available online at https://rsd-watch.wordpress.com/no-margin-for-error/ (accessed 25 May 2015).

RSD Watch. (2008) *No margin for error. Monitoring the fairness of refugee status determination procedures at selected UNHCR field offices in 2007*. Available online: https://rsdwatch.wordpress.com/no-margin-for-error/ (accessed 25 May 2015).

Sandvik, K. B. (2011) "Blurring boundaries: refugee resettlement in Kampala – between the formal, the informal, and the Illegal." *PoLAR: Political and Legal Anthropology Review* 34(1): 11–32. p.15.

Scalettaris, G. (2013) *La fabrique du gouvernement international des réfugiés. Bureaugraphie du HCR dans la crise afghane*. Thèse de doctorat. EHESS Paris.

Thomson, M. J. (2012) "Black boxes of bureaucracy: transparency and opacity in the resettlement process of Congolese refugees", *PoLAR*, 35(2): 286–305.

UNHCR. (1951) *Memorandum by the High Commissioner on Certain Problems Relating to the Eligibility of Refugees*. Geneva: UNHCR.

UNHCR. (1992 [1979]) *Handbook on Procedures and Criteria for Determining Refugee Status*. Geneva: UNHCR.

UNHCR. (2005) *Procedural Standards for Refugee Status Determination under UNHCR's Mandate*. Geneva: UNHCR.

UNHCR. (2011) *Statistical Yearbook*. Geneva: UNHCR.

UNHCR. (2013) *Beyond Proof. Credibility Assessment in EU Asylum Systems*. Geneva: UNHCR.

UNHCR. (2014) *Providing for Protection. Assisting States with the Assumption of Responsibility for Refugee Status Determination. A Preliminary Review*. Geneva: UNHCR.

Valluy, J. (2009) *Rejet des exilés. Le grand retournement du droit de l'asile*. Bellecombe-en-Bauge: Editions du Croquant.

von Känel, A. (2010). *Asylum Makers. The Fabrication of Protection in a North African UNHCR Office*. Master's thesis. University of Neuchâtel.

Weber, M. (1995 [1919]) *Le savant et le politique*. Paris: Union Générale d'Éditions.

7 Accounting for the past: a history of refugee management in Uganda, 1959–64

Ashley Brooke Rockenbach

I am sitting in the compound of an elderly Munyarwanda man named Yonah, who has lived in southwestern Uganda since 1959. 'I was chased', he says, 'by the Hutu'. He and his parents were living in northern Ruanda[1] at the start of the Revolution, a conflict that brought about the end of Belgian colonial rule in Ruanda-Urundi and drove more than 160,000 people – predominantly Tutsi – into neighbouring Uganda, Tanzania, Burundi and Congo. Yet, When I ask Yonah to describe his life as a 'refugee', he is quick to dismiss the label: 'I told you I was *chased* – my neighbours know that. That doesn't make me *empungye* [refugee]'. Gesturing to his wife, who is bouncing their grandchild on her knee, he exclaims, 'My life is here!'

Yonah's rejection of the refugee label complicates UNHCR's contemporary quest for institutional accountability. Since the late 1990s, the Office has endeavoured to promote refugee protection and responsible allocation of donor funds by creating a legible beneficiary population (see Sandvik on results-based management and Lindskov Jacobsen on biometrics in this volume). This approach to accountability ultimately rests on the premise that refugees constitute problems to be first identified (through the standardized collection of reliable population data) and then solved (through the reestablishment of the citizen-state bond). Yonah's story, however, does not fit this problem/solution model. Violently displaced at the age of ten, he and his family sought asylum in Uganda three years before national independence, when domestic refugee and citizenship laws did not yet exist. The British Protectorate government passed the *Control of Alien Refugees Act* (CARA) the following year, in 1960, at which point local authorities reclassified Yonah and his parents as 'refugees'. Despite this relabelling, the family did not move to a refugee settlement (as it had not yet been built) but remained in southwestern Uganda as tenant farmers on rented land. Fifty-five years later, Yonah no longer considers himself 'displaced', having spent his entire adolescence and adult life in 'exile'. Nonetheless, he is also not a citizen due to the fact that CARA, which remained on the books until 2006, expressly forbid refugees the right to naturalize.[2] Yonah's lack of legal recognition as either citizen or refugee leaves him vulnerable to harassment deportation, yet he nevertheless, he remains in Uganda for reasons both simple and profound: His life is now *here* – it is no longer *there*.

Yonah's ambivalent legal status is not unique. Rather, it is a product of the particular social, legal and administrative histories of refugee management in Uganda. Historical analysis is therefore necessary if we are to discern actual protection needs in a country like Uganda, where long histories of migration and population management have blurred the line between citizens and non-citizens. This chapter offers a preliminary venture into this field of inquiry, drawing on newly accessible Uganda archives, UNHCR records and oral histories to demonstrate how, during the first decade of national independence, shifting legal and documentary regimes opened up multiple forms of political and social belonging for displaced people, none of which have proven to be stable over time or have been ultimate guarantors of protection.

I centre my analysis on a case study of Rwandans who came to Uganda during the critical period between 1959, the year the Revolution began, and 1964, the year that the Uganda government, motivated by growing concerns regarding refugee guerrilla activities, shifted from a policy of local integration towards one of mandatory encampment. Scholars of forced migration often situate the emergence of the 'African refugee problem' in the context of decolonization and modern state-building (Zolberg and Suhrke 1989; Loescher, Betts, and Milner 2008), but this narrative presumes a teleological relationship between state formation and the production of non-citizens. it also implies, wrongly, that the refugee category emerged in the immediate post-colonial moment as a singular, coherent concept, one that has remained stable across time and space. This framework provides little explanatory power for the widespread variations in both population management practices, on the one hand, and the experiences of the displaced, on the other hand.

Attention to the historical contingency and multiplicity of the refugee label raises critical questions concerning the ability of UNHCR's Uganda Office to achieve 'accountability' through RBM and improved data collection technologies. Renewed efforts to identify 'refugees' will not service the untold number of long-term, self-settled individuals who, while still requiring political protection, are neither recognized as refugees nor recognizable as such. Indeed, critical discussions of UNHCR's accountability initiatives usually assume that displaced individuals *want* to be counted as populations of concern because the act of registration is imagined to confer legitimacy, a more opportune identity and access to resources. Attention is seldomly given to likely distributive costs and how they may shape alternative perceptions. Just as the imposition of camp-based policies led to the practical redefining of the refugee category in Uganda (Kaiser 2006), so, too, will the current push for 'better' numbers contribute to the political reimagining of what it means to be displaced.

This chapter is organized into five sections. It begins with a review of the literature on encampment and self-settlement, followed by a brief history of the Rwandan Revolution and the resultant diaspora. Part 2 situates the emergence of late colonial Uganda's so-called 'refugee problem' in political and historical context, highlighting the political and administrative considerations that factored into the transitioning government's decision to recognize the Banyarwanda exiles as refugees, rather than as migrants. Part 3 turns to a detailed exploration of the everyday work of defining and managing a refugee population, giving careful attention to the substantial gatekeeping power wielded by local chiefs and the ways that decentralized documentation practices effectively excluded many would-be refugees (particularly women and children) from official government records. Part 4 traces the central administration's halting steps towards mandatory refugee settlement and the consequences of this hesitation for self-settled refugees. A brief conclusion follows.

Encampment, self-settlement and the spaces in-between

Exiles of the Rwandan Revolution (1959–61) and their descendants constitute one of the oldest refugee diasporas in Africa. Displaced on the eve of independence and denied the likelihood of return by a hostile Rwandan government, the vast majority of the so-called '59-ers' were forced to remain in exile for decades. Their protracted displacement has garnered significant attention from forced migration scholars, who have drawn important linkages between political exclusion, refugee militarization and cyclical violence in the Great Lakes Region (Otunnu 1999; Terry 2002; Lischer 2006). These linkages constitute an important field of inquiry in refugee studies, one that demands continued investigation in light of the persistent centrality of the camp to refugee governance programs in Africa today (Schmidt 2003). However, it is equally important to remember that refugee militias represent only one set of responses to exile, and that government efforts to isolate and exclude were never totalizing. The same political context that spurred the formation of militant refugee movements, such as the Rwandan Patriotic Front (RPF), also facilitated various forms of self-settlement, however imperfect or unstable. To understand this phenomenon, it is necessary to shift the focus from refugee militarism and its causes to a larger analysis of the links between evolving population management practices, on the one hand, and the emergence of self-settlement as a risky yet preferable alternative to protracted refugee status, on the other hand.

Scholars have rightly noted the role of encampment policies in limiting the scope of refugee protection in Uganda, with 'refugee' coming to mean only persons who live in settlements, rather than persons in need of legal protection (Kaiser 2006; Hovil 2007). What this scholarship largely overlooks, however, is the fact that the decision to construct settlements was separate from the decision to require all of the refugees to live in the settlements.[3] Government consensus on the matter – which was never total or uncontested – developed slowly, over a period of years.[4] In the interim, refugees, faced with few tenable options, busily made their own way into Uganda's social order, drawing on familial, religious, and economic networks to secure land, housing and local political patrons. Tens of thousands of would-be refugees slipped through the cracks of a rapidly evolving constellation of laws, policies and infrastructure during the 1960s, with government reporting that only 60,000 of an estimated 180,000 Rwandan, Sudanese and Congolese refugees resided in settlements by 1970 (Holborn 1975, p. 1212).

This phenomenon begs further investigation of the relationship between refugees in settlements and refugees outside of settlements. Scholars of refugee studies have generally treated refugee governance and self-settlement separately, rather than in tandem; when scholars have addressed these topics in tandem, they have adopted a comparative approach, treating 'camp' and 'town' as discrete rather than interconnected and mutually constituted spaces (Chambers 1979; Hansen 1990; Malkki 1995). Social scientists and policy experts have exhibited significant energies to debating the merits and failings of camp-based vs. self-settlement approaches and the long-term effects of each (Gallagher, Clark and Stein 1985; Kibreab 1989; Jacobsen 2001; Bakewell 2014), and to presenting the intellectual history behind camp-based policies in Africa and its rootedness in modernization theory and colonial development programs (Schmidt 1998).

In Uganda, however, scholars have managed to publish important studies tracing the movements of self-settled refugees in and out of camps and across changing protection fields. Quantitative data are difficult, if not impossible, to collect, due to the mobility and political vulnerability of self-settled refugees; however, several scholars have built persuasive cases drawing on qualitative research gathered over years of fieldwork. These works challenge common assumptions regarding camp/non-camp binaries, showing instead how refugees inhabit 'overlapping and fluid categories which change over time' (Kaiser 2006, p. 608). This chapter builds on these studies by investigating the historical relationship between evolving camp-based policies and the diversity of exilic experiences.

Displacement at the end of empire

The Rwandan revolution began in November 1959 as a series of localized uprisings against the chiefs who governed on behalf of the Belgian colonial state. Although the majority of these African elites were Tutsi, these early violent episodes were not about ethnicity *per se* – they were about dismantling the infrastructure of an oppressive colonial regime (Newbury 1988; Pottier 2002). More than 350 Tutsi chiefs and sub-chiefs were either killed or removed from office during the first month of the war. The Belgians, in a desperate act of appeasement, responded to the rebellions by reversing their long-standing support of the Tutsi ruling class and appointing more than 300 Hutu chiefs to replace them (Lemarchand 1970, p. 173). They then organized the country's first local council elections in June and July 1960, in which the hyper-nationalist Hutu party, PARMEHUTU, took 2,390 of likely 3,125 seats (Longman 2009, p. 73). The *Mwami* (Tutsi[5] king) permanently vacated the country six months later after a breakdown in peace negotiations with PARMEHUTU leadership and colonial authorities. Hutu nationalists seized the *Mwami's* departure as an opportunity to abolish the monarchy and declare Ruanda a Hutu Republic (Lemarchand 1970, p. 192). On 1 July 1962, the UN Trust Territory of Ruanda-Urundi became the independent states of Rwanda and Burundi.

The overthrow of the monarchy and the sudden upending of power relations resulted in the displacement of nearly 100,000 people by 1962 (Holborn 1975, p. 981). These numbers continued to climb in the wake of sustained unrest and the new PARMEHUTU administration's increasingly oppressive treatment of Tutsi citizenry. By the end of the decade, more than 160,000 people had fled Rwanda, nearly half of whom has sought asylum in Uganda.[6]

The government of Uganda and the UNHCR framed refugees as constituting a national and regional crisis, one that represented a serious break from earlier types of cross-border migration. Chief among their concerns was the fear that refugees posed a threat to regional peace and stability and would lead to the unnecessary entanglement of Uganda in Rwandan affairs. The British regarded the '59-ers as dangerous ideologues, whose monarchist attachments might serve to radicalize the Protectorate's own complicated royalist politics (Long 2012). Unlike the tens of thousands of seasonal workers who cycled through the country every year, people displaced by the revolution came to Uganda with no sense of when they might return.

Protectorate authorities were also concerned that refugees' livestock would reintroduce deadly animal diseases into Uganda and threaten the country's $70 million livestock industry. Unlike migrants, Rwandan refugees sought to bring all of their moveable property with them, namely, their cattle. Refugees brought more than 15,000 head of cattle with them between 1959 and 1962, and Uganda officials feared that the war-induced breakdown in basic government services, such as animal inoculations, would render Rwandan livestock vulnerable to infection.[7]

The third major factor underpinning government anxieties regarding displacement was the costs and logistical challenges of delivering relief aid. Neither the British nor the Belgian Colonial Offices in Europe were willing to offer assistance, on the grounds that they were not responsible for causing or solving Uganda's refugee problem.[8] The UNHCR, while interested in helping, was still in the process of determining its proper role outside of Europe. The Uganda government would ultimately receive substantial assistance from the UN Refugee Agency, beginning with a $50,000 grant in 1962; however, this aid was slow in coming and was not easy to predict.

Thus, the idea of the 'African refugee', as it developed *in situ*, came to reference not only a broken citizen-state connection, but a source of political insecurity, disease and economic underdevelopment as well. Solving the refugee problem, thus, took on a civilizing dimension, with government and international observers readily inserting refugees into the 'savage slot' (Trouillot 2003), as people who needed to be molded into productive members of society through socio-economic and moral development schemes. It is, therefore, not surprising that the Uganda government, in its search for solutions, reached for a model that the colonial state had used before with other supposedly underdeveloped populations: the agricultural settlement.

During the 1940s and '50s, the British Protectorate had organized for the relocation of tens of thousands of Bakiga farmers from the densely populated Kigezi District in southwestern Uganda to more rural areas of neighbouring Ankole, Toro and Bunyoro Districts. The scheme was intended to alleviate population pressures and soil erosion in Kigezi and simultaneously open up 'virgin territory' for agricultural development (Carswell 2007). The arrival of displaced Rwandans in Kigezi after 1959 prompted government authorities to modify their

Bakiga resettlement scheme to address the new crisis at hand (Belshaw 1968). Unlike the squalid refugee camp of post-war Europe, the refugee *settlement* of post-colonial Africa was intended to encourage refugee self-reliance through agricultural development, all the while facilitating greater government surveillance.

British Protectorate authorities began construction on what would eventually become known as Oruchinga Valley Refugee Settlement, the country's first formal refugee settlement for Africans[9] in 1961, one year before national independence. At the time, certain voices in the central and district government argued for the immediate transfer of all Rwandan refugees to the settlement[10]; however, the slowness of the construction process, combined with government fears regarding the political consequences of forcibly relocating refugees, worked to deflate political will on the matter. Until 1964, central authorities repeatedly chose to allow those who were able to settle privately in the border region, all the while refusing to accept the proposition that refugees be granted paths to citizenship.[11]

The following two sections examine the efforts of central and local government actors to craft a legible refugee population through the imposition of new laws and bureaucratic orders. I first trace the development of the *Aliens (Batutsi Immigrants) Rules* and its successor, the *Control of Alien Refugees Act* (CARA); I then explore how local officials interpreted and implemented these new laws. This discussion highlights the pivotal role of chiefs and civil servants in determining the line between citizens and non-citizens (see also Fresia and von Känel on the tension between universalizing norms and local interpretations of citizenship, this volume).

Exceptional movement: creating a refugee category

Displaced Rwandans arriving in southwestern Uganda during the 1960s encountered a diverse and highly mobile borderland, in which the line between 'foreigner' and 'indigene' was far from certain. Tens of thousands of seasonal labour migrants from Ruanda-Urundi and Congo cycled through the country every year (Richards 1954).[12] They were joined by a host of internal migrants from Kigezi and Ankole Districts, among whom were young men in search of cash wages, impoverished Bakiga families en route to government resettlement schemes and church workers connected to Christian mission stations across central Africa (Peterson 2012). The result of these varied movements was that many people in southwestern Uganda were relative newcomers to their place of residence.

Many of the first Ruanda asylum-seekers actually entered Uganda as *de facto* labour migrants and, as such, were not required to furnish identification information or apply for special travel or residency permits.[13] The Protectorate administration had at various times in the past attempted to coordinate pass systems with the Belgian authorities in Congo and Ruanda-Urundi[14]; however, each attempt had ended in failure. The border was too long and too mountainous, and the Protectorate's need for migrant labour too great, to implement a more stringent policy.[15]

The Protectorate government initially pursued a path of non-intervention with regard to the refugees, arguing that the crisis in Ruanda was a purely domestic affair, to be managed by the Belgian authorities. They were soon forced to modify their stance when it became evident that the war was beginning to draw southern Uganda into its orbit. Chiefs from the border region sent alarming messages to their District Commissioners, informing them that they could see huts burning just inside Ruanda and that unknown parties were entering Uganda by night to loot and kidnap.[16] Partly in response to these reports and partly in response to requests from Belgian officials,[17] the Protectorate officials made moves in late November to intercept refugees and deport them in an operation known as the 'Rwanda Resettlement Plan'.[18] These efforts were largely unsuccessful because few refugees were willing to return and the Protectorate was not prepared, for reasons largely political, to forcibly remove them from the border region.[19] Shifting tactics, the Governor introduced the *Aliens (Batutsi Immigrants) Rules* in late December 1959, which aimed to regulate the mobility and settlement of 'African[s] of the Batutsi tribe ordinarily resident in Ruanda'. The *Rules* were applied retroactively to all 'Batutsi', who came to Uganda on or after 1 November of that year, and required all persons subject to the law to apply for special residency permits.[20] Rapid repatriation remained the ultimate objective; however, the *Batutsi Rules* signalled the Protectorate administration's begrudging acknowledgement that most 'migrants' would need to remain in Uganda until peace returned to Ruanda-Urundi.

The government officials identified Batutsi immigrants following what might best be described as *prima facie* status determination, although this process was not how lawmakers framed it at the time. The law applied to a circumscribed group, defined by an assumed social identity (Batutsi) and specific temporal limits (on or after 1 November 1959). Persons who were subject to the *Batutsi Rules* were not granted individual eligibility hearings nor did they have legal recourse to contest the decision of the government official. Instead, authorized government personnel could record any individual as a 'Watutsi immigrant' who, *prima facie, appeared* to belong to a particular group as defined by the law.

In June 1960, just six months after the passage of the *Batutsi Rules*, the Protectorate was faced with a new potential crisis, i.e. independence in the Belgian Congo. Fearful that Congolese independence on 30 June would result in massive refugee flows of both Belgians and Africans to Uganda, the Protectorate government believed it had to move quickly. Discarding earlier piecemeal immigration legislation, the Uganda Legislative Council (LegCo) drafted and passed the comprehensive *Control of Alien Refugees Act* (CARA). The Governor of Uganda, Sir Frederick Crawford, operationalized the law on 13 July 1960.[21]

CARA provided neither specific criteria nor procedural instructions for determining refugee status. Instead, it authorized the Governor (after 1962, the Minister) to declare 'any person being one of a class of aliens … to be refugees' on a case-by-case basis. He had unilateral authority to determine who was a refugee and who was not; his pronouncements, published in the *Uganda Gazette*, served as the legal instruments for determining refugee status. Unlike the 1951 Convention/Protocol or the later 1969 OAU Convention, which defined 'refugee' using a combination of subjective and objective criteria, CARA enabled the Governor/Minister to define refugees on the basis of objective criteria alone. A person who wished to be recognized as a refugee in Uganda had to demonstrate that he or she belonged to a scheduled refugee group; individual asylum-seekers did not need to demonstrate a 'well-founded fear of persecution' before the officer hearing their case issued a refugee permit. Group membership, not individualized fears of persecution, was what mattered.

Determining refugee status on the basis of an individual's membership to a circumscribed group served the interests of the Ugandan state in two distinct ways. First, and most importantly, it allowed the government to avoid politically sensitive questions regarding persecution. The refugees were a source of embarrassment in the context of independence because their presence suggested that an African government was persecuting its own people. Ugandan political leaders had supported the refugee label for people fleeing Belgian Ruanda-Urundi[22]; they were reticent to use it for people fleeing the independent Republic of Rwanda. *Prima facie* refugee status determination, thus, provided a means of saving face, allowing the host governments to recognize refugees without delving into the domestic affairs of another independent state.

Second, receiving refugees on a *prima facie* basis allowed a limited administrative system to process large numbers of asylum-seekers in a short period of time. Assessing individual claims of persecution or fears of persecution was (and is) a time- and labour-intensive process. The Ugandan administration, already stretched thin by the demanding transition from colonial rule, did not have the resources needed to design and implement such intensive eligibility procedures. Persons granted asylum on the basis of group membership were still individually screened; however, the officer adjudicating their case was only concerned with determining the applicant's membership to a refugee group.

The *prima facie* concept also served the interests of the UNHCR. Like the Uganda government, the Office aimed to circumvent the politics of labelling displaced Rwandans as refugees, for fear of upsetting either the exiting colonial power, Belgium, or the United Nations, which had entrusted the Mandate Territory of Ruanda-Urundi to Belgium. The Office was further cognizant of the fact that its authority to intervene in Africa was questionable and not universally accepted due to discrepancies between the UNHCR Mandate and the 1951 Convention. The Mandate gave the Office jurisdiction over all refugee situations, both in Europe and outside; however, the 1951 Convention Relating to the Status of Refugees limited the definition to include only persons displaced before 1951 – i.e. refugees of the Second World War. This ambivalence over the UNHCR's prescribed jurisdiction created significant confusion regarding the reach of the Office's Mandate, even among the members of its own Executive Committee. Great Britain, for example, refused to make requests for international assistance on behalf of its own Uganda Protectorate.[23] Lacking a clear and universally accepted mandate, the UNHCR's move into central Africa refugee issues was therefore cautious and exploratory, rather than visionary. The *prima facie* label allowed the High Commissioner for Refugees to justify his activities on the grounds that the objective evidence of the situation in Ruanda made it clear that at least several persons displaced by the revolution were fleeing fears of persecution and, thus, might be considered to be refugees according to the Mandate.

The decision to exceptionalize certain types of cross-border mobility presented the transitioning Ugandan government with a new challenge, i.e. to create a legible refugee population out of a diverse and highly mobile border region. Without the availability of a controlled settlement, the government officials had to rely on a still-developing system of permits and ration cards to identify refugees from residents. Even a person's own testimony could not be used to aid in the sorting process because the law was not concerned with individual experiences or perceptions.

The following section examines the everyday work of implementing changing immigration law in southwestern Uganda. In theory, *prima facie* RSD procedures were supposed to expedite administrative processes by lowering the burden of proof required for establishing refugee eligibility. The problem with this approach was that refugee groups were recent inventions, not obvious, but overlapping with other social and linguistic groups, making the work of differentiating between refugees and non-refugees exceedingly difficult. Additionally, the difficulties in communication across large rural areas forced district governments to be extremely conservative in their allocation of vehicles and fuel, staff and time. Many asylum-seekers in Uganda likely were unregistered as a result, with the UNHCR Representative in Kampala reporting that 'the large majority of refugees' arriving at his door 'were not only without identity papers as required by the law ... but [were] also fully unaware of the existence and necessity of such a document'.[24]

Crafting a refugee population

District Commissioners (DCs) were the sites for local implementation and operational oversight.[25] At the most mundane level, they decided what information to collect on refugees and how to file and store it. They designed the physical permit forms and decided in what language(s) to produce them, and they incurred the printing costs. Clerks of various pay-grades translated the messages from the chiefs to the British personnel and back again, in a process that often resulted in the blurring of legally distinct categories. This everyday bureaucratic labour contributed significantly to the localization of refugee management, as labels created by central authorities took on new meaning through local application. With limited staff and communication resources, DCs made conservative choices regarding how and when they would issue permits and how they should educate asylum-seekers regarding their responsibilities and obligations under the law.

Each District was responsible for developing its own permitting system, and this localization of record-keeping responsibilities resulted in significant variations in refugee documentation work.[26] Although I have not been able to locate a succinct description of refugee permitting procedures for this early period, it is evident from inter-district correspondence that refugee data collection and permit issuance were performed by at least the following three different sets of local government agents: the police, the DCs and all grades of African chiefs. The refugees might receive permits when they arrived in a village in search of a place to stay, or they might simply have their names recorded by the *muruka* chief, who would then request the District Office to send an assistant DC to issue permits at a later date. Several asylum-seekers arrived in large groups and established their own camps near the border, in which case the local police station might send a deputy to record their names. Unsurprisingly, the multiplication of bureaucratic sites resulted in conflicting numbers. For example, the Refugees Officer (RO) reported that the police had counted 35,000 Rwandan refugees in Uganda as of April 1962, whereas his office could only account for 24,000 of those refugees. The RO hypothesized that the difference in figures was due to the large numbers of people his office had not counted – i.e. those 'staying with friends' and those who had left Uganda and then re-entered.[27]

As with the *Batutsi Rules*, CARA required the refugees to apply for and receive a permit from an 'authorized officer'. The authorized officers had complete authority to both issue and refuse permits to asylum-seekers, and they did not need to offer an explanation in the case of refusal. This power asymmetry was further exacerbated by the fact that asylum-seekers could not appeal the decision nor did they have access to the courts. The law did stipulate that an officer should not refuse to issue a permit to someone whom they believed would, 'on returning to the territory from which he came … be tried or punished for an offence of a political character or be subject to physical attack' (CAP. 64, Article 6, Section 2). The lack of an appeals process, however, meant that the applicants were dependent on the good will of the officer overseeing their case.

The chiefs often provided the first round of screening, recording the names and ages of newcomers to their jurisdiction and sending them to the District Office. The chiefs were assumed to be in the best position to identify outsiders, given their proximity to the local populace.[28] One chief wrote to the DC Kigezi in September 1961 to report the arrival of 22 refugees to his sub-county, all of whom came 'before the 1st November, 1959, and do not have permits to confirm them to be in Uganda'.[29] The chief was not alone in his confusion. The DC Kigezi had to order an entirely new census that year when initial returns revealed that many chiefs 'either counted Watutsi [sic] who were not refugees or that there are a large number of Watutsi in Kigezi who are not in possession of valid permits to remain in Uganda'.[30]

Confusion about the meaning and purpose of refugee permits – and, by extension, the meaning and purpose of refugee status – extended to all levels of government. Refugee Officer (RO) I. M. Sanderson, who was the officer in charge of all field operations and directly responsible to the national Director of Refugees, wrote a memo to his boss in late 1962 stating that he thought it was unnecessary to renew the permits of refugees who were 'self-supporting' and no longer in need of government assistance. He was likewise opposed to issuing new permits to 'refugees living outside the Resettlement areas', arguing that such persons 'should be treated as people of the District in which they live … [since] most of them have been in the area for over a year and have had a good opportunity to settle down'. Sanderson clearly believed that the primary purpose of issuing permits was to control the distribution of relief items, not to facilitate government surveillance (and certainly not to confer legal protection). If the refugees were able to take care of themselves, he reasoned, then they were no longer of practical concern to the government. He had come to this conclusion through his conversations with the DCs in Kigezi and Ankole, who were at that moment addressing unprecedented refugee flows from Congo and Rwanda. In his effort to conserve extremely limited government funds, time and energy, the RO conflated permits with ration cards.

An embarrassment of categories

The RO's conflation of permits (proof of legal residence) with ration cards (access to material assistance) was incorrect in terms of the law because refugees were legally required to hold valid permits. Sanderson's argument made sense in view of ongoing conversations among government personnel regarding how best to organize mobile populations. Between 1959 and 1964, District and Central authorities issued repeated requests to the chiefs to conduct refugee censuses, often with special instructions to sub-categorize refugees by date of arrival, need and property. The chiefs' responses demonstrated varying interpretations of these orders; more importantly, these orders hinted at the number of ways that refugees – whether recognized or not – made their way across the Uganda – Rwanda border.

Old batch vs. new batch vs. newest batches

In government correspondence and casual parlance, the immigrants-cum-refugees came to be known as 'old batch'. Old batch refugees were based in Kigezi District and had, like Yonah and his family, been allowed to settle privately. By contrast, the Protectorate agents referred to persons who arrived after July 10 as 'new batch'. New batch refugees, unlike the old batch, were largely dependent on government rations.[31] The DC Kigezi informed his chiefs that they needed to keep three separate lists, one for each 'batch', as follows: 1) those who entered Uganda on or after 10 July 1960; 2) those who received permits under the *Batutsi Rules*; and 3) future refugees.[32] The following year, the newly appointed Director of Refugees provided an update on the status of 'old batch' refugees. Old batch refugees were largely allowed to remain as they were and were considered by many senior Uganda officials to be permanent residents.[33]

Increasing levels of border insecurity, however, pressed the Protectorate state – then on the verge of independence – to reconsider its stance on self-settlement. By May 1962, after a serious border violation by Belgian security forces, the Minister of Community Development, who held the refugee portfolio, ordered a census of all of the refugees who were either 'settled with friends or relatives' or 'who are accepted as having settled permanently' within five miles of the border.[34] The government had allowed these 'old batch' refugees to settle privately; however, now central authorities were prepared to order their removal, regardless of public opinion.

At the last moment, however, the Minister rescinded his order to sweep the border, deciding instead that all 'permanently settled' refugees should be allowed to remain where they were. This category – 'permanently settled' – was not found anywhere in Ugandan law. It was, instead, a phrase that the Minister devised to help differentiate between refugees who were self-sufficient and those who were still dependent on government rations for survival. This differentiation was not about protection or legal status but about perceived levels of need.

The phrase was sufficiently confusing that the DC Kigezi felt obliged to define it for his chiefs: '"Settled permanently" means refugees who are farming on their account on their own land'. He further stressed the importance of distinguishing between 'old' and 'fresh' refugees in the following manner:

> It must be clearly understood that [permanently settled] applies only to those refugees who are already staying with friends or relatives or who are already settled permanently. Fresh refugees entering the district will not be allowed to remain on the border and you must notify me at once when fresh refugees enter your area, giving me details of their names and numbers and where they are living.[35]

Women and children: the meaning of a tally mark

As a general rule, the DC and his Assistant DCs issued permits to 'heads of families', not to individuals. This meant that only men – the presumed household heads – were named in official documents, except when a woman could demonstrate that she had neither husband nor adult male relative who might claim her as a dependent. Adult men without dependents were also considered to be household heads and they were issued permits, despite the fact that they were alone. Generally, adult women and teenage boys were categorized as 'women dependents' and 'male dependents' and were noted with a tally mark in the appropriate column. Children might be counted together or divided by gender, depending on the inclination of the official recording the information, and were likewise represented by a tally mark.

That government officials endeavoured to organize displaced Rwandans into male-headed nuclear family units is hardly surprising. In previous decades, the Protectorate had managed the Ugandan populace in similar fashion, collecting taxes and labour by household rather than individual. The chiefs and district officials would have good reason for collecting the names of adult male refugees, precisely because they viewed these men as potentially a new source of revenue. From as early as January 1960, central and local authorities regularly questioned whether the refugees might be taxed. Between 1962 and 1963, a broad consensus emerged across all levels of government that the 'older refugees' (meaning, those who had arrived in 1960) who were self-settled should be treated as ordinary residents.

The decision to only record the names of adult men also reflected the perceived security interests of the state. Although public campaigns led by the British Red

Cross of Uganda and other voluntary agencies emphasized the plight of refugee women and children, government correspondence from this period was concerned nearly entirely with the whereabouts, networks, and political organization of refugee men. The spectre of the 'Refugee Warrior' – a figure always cast as the angry black male youth, radicalized in the crucible of exile, vulnerable to the seductions of the Communist bloc[36] – haunted every government meeting, policy and law intended to address the country's 'refugee question'. Connected to this, government officials sought to engage refugee men in meaningful, productive labour to prevent dependency and boredom, which Uganda authorities viewed as the seeds of political radicalization.

Whatever the logics behind the government's focus on refugee men, the practice of naming refugee men and tallying women and children meant that the vast majority of 'documented' refugees are unnamed in official records; they were visible, yet anonymous. For several refugees, the anonymity afforded by the tally mark allowed several women and children the opportunities to shed their political status more readily than men.[37] However, the lack of personal recognition could also prove to be detrimental to a woman's ability to move freely and access resources. Government officials reported on women who had either been abandoned or separated from their male relatives, who carried the family permit.

Towards a policy of mandatory settlement

By the close of 1963, Uganda officials estimated that more than 12,000 refugees were settled as private residents in the southwest.[38] The government had initiated the construction of the country's first refugee settlement two years prior; however, the intent had been to facilitate aid distribution and provide adequate space for cattle quarantines. Whether refugees should be required to live in the settlements was a separate question altogether, one that deeply divided parliament and the Cabinet of Ministers. On the side of encampment, the Minister of Security and External Relations (later, the Minister of Foreign Affairs) viewed displacement through the prism of national security and vigorously advocated for settlement. He was supported by the DC Kigezi, whose District served as the primary gateway into Uganda for both Rwandan and Ugandan refugees. The Minister's colleagues, however, voiced caution. Encampment would be a costly endeavour, and it was not clear whether the international community would be willing to foot the bill. Even with outside funding, the actual implementation of mandatory settlement would require more personnel from district governments and the central ministries than the state could spare. Politically, the Cabinet members, as elected parliamentarians, had to consider their own jobs: Forcibly relocating refugees was a risky move in certain regions, and voters were certain to express their displeasure at the ballot box. Thus, the Cabinet as a whole remained committed to a diplomatic solution throughout the early 1960s, believing that refugee solutions could be achieved through direct talks with the Rwanda government.[39]

Meanwhile, the security situation along the Uganda – Rwanda border continued to deteriorate, with local authorities reporting on cross-border raids, kidnappings and arson with increasing frequency. Intelligence sources embedded in the refugee settlements had become aware of a Rwandan refugee organization known to them as *Inyenzi*,[40] which they believed to be a terrorist group with support from the exiled Rwandan government and likely the Soviets.[41] Between 1962 and 1967, this faction launched a series of border raids into Rwanda with the aim of overthrowing the Hutu Republic and reinstating the exiled Mwami.

The worst of these assaults came in December 1963 when 500 refugee guerrillas invaded from Uganda in concert with another militia of 200 refugees from Burundi. The result was catastrophic. The Rwandan Army, with its superior firepower, quickly repelled the attack. They used the invasion as a pretext to hunt down alleged spies and sympathizers. Thousands of unarmed civilians – for the most part, Tutsi peasants who had managed to remain in Ruanda during the revolution – were massacred in the pogroms that followed.

The unprecedented bloodshed of the invasion left a profound impact on the Rwandan diaspora as well as their countries of asylum. For many, 1963/64 marked the point of no return. Kayibanda's administration, which had previously paid lip service to the likelihood of mass repatriation, now made its hostilities to the diaspora explicit. The Ugandan government abandoned hopes of reaching a bilateral agreement with the Rwandan authorities for mass repatriation of refugees.

The invasion gave the pro-encampment contingent the political capital they needed to push forward their plan for refugee settlement. Beginning 31 January 1964, on the orders of M. Davies, the Minister for Internal Affairs, police and military personnel initiated a clearance of the Uganda – Rwanda border in Kigezi and Ankole Districts without seeking approval from the Prime Minister or the Cabinet.[42] First-hand accounts reported chiefs and police officers used their participation in the operation as an opportunity to exact revenge on their personal and political foes, putting persons they knew to be Ugandan citizens on lorries headed for Oruchinga. The refugees who had settled there for several years and who had built houses, planted fields and even gotten married found themselves uprooted once again.

The Cabinet expressed outrage at the Minister's actions but curiously did not seek to reverse the move. Instead, the Minister of Community Development introduced a bill in December 1964 to amend the *Control of Alien Refugees Act* with a prohibition against refugee self-settlement. 'Many refugees come and do not report to the authorities', explained the Minister in his speech before Parliament. 'They merely go to stay with their relations … with the result that although we say there are so many hundred thousand refugees in Uganda at the moment, we actually do not know the exact number …'. The Minister warned that the government's inability to 'see' the refugees would lead to increasing instances of 'subversion', as well violent crime, gun-running, and economic stagnation.[43] The Bill would, in theory, wrest some of the gatekeeping power that local communities had accrued between 1959 and 1964, giving central authorities greater control over their borders. The Bill passed easily through Parliament, becoming law on 24 December 1964.

Unsurprisingly, the passage of the 1964 amendment against 'harbouring refugees' did little to change the situation on the ground, even if it served as a major step towards mandatory encampment and the subsequent criminalization of self-settlement. The inability of the decolonizing government to impose a new political imaginary on the country, one in which citizens and refugees existed as discrete categories, was indicative of the many political possibilities that emerged in the transition to independence.

Conclusion

In October 1990, a refugee militia, composed primarily of second-generation refugees and calling itself the Rwandan Patriotic Front (RPF), invaded northern Rwanda in a move eerily reminiscent of the border raids in the 1960s. Unlike the guerrilla movements of their parents' generation, however, the RPF ultimately succeeded in taking over Kigali, but only after engaging in a protracted struggle that culminated in genocide. During my fieldwork (May–July 2011, January–November 2013 and May 2015), many persons I interviewed identified the RPF invasion as the moment when refugees finally 'went home'. This perception is reflected in scholarly accounts as well, with Mamdani (2001) characterizing the attack as an attempt by the Ugandan government to export its crisis of citizenship through 'armed repatriation'.

Yet, people like Yonah remain, and their continued efforts to remain in Uganda invite careful reconsideration of scholarly preoccupation with the nexus between political exclusion and refugee militancy. Not to downplay or apologize for the very real history of repressive refugee management practices and policies, this situation is instead a call to investigate how refugee management practices in Uganda have opened up multiple, simultaneous and contingent types of inclusion and exclusion. To this end, I have endeavoured to present refugee management as a process, as a shifting constellation of laws, policies, spaces and people that has produced over time an inconsistent and variegated protection landscape.

The argument in this chapter is motivated by the idea that considering past protection measures can help UNHCR think critically regarding its present responsibilities to refugees, host governments and donors. I have suggested that framing refugees as ahistorical problems to be solved fails to illuminate the processes by which certain individuals have been imagined as refugees, but not others. Forced migration scholars have helpfully pointed to the role of encampment policies in shaping Uganda's particular protection landscape; however, I have argued that these observations do not go far enough. Attention to process – to change over time – is necessary if we are to understand how tens of thousands of would-be refugees settled across southwestern and central Uganda during the first decade of national independence.

Notes

1 Before independence, the official spelling for Rwanda was 'Ruanda', and it was part of the conjoined League of Nations/UN Trust Territory of Ruanda–Urundi. Throughout this chapter, I adopt the spelling that corresponds to the time period under discussion.
2 Uganda Control of Alien Refugees Act, Laws of Uganda, Chapter 62, 1960 (1964).
3 Articles 7 and 8 of the Control of Alien Refugees Act state that authorized government officers *may* direct refugees to live in settlements.
4 UNA *Confidential Office of the President* (hereafter COP), Box 79, File CM/21, 'Ministry of culture and community development policy review', 17 June 1966.
5 The UNAR argued that the *Mwami*, while Tutsi, was king for all Banyarwanda.
6 United Nations. (1971) *Yearbook for the United Nations, 1968*, v. 22, p. 530. New York: UN.
7 Director of Veterinary and Animal Industries to the Director of Refugees. (1965) 'Movement of cattle-owning refugees' (Confidential), 28 May 1962, in B. L. Jacobs, *Administrators in east Africa: six case studies*, p. 41. Entebbe: Government Printer.
8 UNA COP, Box 44, File EC.8780i, Cabinet Memorandum CT. (1962) Minister of Finance, 'Rwanda-Burundi refugees finance', 2 November 1962, p. 277.
9 The British Protectorate had established two settlements for Polish refugees and POWs during the Second World War (S. Lwanga-Lunyiigo 1998).
10 UNA COP, Box 68, File S.10484. (1961) 'Ruanda refugees: note of decisions taken at the meeting in Mbarara', 3 October 1961.
11 UNA COP, Box 68, File S.10484. (1962) 'Extract of Cabinet minute', p. 634.
12 Uganda Labour Department. (1959) *Annual Report of the Labour Department*, p. 7. Entebbe: Government Printer.
13 KigDA Immigration, Box 8, File MIG 1vi. (23 April 1958) DC Kigezi to M. L'Administrateur de Territoire, Rutchuru, Ruhengeri, and Biumba; KigDA Immigration, Box 1, File LAB 1/3i. (25 May 1949) Provincial Commissioner, Western Province, to Labour Commissioner.
14 Ibid.
15 KigDA Immigration, Box 8, File MIG 1vi. (25 July 1958) DC Kigezi to OC Police, Kigezi.
16 KigDA Immigration, Box 1, File LAN 5i. (10 November 1959) Mutwale Bufumbira to Secretary General, Kigezi District Council.
17 KigDA Immigration, Box 1, File LAN 5i. (4 December 1959) Chief Secretary C.H. Hartwell to Abanyaruanda na Abarundi Abadahemuka.
18 KigDA Immigration, Box 1, File LAN 5i. (15 December 1959) Police Kisoro to Police Kabale.
19 UNA COP, Box 32, File 007. (27 March 1962) Cabinet minute, p. 72.
20 Legal Notice No. 311 of 1959. (24 December 1959) 'The aliens (Batutsi immigrants) rules, 1959', pp. 658–659, *Supplement to Uganda gazette*.
21 Legal Notice No. 136 of 1960. (13 July 1960) 'The control of alien refugees ordinance, 1960', p. 314, *Supplement to Uganda gazette*.
22 ULC Deb. 40s. (28 February 1960) pp. 164–173.
23 UNA COP, Box 44, File EC.8780i. Cabinet Memorandum No. 277. (n.d.) 'Refugee finance'.
24 UNHCR Representative, Kampala, to UNHCR, Geneva, 'Identity papers for refugees in Uganda', 27 April 1967; 6/1/UGA: Protection – Uganda (v. 1), 1964–69; Series 1, Classified Subject Files; Fonds 11, Records of the Central Registry; Archives of the United Nations High Commissioner for Refugees (hereafter Series 1, Fonds UNHCR 11). This would prove to be a continuing problem through the early 1970s. See, for example, Rorholt, A. (28 October 1968) 'The control of Aliens Refugee Act of 1960 and its effect on the status of refugees in Uganda (and Tanzania)', 6/1/

UGA: Protection-Uganda (v. 2) 1967–70; 6/1/UGA: Protection – Uganda (v. 2), 1967–70; Series 1, Fonds UNHCR 11.

25 KigDa Immigration, Box 3, File ADM 23ii. (, 6 October 1961) Richard Posnett, Director of Refugees, to the Provincial Commissioner, Western Region and the District Commissioners for Ankole, Bunyoro, Kigezi, and Toro Districts.

26 UNA COP, Box 32, File 007. (29 May 1962) Cabinet minute 65 (CT 1962).

27 KigDa Immigration, Box 3, File ADM 23/1i. (30 April 1962) 'Record of a meeting of the refugee co-ordinating committee'.

28 KigDA Administration, Box 62, File ADM 23iv. (9 January 1967) Minister of Regional Administrations to All Chief Executive Officers, Kingdom Governments, and District Administrations.

29 KigDa Immigration, Box 3, File ADM 23ii. (21 September 1961) Gombolola Chief, Kayonza, to the District Commissioner, Kigezi.

30 KigDa Immigration, Box 3, File ADM 23ii. (20 September 1961) Circular, DC Kigezi to all Gombolola Chiefs.

31 UNA COP, Box 68, File S.10484. (3 October 1961) Director of Refugees, 'Ruanda refugees: note of decisions taken at the meeting in Mbarara'.

32 KigDa Immigration, Box 3, File ADM 23ii. (26 September 1960) District Commissioner, Kigezi, to all Gombolola chiefs, 'Batutsi Refugees'.

33 UNA COP, Box 68, File S.10484, (11 February 1964) 'Extract from minute 79 of Cabinet meeting'.

34 UNA COP, Box 68, File S.10484. (1962 CT) Extract of Cabinet Minute 65.

35 KigDA Immigration, Box 3, File ADM 23. (16 July 1962) DC Kigezi to Saza, Gombolola Chiefs, 'Refugees from Ruanda'.

36 It is unclear whether *Inyenzi* was actually receiving aid from the USSR. Belgian authorities believed they were, but British intelligence sources dismissed Belgian intelligence as 'rumours and hearsay' (KigDA Administration, Box 94, File S.INT.1B. (23 January 1962) *Ruanda and Congo, 1962–83*; Commissioner of Police, Report on the 'Ruanda liaison meeting'). Lemarchand claimed that certain UNAR factions did receive military training from the Chinese, however. (See Lemarchand, R. (1970) *Rwanda and Burundi*, pp. 37–8. New York: Praeger Publishers.)

37 Interview with Amelia, K., Mbarara District, 18 February 2013.

38 UNA COP, Box 68, File S.10484. (11 February 1964) 'Extract from Minute 79 of Cabinet meeting'.

39 UNA COP, Box 68, File S.10484. (20 August 1963) 'Cabinet minute 446 (CT 1963), Ruanda refugees: resettlement and finance'.

40 *Inyenzi*, the Kinyarwanda word for 'cockroaches', was a derisive slur initially used by the Kayibanda regime. The term was revived in 1990 in reference to the Rwandan Patriotic Front, which invaded Rwanda in October of that year. During the 1994 genocide, the participants in the slaughter used the term to reference civilian Tutsi, whom they accused of being the RPF's fifth column. See des Forges, A. *Leave none to tell the story: genocide in Rwanda* (Human Rights Watch, 1999), p. 54, n. 34.

41 It is unclear whether *Inyenzi* was actually receiving aid from the USSR. The exiting Belgian authorities believed they were, but British intelligence sources dismissed Belgian intelligence as 'rumours and hearsay'. KigDA, File S.INT.1B. (23 January 1962) Commissioner of Police, Report on the 'Ruanda liaison meeting'.

42 KigDA Justice, Law, Order, Box 3, File S.INT.5. D.W.K. Sempa, Security and Intelligence Report from Ankole District for the period 7th January to 5th February 1964.

43 Uganda National Assembly. (22 December 1964) *Uganda parliamentary debates (Hansard), Vol. 38, Third Session, 1964–5*, pp. 617–618.

References

Bakewell, O. (2014) 'Encampment and self-settlement', in E. Fiddian-Qasmiyeh, G. Loescher, K. Long and N. Sigona (eds.), *The Oxford Handbook of Refugee and Forced Migration Studies*, pp. 127–38. Oxford: Oxford University Press.

Belshaw, D. G. R. (1968) 'An outline of resettlement policy in eastern Africa', in R. Apthorpe (ed.), *Land Settlement and Rural Development in Eastern Africa*. Kampala: Transition Books.

Carswell, G. (2007) *Cultivating Success in Uganda: Kigezi Farmers and Colonial Policies*. Oxford: James Currey.

Chambers, R. (1979) *Rural Refugees in Africa: What the Eye Does Not See*. Brighton: Institute of Development Studies.

des Forges, A. Liebhafsky. (1999) *Leave None to Tell the Story: Genocide in Rwanda*. New York: Human Rights Watch.

Gallagher, D., L. Clark and B. N. Stein. (1985) *Older Refugee Settlements in Africa: Final Report*. Washington, DC: Refugee Policy Group.

Hansen, A. and A. Oliver-Smith. (1982) *Involuntary Migration and Resettlement: The Problems and Responses of Dislocated People*. Boulder, CO: Westview Press.

Hansen, A. (1990) *Refugee Self-Settlement versus Settlement on Government Schemes: The Long-Term Consequences for Security, Integration and Economic Development of Angolan Refugees (1966–1989) in Zambia*. Geneva, Switzerland: United Nations Research Institute for Social Development.

Holborn, L. (1975) *Refugees: A Problem of Our Time: The Work of the United Nations High Commissioner for Refugees, 1951–1972*. Metuchen: The Scarecrow Press, Inc.

Hovil, L. (2007) 'Self-settled refugees in Uganda: an alternative approach to displacement?', *Journal of Refugee Studies*, 20(4): 599–620.

———. (2010) *A Dangerous Impasse: Rwandan Refugees in Uganda*. New York: International Refugee Rights Initiative.

Jacobsen, K. (2001) *The Forgotten Solution: Local Integration for Refugees in Developing Countries*. Geneva: UNHCR.

Kaiser, T. (2006) 'Between a camp and a hard place: rights, livelihood and experiences of the local settlement system for long-term refugees in Uganda', *The Journal of Modern African Studies*, 44(4): 597–621.

Kibreab, G. (1989) 'Local settlements in Africa: a misconceived option?', *Journal of Refugee Studies*, 2(4): 468–490.

Lemarchand, R. (1970) *Rwanda and Burundi*. New York: Praeger Publishers.

Lischer, S. Kenyon. (2006) *Dangerous Sanctuaries: Refugee Camps, Civil war, and the Dilemmas of Humanitarian Aid*. Ithaca: Cornell University Press.

Loescher, G., A. Betts and J. Milner (2008) *The United Nations High Commissioner for Refugees (UNHCR): The Politics and Practice of Refugee Protection into the Twenty-First Century*. New York [u.a.]: Routledge.

Long, K. (2012) 'Rwanda's First Refugees: Tutsi exile and international response.' *Journal of Eastern African Studies*, 6(2): 211–229.

Longman, T. P. (2009) *Christianity and Genocide in Rwanda*. Cambridge: Cambridge University Press.

Lwanga-Lunyiigo, S. (1998) 'Uganda's long connection with the problem of refugees: from the Polish refugees of World War II to the present', in A. G. G. Gingyera-Pinycwa (ed.), *Uganda and the Problem of Refugees*, pp. 19–34. Kampala: Makerere University Press.

Malkki, L. (1995) *Purity and Exile: Violence, Memory, and National Cosmology Among Hutu Refugees in Tanzania*. Chicago and London: The University of Chicago Press.

Mamdani, M. (2001) *When Victims Become Killers: Colonialism, Nativism, and the Genocide in Rwanda*. Princeton, NJ: Princeton University Press.

Newbury, C. (1988) *The Cohesion of Oppression: Clientship and Ethnicity in Rwanda, 1860–1960*. New York: Columbia University Press.

Otunnu, O. (1999) 'Rwandese refugees and immigrants in Uganda', in Howard and A. S. Adelman (eds.), *The Path of a Genocide: The Rwanda Crisis from Uganda to Zaire*, pp. 3–30. New Brunswick and London: Transaction Publishers.

Peterson, D. R. (2012) *Ethnic Patriotism and the East African Revival: A History of Dissent, c. 1935–1972*. Cambridge: Cambridge University Press.

Pottier, J. (2002) *Re-imagining Rwanda Conflict, Survival and Disinformation in the Late Twentieth Century*. Cambridge: Cambridge University Press.

Richards, A. I. (1954) *Economic Development and Tribal Change: A Study of Immigrant Labour in Buganda*. Cambridge, UK: W. Heffer.

Schmidt, A. (1998). 'How camps become mainstream policy for assisting refugees.' Paper presented at the 6th IASFM-ARAP Conference, Jerusalem, December 13–16.

Schmidt, A. (2003) 'FMO thematic guide: camps vs. settlements'. Oxford, UK.

Terry, Fiona. (2002). *Condemned to Repeat? The Paradox of Humanitarian Action*. Ithaca: Cornell University Press.

Trouillot, M.-R. (2003) *Global Transformations: Anthropology and the Modern World*. New York: Palgrave Macmillan.

Verdirame, G., B. E. Harrell-Bond, Z. Lomo and H. Garry. (2005) *Rights in Exile: Janus-Faced Humanitarianism*. New York: Berghahn Books.

Zolberg, A. R. and A. Suhrke (eds). (1989) *Escape from Violence: Conflict and the Refugee Crisis in the Developing World*. New York: Oxford University Press.

8 How accountability technologies shape international protection: results-based management and rights-based approaches revisited

Kristin Bergtora Sandvik

The Office of the United Nations High Commissioner for Refugees (UNHCR) holds itself not only accountable to donors, refugees, the international community and the sanctity of international law but also to the fulfilment of its specific mandate, namely, to provide international protection to refugees and other people of concern.[1] Since the 1980s, UNHCR has undergone five reorganizations, with the goal of improving its operations (Espinoza 2009); thus far, there has been little scholarly interest in how these initiatives have shaped institutional notions of international protection or accountability.

To begin to bridge this knowledge gap as well as contribute to the general exploration of accountability undertaken in this volume, this chapter takes a sociolegal approach towards exploring how two types of organizational reform – rights-based approaches (RBA) and results-based management (RBM) – are used and understood as 'accountability technologies' within UNHCR. To this end, the chapter considers selected UNHCR policy documents, official statements from UNHCR officials, evaluation reports, reports from nongovernmental organizations (NGOs) and academic literature. The analysis builds on general insights and observations I developed during fieldwork on UNHCR resettlement in Uganda.

At first glance, RBM and RBA, both of which UNHCR implemented in the late 1990s, would appear to be opposites: RBM is part of a wave that swept development and humanitarian aid in the late 1980s and 1990s, emphasizing effectiveness, efficiency and 'value for money'. As such, it is typically viewed – both in the literature and within UNHCR – as a tool for ensuring upward accountability (e.g. to donors and the UNHCR Executive Committee). RBA, in contrast, has been viewed as a tool for achieving downward accountability (to affected populations), thereby improving the standing of an international humanitarianism that was wounded in the early 1990s by a series of moral and ethical failures.

Despite their disparate origins and orientations, UNHCR clearly sees both RBM and RBA as being capable of producing accountability. In an article titled 'Strengthening accountability in UNHCR', Volker Türk, UNHCR's director of international protection, and Elizabeth Eyster, senior change management officer and focal point for management accountability at UNHCR, suggested that RBM 'provides a methodology for UNHCR to enhance its responsiveness and thereby its accountability to the populations it serves' (Türk and Eyster 2010). In a more general statement, the Office of the High Commissioner for Human Rights noted that 'the raison d'être of the rights-based approach is accountability' (Klasing, Moses, and Satterthwaite 2011).

Protection is increasingly being talked about as a governance issue.[2] Hence, the chapter reflects on how RBM and RBA can be perceived as part of the humanitarian governance task.[3] This perspective is congruent with UNHCR's own views of RBM and RBA as governance tools. In a 2007 report on UNHCR's use of RBM, the United Nations Office of Internal Oversight Services (OIOS) described RBM as 'a paradigm of organizational governance' at UNHCR – one that is focused on results (OIOS 2007). Six years later, in a speech to the 64th session of the UNHCR Executive Committee, Türk noted that 'the time has perhaps come to reframe protection as a broader governance issue'. In that same speech, Türk described a rights-based approach to the delivery of services and assistance as 'inherent to UNHCR's protection mandate' (Türk 2013).

To make sense of this type of humanitarian governance, it is necessary to focus on how soft law-like initiatives (such as RBM, RBA, manuals, codes of conduct and indicators) travel and are translated as they move from the global to the local levels and back again. Such explorations are important for understanding what humanitarian accountability initiatives may more broadly represent. To unpack the distributive effects that such initiatives have on power, there must be emphasis on empirical investigation of particular cases (Davis *et al.* 2012). As I have observed elsewhere, such soft initiatives are both constitutive of and constituted by everyday practices of refugee management (Sandvik 2008, 2009, 2011, 2013).

UNHCR's willingness to accept more governance tasks is reflected in the continued expansion of the agency's portfolio and its burgeoning budgets (Hammerstad 2014, p. 79). Discussions of such expansion, however, are characterized by references to a 'protection gap',[4] that is, the moral and technical failure, on the part of humanitarian actors, such as UNHCR, to protect affected people and communities (DuBois 2010; Darcy 2013).

The first two parts of the chapter examine the ways in which RBA and RBM have been marshalled to improve UNHCR's accountability. After presenting the rationale behind these two initiatives, I identify conceptual and empirically rooted criticisms that arose in the wake of their introduction. To indicate several issues that have emerged at the level of implementation, I reflect on the ambiguous role of RBA in refugee resettlement narratives and the early challenges associated with the rollout of the Focus software, a key UNHCR RBM initiative.

The third part of the chapter uses a cross-cutting perspective to examine how RBA and RBM shift the content and direction of accountability efforts; it also explores likely shifts in UNHCR's notions of upward and downward accountability. Concluding with a reflection on what RBA and RBM mean for our understanding of international protection, the chapter offers several suggestions for empirical research into UNHCR's implementation of RBA and RBM initiatives.

RBA: accountability through moral improvement

In the late 1990s, several observers conceived of the move from needs to rights as a way to formally improve the conceptual framework of humanitarianism (Minear 2002). Slim (2002, p. 15), for example, suggested that rights 'make people more powerful as rightful claimants rather than unfortunate beggars. Rights reveal all people as moral, political and legal equals'. By the early 2000s, as a strategy for moral improvement, human rights had become a staple of humanitarian rhetoric and the subject was well established in numerous handbooks, manuals and codes of conduct (Sandvik 2010).

Although there is no scholarly consensus on when RBA first appeared, reference is often made to the 1993 World Conference on Human Rights, the 1995 Women's Conference in Beijing and the 1997 call by Secretary-General Kofi Annan for the UN to 'fully integrate' human rights into its peace and security, development and humanitarian programming. Large international nongovernmental organizations (NGOs), such as CARE and Save the Children, in addition to development agencies, such as the United Kingdom Department for International Development (DFID), the Swedish International Development Agency (SIDA) and the Norwegian Agency for Development Cooperation (NORAD), heeded the call. In 2003, the UN Children's Fund, the UN Development Programme and the Office of the High Commissioner for Human Rights adopted the UN Statement of Common Understanding on Human Rights Based Approaches to Development Cooperation and Programming (known as the Common Understanding) (HRBA Portal n.d.).

Although RBA as implemented in development contexts shares several important features with RBA in humanitarian contexts, the following key differences exist:

- In the development context, human rights primarily concerns the relationship between the individual and the state during peacetime; as such, it implies the existence of a social contract, under which the state is expected to provide services and protection. Humanitarian action, in contrast, assists individuals in crisis when the state is unable or unwilling to so; thus, humanitarian actors substitute for the state, either in the short or long term, in providing services and protection (Slaughter and Crisp 2009).
- Whereas humanitarian action is thought of as being underpinned by international humanitarian law and an ethical-moral framework of humanitarian imperatives and principles (neutrality, impartiality and universality), development practice has always been premised on a distinction between legalistic and pragmatic perspectives.
- In the development sector, RBA was an attempt to 'rescue' the values of participation and empowerment from top-down, managerial development initiatives. In the humanitarian context, these values had not traditionally played an important role and were essentially brought on board as humanitarian values through RBA.

Thus, in the case of UNHCR, RBA should be understood in the context of the agency's relationship to human rights.

Beginning in the mid-1970s, the UNHCR Executive Committee began to periodically express concern regarding the violation of refugees' human rights. Only in the mid-1990s, however, did UNHCR begin to call itself a 'human rights organization' and describe its work as including the promotion of human rights. In 1993, for example, Sadako Ogata, the High Commissioner for Refugees, observed that 'humanitarian assistance is much more than relief and logistics. It is essentially and above all about protection – protection of victims of human rights and humanitarian violations'. The following year, Ogata stated in her address to the 50th session of the UN Commission on Human Rights that 'UNHCR today is very much an operational human rights organization, albeit for certain categories of people' (Kenny 2000, p. 4). Finally, in 1995, Ogata noted that 'human rights concerns go to the essence of refugee movements, as well as to the precepts of refugee protection and the solution of refugee problems' (Kjaerum 2002).

With regard to this reframing of the organization's mission, Chandler (2001, p. 678) offered a critical insight: In response to what he described as the 'new humanitarian consensus' on the permissibility of humanitarian interventions, UNHCR had begun to downplay its role of providing aid to refugees, in favour of a new – and more invasive – role as a human rights actor. Importantly, this reframing allowed UNHCR to undergo a species of transformation: It could now act not only as administrator but as advocate, continuing its asymmetrical relationship with whom it served.

A degree of misrecognition was also intrinsic to this transformation. For example, according to a 1995 UNHCR manual on human rights, the following text appears:

> placing greater reliance on human rights standards as a basis for UNHCR's work does not jeopardize the humanitarian character of our activities, since international human rights law is itself non-political and non-partisan: international human rights law treats all countries equally by imposing the same standards and obligations on each state regardless of the ideology of any particular government; and many provisions of international human rights law have been universally accepted and/or specifically undertaken by states, and advocating their implementation is not 'political' but simply asking governments to live up to their obligations. (UNHCR 1995, chap. 1, sec. B, para. 1)

Despite such claims regarding the apolitical nature of human rights work, RBA is, in practice, politically contentious. For example, a 2013 review of UNHCR's role in disaster response cited the view, among many disaster responders, that a human rights lens unnecessarily politicizes the otherwise purely 'humanitarian' nature of disaster relief and further notes that precisely because of this issue, humanitarian actors in several countries, such as Indonesia and Pakistan, avoid any overtly human rights-based approach to disaster response (UNHCR 2013).

An RBA typology

Reflecting an emerging consensus among scholars of humanitarian studies, Stevens described RBA as 'a contested and contestable concept' (2015, p. 10). At UNHCR, for example, the precise meaning and scope of RBA vary with the context. Nevertheless, I think it is important to shed light on several ways in which UNHCR uses and understands RBA. To that end, on the basis of my reading of UNHCR policy statements on RBA, I have developed the following, four-part typology.

First, RBA is viewed as a conceptual framework that integrates the norms, standards and principles of the international human rights system into the policies, programs and processes of development and humanitarian actors (UNHCR 2008b). This perspective may entail linking the obligations of the 1951 Convention relating to the Status of Refugees and accompanying Optional Protocol of 1967 to the human rights framework[5]; it may also entail matching specific groups of people of concern with specific rights. For example, when UNHCR talks about trafficking, it does so 'emphasizing a rights-based approach, including the right not to be subjected to slavery or servitude' (UNHCR 2008).

Second, RBA is envisioned as a source of empowerment and participation. For example, the *Practical Guide to the Systematic Use of Standards & Indicators in UNHCR Operations* noted the following:

> The RBA brings together core elements of human rights, community development, and empowerment of asylum-seekers and refugees as holders of rights. When adapting a RBA to planning and implementation, the rights and standards need to be linked to participation and involvement of persons of concern, thereby leading to their empowerment. (UNHCR 2006, p. 17)

Similarly, the UNHCR community manual explained that the 'rights-based approach is founded on the principles of participation and empowering individuals and communities to promote change and enable them to exercise their rights and comply with their duties' (UNHCR 2008b). In its 2008 Note on International Protection, UNHCR reported that it strives to perform the following:

> fulfil its responsibility to integrate a rights- and community-based approach into its work, including by working to ensure an inclusive and participatory approach to mainstreaming ... and thereby promote the equal enjoyment of rights by all of concern.

In the same document, the organization also referred to 'a participatory, rights-based approach' as having been 'integral to UNHCR's efforts to protect IDPs [internally displaced persons]' (UNHCR 2008).

Third, RBA has been used to serve two functions related to mainstreaming: (1) as a mechanism for accomplishing mainstreaming; and (2) as an example of mainstreaming. As an example of the first function, RBA has explicitly extended itself to various subgroups among people of concern. In 2007, for example, the UNHCR Executive

Committee stated that a rights-based approach was fundamental to child protection (UNHCR 2008b). With regard to the second function, UNHCR has pointedly presented its implementation of RBA as an example of mainstreaming – as evidenced from its 2009 Note on International Protection, in which UNHCR indicated that it was continuing the following:

> its efforts to integrate human rights into all areas of work, including by promoting the integration of people of concern and relevant humanitarian issues into the evolving legal human rights framework; intensifying cooperation with human rights mechanisms; and capacitating staff to effectively use human rights standards as the basis for planning, policy, guidance and advocacy. The Office leveraged human rights mechanisms to strengthen refugees' and IDPs' equal access to rights. (UNHCR 2009)

Finally, RBA is conceived as an organizational strategy, which in practical terms means that by attaching rights-based discourse to its initiatives, UNHCR can use the human rights machinery to strengthen them. For example, the 2008 Note on International Protection proposed the likelihood of using RBA, drawing on standards of international human rights law and the human rights machinery, to reinforce UNHCR's own initiatives. Similarly, the 2010 Note on International Protection exemplified a deliberate effort to use RBA to reinforce UNHCR's role as a player in disaster response, specifically by identifying a likely role for protection actors in cases where the host governments may 'require support to coordinate protection-related activities or to map out strategies aimed at protecting victims and adopting a rights-based approach in the relief and rehabilitation response' (UNHCR 2010, para. 63).

This typology suggests that RBA not only performs different conceptual functions but also co-produces a range of knowledge concerning protection. As will become clear in subsequent sections, inconsistencies within or tensions between these types of knowledge may have implications for RBA as a vehicle for delivering accountability to people of concern. Subsequent consideration of how protection officers and displaced persons negotiate the use and meaning of RBA will raise additional questions regarding RBA as a vehicle for empowerment and participation.

Criticisms of RBA

The use of RBA in humanitarian action has been the subject of a variety of general criticisms. One argument, for example, holds that rights-based humanitarianism suffers from an inbuilt tension between the limited goal of alleviating suffering and the broader agenda of addressing structural injustice by appealing to human rights. According to Fox (2001), the intent of humanitarian action should be to meet needs; however, when humanitarianism becomes part of an imperial transformative project, RBA has the potential to render relief conditional and to lead to the abandonment of neutrality.

Other critics have argued that because the integration of RBA into humanitarian work originated in the need, in an increasingly competitive and sceptical world, to periodically invent a new identity, it failed to actually change what humanitarian agencies do (Duffield 2001), and instead led to instrumentalization, co-option by political actors and inflated aims (Darcy 2004). The reviews of RBA practice have also noted endemic problems with respect to how rights are conceptualized, their exact role in improving humanitarian action and failure to adequately consider how difficult it can be to apply RBA in conflict situations (Kenny 2000; Leebaw 2007; Benelli 2013).

In my view, UNHCR's efforts to incorporate RBA into its operations have been characterized by various problems, including conceptual confusion, bureaucratization, legalism, lack of compliance with RBA guidelines and the difficulty of proving value. As Stevens has observed, for example, agencies and organizations habitually improvise in their effort to define what constitutes a rights-based approach; moreover, she noted that 'in the quest to fashion a set of norms and principles that are perceived as being comprehensible as well as workable by those working for NGOs there is a tendency for definitions to become overly reductive' (2015, p. 10). Hence, RBA may be reduced to mere slogans or may be defined in such broad terms that it gives rise to an unworkable number of interpretations. In the confusion that results, RBA may become the site of struggles between an organization and the people it is meant to serve.

Ambiguous role of RBA in resettlement narratives

On the basis of my field research, I would maintain that the highly ambiguous role of RBA in refugee resettlement narratives illustrates several broader challenges associated with RBA. In particular, it illuminates an important but little-discussed conundrum, namely, the ways in which UNHCR's rights discourse, including attendant pronouncements on empowerment and participation, run up against the refugees' use of rights discourse. In the case of resettlement (one of UNHCR's three 'durable solutions', in addition to local integration and return), refugees are selected for transfer from a state in which they have initially sought protection to a third state that has agreed to award them permanent resident status (see Garnier in this volume). Refugees do not have specific rights to any of the durable solutions. Resettlement is primarily envisioned as a solution for refugees with legal and physical protection needs, meaning that their fundamental human rights are at risk in the initial country of refuge.

Beginning in the late 1990s, resettlement procedures gradually became more formalized to ensure that only 'real' victims were resettled and enable the process to become more transparent and effective. Both the *UNHCR Resettlement Handbook* and the protection officers whom I interviewed in the field asserted that resettlement should be and is offered only to 'real' victims. In reality, however, refugees actively participate in the processes that determine who is (and is not) a 'real' victim. Thus, qualifying for resettlement requires substantial individual entrepreneurship. On the basis of insights gleaned from fieldwork on how refugees in

Uganda negotiate with UNHCR to obtain access to resettlement, I have found that the ways in which refugees try to use rights discourse, including identity labels, sit uneasily with UNHCR's view of RBA (Sandvik 2008, 2011).

In 2005, as a consequence of regional conflicts plaguing the region (see Rockenbach in this volume), Uganda was home to approximately 270,000 refugees. Under UNHCR's framework, refugees cannot 'apply' for resettlement; instead, UNHCR staff or NGO partners identify suitable candidates during general screening. In the subsequent resettlement interview, protection officers evaluate the refugees' personal history in relation to the various requirements of the selected resettlement category (e.g. legal and physical protection, women-at-risk and medical needs) and subject the refugees' rendition of biographical data, history prior to flight and their situation in Kampala to thorough credibility assessments.

For UNHCR, it is important that refugees understand that resettlement is not a right to be applied for or informally negotiated; in practical terms, however, there is room for bureaucratic discretion. When I asked Thomas, a former protection officer, how he evaluated personal histories that drew on rights language, he replied, 'I have a checklist, which is the procedures of UNHCR', but 'in order to put labels, the story itself, with a credible language of suffering, was enough'.

As the humanitarian enterprise has come to place increasing emphasis on testimony, the refugees' use of 'stock' testimonies has increased in tandem. Relying on information from authoritative global media, such as human rights reports, and applying elements of human rights discourse (including reference to gender, racial or sexual identity), refugees develop testimonies that are designed to maximize their chances of resettlement. Although UNHCR is aware that refugees use such resources, as well as coaching and rehearsal, to develop their testimonies, and regards such behaviour as 'cheating', these methods are an integral part of the complex, informal negotiations that play out between refugees and the UNHCR bureaucracy.

The construction of a resettlement identity that reflects evolving representations of the humanitarian subject as a human rights bearer relies heavily on sufficient command not only of human rights discourse but of what I will call 'the performance of credibility'. The key elements in such performance are as follows: (1) maintaining the immediacy of pain in the narrative; and (2) displaying an appropriate – and appropriately deferential – demeanour. It appears preferable, for example, to present oneself as a victim who has experienced tangible forms of physical or psychological trauma than to assume the more abstract persona of a rights bearer. Moreover, a refugee who demands his or her rights may be perceived as having a sense of entitlement, which can undermine any sense of urgent vulnerability.

The refugees most likely to be categorized as being in need of legal and physical protection are those who have been persecuted (e.g. subject to threats, harassment, insecurity and arbitrary detention) for promoting civil or political rights. For these refugees, the performance of credibility involves striking an appropriate balance, both in speech and demeanour, between Western conceptions of the human rights defender as a liberal, heroic agent, and less openly acknowledged notions of what constitute appropriate displays of Third World victim status. Although the attempts to establish a bond through a shared commitment to liberal humanity often pay off, refugees who suggest, through human rights language, that they see themselves as human rights bearers risk being observed as opportunistic.

For Thomas, the former protection office, the resettlement seekers who used rights language – whether, for example, they were seeking to be classified as human rights defenders or as vulnerable women – tended to be unconvincing. Thomas also saw the appropriation of rights language as an expression of entitlement. Such perceptions regarding agency and 'ownership' of RBA create difficulties for refugees with some legal literacy, who evaluate the criteria and determine that they meet them. UNHCR's insistence on resettlement as an instrument of human rights protection was also bewildering for refugees who had encountered corrupt humanitarians in Uganda or who had heard about the many scandals surrounding resettlement in East Africa (Sandvik 2008).

The experiences of refugees in Uganda raise several broader questions concerning the tensions between UNHCR's emphasis on empowerment, its RBA narrative and the agency's actual practice. Although UNHCR policy links RBA to the agency's quest for downward accountability, UNHCR resettlement processes in Uganda suggest that a 'rights-based' approach to protection may require refugees to surrender agency in their effort to establish credibility, thereby interfering with their existential struggle to find a solution to their own displacement.

Hastrup has expressed concern that the rights-based conceptions of justice may distort our understanding of suffering and pare down social and moral narratives, creating a 'censorious rights-based regime of truth' (2003, p. 309). The recent history of resettlement indicates progressively expanding categories of recognized suffering (e.g. based on gender identity or on the experience of particular types of torture) that have developed as a result of transnational human rights activism on behalf of particular identity categories and ethnic groups. It is important to recognize that the stories refugees tell humanitarians reveal both their predicament and the institutionally imposed imperative to conform to explicit and implicit expectations of suffering; in the UNHCR context, these stories must be articulated in such a way as to reflect and confirm membership in defined categories.

RBM: accountability through management

RBM entered the humanitarian realm as an element of new public management (NPM). The goal of NPM was to improve the quality of public sector service delivery by improving public choice; this perspective entailed viewing the public as a consumer operating within a free-market system, as opposed to viewing the public as a captive market that had no option but to accept poor services. The ideal service delivery mechanism would be s smaller decentralized government, which would implicitly 'ensure accountability and transparency to the tax-payer' (Larner 2000, as cited in Morris 2014, p. 41).

Although NPM emerged in the 1980s and its predecessor approaches, such as management by objectives (MBO) and total quality management (TQM), had existed since the 1950s (Ramalingam *et al.* 2009, p. 14), its influence first became evident in the humanitarian and development realms in the early 1990s when Western donor countries introduced RBM to those sectors. The turn to RBM was accelerated, in part, by serious and endemic accountability flaws that came to light in the early to mid-1990s when a series of audits and subsequent reports undertaken by the OIOS, the UN's internal watchdog, called into question UNHCR's financial management practices.[6]

A series of UN reforms undertaken in the late 1990s reflected the importance of RBM: for example, Secretary-General Kofi Annan stated that the reform programme that he had initiated in 1997 was intended to shift the focus from how things are done to what is accomplished. Despite the fact that it is referred to frequently in UN documents, however, there is no single, authoritative – or even commonly understood – definition of RBM (Flint 2003). For example, what one agency calls an outcome may be another's output, intermediate outcome or impact.

For humanitarians, RBM offers a host of ways of talking about accountability, including the following:

- As a means of assuring donors and political constituencies that programmes are yielding value for money;
- As a means of optimizing international protection (and thereby achieving value for money);
- As a more reliable and effective toolbox (and therefore a means of improving protection); and
- As normatively more attractive than traditional management approaches: the assumption here is that by providing better protection, RBM automatically provides accountability to people of concern.

UNHCR adopted RBM in 1998 (UNHCR 2006). As of 2010, the agency was defining RBM rather loosely as 'a philosophy that emphasizes the achievement of results as the essential task of management' (UNHCR 2010). That same year, Türk and Eyster stated that RBM is the right platform for achieving 'the right results in the most efficient and effective manner' (Türk and Eyster 2010, p. 168). RBM can help UNHCR realize its protection mandate and that through RBM, 'accountability is being strengthened through an emphasis on global coherence, transparency, participation, impact, and performance measurement and analysis' (Türk and Eyster 2010, p. 169).

The incremental introduction of RBM, beginning with the introduction of log frames, led to a number of in-house initiatives designed to improve UNHCR's ability to demonstrate not only how its resources were being used but with what result (Kelley *et al.* 2004). In 2002, for example, UNHCR launched the Standards and Indicators Initiative to support the planning, implementation and assessment of operations as well as Project Profile, a campaign to modernize registration.

In 2006, the agency moved beyond a piecemeal approach focused on indicators and standards, initiating a far-reaching internal reform process to increase efficiency and improve service delivery. One result of this effort was a comprehensive package of six RBM-related concepts and related initiatives: the Comprehensive Needs Assessment, Initial Budget Targets and the prioritization process, Global Strategic Priorities, the Results Framework, the implementation of Focus software and a new budget structure (UNHCR 2010b). Despite being formally framed in language that signals a unitary vision of the objectives of RBM and the desirability of improving RBM, however, these initiatives have also espoused highly heterogeneous notions of accountability.

Criticisms of RBM

A number of general criticisms have been levied against RBM. Given the changes in local context and priorities, the plans that are the very core of RBM can never be completely accurate; as a result, unintended consequences are inevitable. Moreover, these plans, which focus on short-term, quantitative results, require elaborate matrixes and rely on assumptions of linear causality, can be time-consuming, irrelevant or even disruptive. RBM methodology may also be ill suited for documenting the results of complex interventions (Ebrahim and Rangan 2010, p. 12; Ramalingam *et al.* 2009). For example, under RBM, accountability does not depend on reviewing outcomes but is a matter of determining that no negligence, misconduct or breach of rules and regulations has occurred. RBM's emphasis on control may also skew the direction of accountability by focusing on how the lower parts of the system (field offices) document, aggregate and represent results to the higher parts of the system (headquarters and donors) (Ortiz and Taylor 2009, p. 30).

A 2008 OIOS study of RBM among UN agencies suggested that a formalistic approach to codifying how to achieve outcomes, which is inherent to RBM, can stifle the very innovation and flexibility that are required to achieve those outcomes; the study also found that RBM often makes no or little contribution to strategic decisions. Finally, because several important goals can be difficult to measure, certain projects may be forced off priority lists and replaced by initiatives that are more amenable to quantitative documentation (Ramalingam *et al.* 2009; OIOS 2008).

Evaluations of UNHCR's RBM efforts have identified a specific set of challenges to successful implementation, all of which centre around UNHCR's particular operating environment. A 2007 OIOS report noted that in addition to often functioning under emergency conditions, UNHCR is affected by the inherent unpredictability of population movements and national government policies; the expansion of target populations to include IDPs, other people of concern and 'traditional' refugees; and the proliferation of actors in the field. In light of these challenges, the report noted that UNHCR has a particular need for greater coordination of effort and 'needs to shape its approach to RBM based on the unique needs and characteristics of the organization' (OIOS 2007; see also UNHCR 2010b and Bradley in this volume).

Another challenge arises from the need to provide quantitative data on UNHCR's output and impact in areas, such as protection, advocacy, capacity building and legislative reform, which are less easily quantified than, for example, service delivery (UNHCR 2010). Data needs, in turn, raise the issue of data accuracy. A 2010 UNHCR evaluation report noted the difficulties associated with 'ensuring that country-level data is collected in an accurate, comprehensive and consistent manner, and in a way that enables the establishment of meaningful cross-country comparisons and aggregated global results' (UNHCR 2010b, p. 2).

That same report also found that given the many other variables that determine the well-being and level of protection afforded to the populations that UNHCR serves, it is difficult to attribute changes in the situation of persons of concern to UNHCR programmes and activities (UNHCR 2010b). A related problem is the difficulty of identifying the actual impact of the agency's RBM efforts, according to a 2011 assessment conducted by the Multilateral Organisational Performance Assessment Network (MOPAN), as shown below:

> UNHCR has operationalized results-based management (RBM) through a complex system that has several limitations. UNHCR is perceived to make contributions to humanitarian results, but neither its reports nor its performance measurement systems provide a clear and complete picture of how it is improving the circumstances and well-being of persons of concern. (2014, p. x)

More broadly, the report observed that UNHCR's results frameworks failed to fully define, communicate, guide or monitor the ways in which the organization's mandate is translated into organization-wide results (MOPAN 2014).

Finally, RBM, at least as undertaken by UNHCR, suffers from a discrepancy between intent and implementation. On the one hand, one of the rationales for RBM is that it yields performance information, which can be used to make decisions about a project. According to the *Practical Guide to the Systematic Use of Standards & Indicators in UNHCR Operations*, RBM ensures 'accountability of individuals, teams and partners based on continuous feedback to improve performance' (UNHCR 2006, p. 23). Although OIOS found that UNHCR staff spent a large portion of their time collecting data and monitoring and reporting on performance, the staff reported feeling that 'there is little payoff to these activities, as feedback is rarely given on the information they produce and performance data are rarely seen being used in actual decision-making' (OIOS 2007, p. 24).

Bottom-up RBM: early days of Focus

Focus is an operations' management support software designed to assist UNHCR's offices in recording operational objectives, defining performance indicators, preparing programme budgets and reporting on the progress made in achieving results (OIOS 2010). In an interesting exchange regarding the challenges of introducing the Focus software, documented in the 2007 OIOS report, OIOS urged UNHCR to 'thoroughly address as many remaining technical anomalies in the [Focus] software as possible before bringing it to scale throughout the agency' (OIOS 2007, p. 25). In its response, UNHCR indicated that OIOS's reference to 'technical anomalies' unfairly implied that 'UNHCR might consider putting a product out that did not work well'. UNHCR claimed that it would not release a substandard product (25). Nevertheless, a 2010 OIOS audit indicated that security requirements had still 'not been clearly defined and documented for the Focus system' (OIOS 2010, p. 9) and that there was inadequate control over the system development, noting that 'the developers of the Focus system were performing tasks that were inconsistent with their role, such as granting and managing user access to the system' (OIOS 2010, p. 10).

The development of Focus started in 2005–2006. Focus was rolled out in 2009, through 30 workshops, each lasting five days, at the regional and country levels; all of the operations were expected to use it to plan for and prepare their 2010 budgets. UNHCR's experiences with Focus software exemplify both the promise and challenge of RBM. Türk and Eyster (2010, p. 169) noted that Focus allows UNHCR to 'generate a global overview for the purpose of strategic analysis', enabling the organization to 'plan, articulate, analyze and measure results being pursued on the micro as well as the macro level'. A 2010 UNHCR evaluation report described Focus as 'the tool that brings together the different elements of RBM in UNHCR' (UNHCR 2010b). However, according to the report, staff members felt that 'RBM has little utility whatsoever in a humanitarian or United Nations field setting', in part because of certain 'rigidities' (OIOS 2007, para. 32). Moreover, staff enthusiasm for Focus had 'been dimmed by the well-documented technical difficulties and demands associated with Focus since its introduction' (UNHCR 2010b).

The adoption of Focus was premised on the assumption that the software is programmed to facilitate needs assessments. In practice, however, needs assessments are generally conducted through research, interviews, and discussions with colleagues, the results of which are subsequently entered into Focus. According to the 2010 evaluation report, staff members felt that the software itself provided insufficient guidance to the needs assessment process. As noted earlier, UNHCR operations often occur under difficult and dangerous conditions. Emergency operations staff expressed particular frustration with the fact that limited access to rapidly moving populations prevented them from conducting meaningful, comprehensive assessments. In fact, their assessments were generally extrapolated from existing (and often outdated) information (UNHCR 2010b). Furthermore, staff described the problem analysis function in Focus as 'superficial and misleading'. Through a standard, drop-down options list, Focus first proposed causes for the problems that have been identified and subsequently offered solutions to those causes. The available options for 'causes', however, were so vague that the proposed solutions were often irrelevant to the problem at hand (UNHCR 2010b, p. 24).

Although Focus is intended to be a 'live' planning tool, the specific characteristics of UNHCR's operations, in particular, limitations on bandwidth and on the availability of technically proficient staff, have significant practical implications. For example, plans were often developed offline and were subsequently entered into the system by the staff who had the technical expertise to do so. The sub- and field-office staff had little access to Focus and occasionally had to travel to the main office to enter their plans and budgets. Although the sub-offices of larger operations did have access, they had to rely on complicated arrangements involving phone calls and scheduled access days (UNHCR 2010b, p. 25). Finally, consistent with the criticisms outlined in the previous section, the staff expressed concern that RBM's focus on outcomes that are easy to measure risks lessening attention to outcomes that are equally or more important but that require alternative assessment methods (UNHCR 2010b, p. 18).

A cross-cutting perspective: RBA, RBM and accountability

So far, this chapter has considered the ways in which UNHCR's overly broad (and occasionally inherently contradictory) understanding of RBA makes it difficult to operationalize, engendering conceptions of protection that are difficult to achieve. RBM, for its part, can distort protection efforts by favouring objectives whose outcomes lend themselves to quantitative measurement, while giving short shrift to those that are less easily measured. This section turns to the ways in which RBA and RBM, in their dual quest for 'the right result' and a 'rights result' impinge on each other, potentially skewing accountability.

Just as RBA and RBM are interpreted differently in various contexts and by various actors, so is the relationship between the two. Although several observers maintain that the interactions between the two bear additional scrutiny, others view RBA and RBM as working in tandem. An analysis of child protection undertaken by a European Union agency for fundamental rights reflects the first perspective, noting that 'further dialogue is necessary between child well-being indicator research and rights-based approaches (FRA 2009). The 2006 *Practical Guide to the Systematic Use of Standards & Indicators in UNHCR Operations*, in contrast, reflects the second perspective, claiming that 'RBM and a RBA are linked and allow UNHCR to set up objectives systematically formulated in terms of rights' (UNHCR 2006).

Explorations of tensions between RBA and RBM have pointed to the potential for adverse interactions. For example, human rights protection may be among the hard-to-measure goals that may be given short shrift because of RBM's focus on measurable impacts (Hofmann *et al.* 2004). Kindornay *et al.* (2012, p. 497) noted that one of the reasons that RBA is in trouble is that donors are increasingly keen to support projects that can quickly demonstrate value for money and that offer clear, measurable results, that is, projects that match up with the goals and methods associated with RBM.

Another issue concerns the ways in which RBM and RBA are altering notions of upward and downward accountability. Although RBM has traditionally been associated with upward accountability, I would argue that UNHCR now views it as indispensable to downward accountability because of its presumed impact on the agency's ability to provide effective and efficient international protection. A consideration of these effectiveness and efficiency claims reveals, however, that RBM has faced considerable challenges at UNHCR, first because of the contradictory ways in which it has been implemented, and second regarding the meaning of delivering accountability through RBM.

Since 2006, UNHCR has been attributing significant transformative capacity to RBM (including as a vehicle for accountability); this view is incongruent, however, with a more technically oriented view of RBM. For example, a 2010 UNHCR evaluation report observed that tension exists between RBM's role in 'the effective and efficient delivery of UNHCR's mandate' and the view that RBM is 'primarily a matter of compliance with planning and budgeting systems and the introduction of new information technology' (UNHCR 2010b, p. 1; see also Lindskov Jacobsen in this volume). According to Türk and Eyster (2010, p. 170), while 'UNHCR has shown a longstanding determination to shift fully to a results-orientation ... RBM is not the "magic bullet" for accountability'. This perspective echoes a concern expressed by Wigley (2006, p. 22), who cautioned against a lack of precision in conceptualizing accountability, 'as though RBM will take care of accountability in its entirety'.

In 2004, commenting on the use of RBM in UN organizations, the UN Joint Inspection Unit observed that RBM risked being turned into a bureaucratic process in itself (JIU 2004/6), that it had been difficult for UN agencies to develop a culture that promotes 'high performance and accountability' and that the focus of RBM had too often been on the budgeting and programming aspects of management (JIU 2004/5). Wigley (2005) has argued, specifically with respect to UNHCR, that the agency will need to guard against transforming accountability into a bureaucratic exercise detached from its original meaning and purpose.

For its part, UNHCR has expressed a clear understanding of likely tensions between RBM and accountability to persons of concern, and the risk this might entail. A 2005 statement made by the acting High Commissioner suggested a more comprehensive understanding of accountability as follows: 'building sustainable and meaningful accountability into the system goes beyond oversight, audits, and reporting on weaknesses' (UNHCR 2005b). Writing in 2013, Türk noted that focusing principally on people of concern is critical to UNHCR's accountability to 'those we serve, but also keeps us on our toes'. He suggested that such a focus 'is the antidote to what could otherwise become an administration of misery or a bureaucratic, process-oriented culture' (Türk 2013).

With respect to the role of RBA within UNHCR, I would argue that it is most meaningfully described today as an upward accountability mechanism. My reasoning is as follows: UNHCR's understanding of RBA is characterized by a conceptual split that essentially negates any form of downward accountability. On the one hand are UNHCR's multiple, simultaneous, and difficult-to-operationalize definitions of RBA (described in the typology earlier in the chapter) and on the other hand is a legalistic, relational definition of RBA that presupposes a rights holder (person of concern) and a corresponding duty holder (UNHCR).

With respect to the meaning of 'international protection' for UNHCR, Stevens (2015, p. 21) noted that 'protection is expected to achieve much ... protection is now heavily associated with rights'. She also noted, however, that a rights-based definition of protection is inherently confusing because the concept of protection is so malleable, a point that is consistent with my observations regarding competing conceptualizations of RBA. Importantly, Stevens suggested that a rights-based definition of protection conjures up a scenario of continuous failure: 'who is seen as the lead protection provider – state or UNHCR – will have a huge bearing. If "protection" is to be all-encompassing, delivery will be rare, and failure frequent' (Stevens 2015, p. 17).

Despite this caveat, I think that UNHCR's conceptualization of rights-based protection can usefully be viewed as dynamic, i.e. continuously contracting and expanding in response to an unstable emergency context. It is this dynamic quality that defines RBA as a humanitarian governance tool.

Paradoxically, one way of conceptualizing RBA is to do so without much emphasis on human rights. The Humanitarian Accountability Partnership International, for example, defines accountability as 'the means through which power is used responsibly', a view that incorporates the recognition that in crisis situations, humanitarian organizations often wield immense power, independent of the state (HAP n.d.). The focus of this definition is not human rights, per se, but ensures that people of concern can have their needs met by humanitarian agencies (Klasing, Moses and Satterthwaite 2011).

Another option is an idealistic, rhetorically expansive version of RBA. Such broad conceptualizations have been criticized for positing humanitarian agencies as duty bearers, but within a voluntary context, which effectively eliminates downwards accountability (Darcy 2013). A third option is the one that UNHCR appears to have chosen, namely, to operate under both expansive and legalistic perspectives and when prodded about the content of expansive definitions, to retreat to legalistic ones, which do much less rhetorical work with respect to UNHCR's quest for accountability but which are also less burdensome.

The human rights law requires that individuals have access to accountability mechanisms, including the means for obtaining binding legal redress through state institutions (Klasing, Moses and Satterthwaite 2011). UNHCR's legalistic version of RBA is premised on the notion that the rights holders (that is, persons of concern to UNHCR) are entitled to hold the duty bearer accountable (principally, the state and its agents). In accordance with this view, UNHCR seeks to strengthen the capacities of the rights holders to make their claims and of duty bearers to satisfy those claims. UNHCR must consider 'rights-holders with legal entitlements' (UNHCR 2008b, p. 16), but does not see itself as accountable for the fulfilment of those rights – or even for advocating on behalf of 'poor and disadvantaged people', regardless of whether it seems to be exercising governance functions, as in the case of determining refugee or resettlement status (see Fresia and von Känel in this volume). Instead, UNHCR articulates what I see as a rather 'thin' vision of RBA, namely, a process in which the agency supports broad societal change but is not directly accountable to persons of concern for anything beyond 'strengthening capacity'.

Conclusion

Although the effects of RBA and RBM and their constitutive relationship to accountability are significant both for UNHCR's operations and humanitarian action more generally, as of yet no research has been conducted to identify cross-cutting issues in the RBA and RBM agendas or the interfaces, ideological overlaps and tensions that characterize these initiatives. Instead, such issues seem to have passed under the radar of scholars who are more broadly concerned either with refugee management or humanitarian governance.

This chapter examines how RBA and RBM function as 'accountability technologies' at UNHCR – and, by doing so, helps fix and fixate international protection as an object of value. Although the picture that emerges of the production of accountability for international protection is complex, it illuminates the ways in which both RBA and RBM constitute a type of humanitarian governance by producing accountability.

One of the key challenges associated with both RBA and RBM is that the problems they are deployed to solve are not technical but political. The chapter shows that by making RBA and RBM more 'governance-like', UNHCR has used them as tools for making international protection efforts more accountable. The notion of protection as 'governance', however, indicates a key dilemma: When UNHCR retreats from a broader vision of accountability to a narrower conceptualization, in which the agency as duty holder is largely removed from the equation, something seems to be lost. Simultaneously, the broad vision of accountability has a significant drawback: Ultimately, it is a matter of voluntary commitments, outside the binding structures of the human rights law or the democratic contract between a state and its citizens.

Another way of gauging the role of RBA and RBM in UNHCR's accountability efforts is by thinking of these initiatives as ways of producing knowledge regarding norms and rules. In this view, the two initiatives represent different and occasionally competing ways for interpreting and structuring information and interactions.

Critics tend to see both initiatives as defunct transplants from the neoliberal state to the global emergency zone and explain their failure as stemming, in large part, from their unsuitability to the new, emergency context. At the same time, critics insist that despite being defunct, these initiatives can work to depoliticize and technicalize humanitarian action. I would counter that as RBA and RBM are imported into new contexts, they will evolve, adapt and be taken up by new actors. By focusing on these changes, we can understand how RBA and RBM function as accountability technologies.

The relationship between RBA, RBM and accountability is mutually constitutive but uneven. Examining these three concepts from new vantage points (and in relation to each other), however, can reveal the ways in which resources and power are produced, distributed and appropriated *through* but also *for* these accountability technologies. From a sociolegal perspective, capturing the power exercised through the humanitarian governance apparatus will require more empirical and analytical focus on the interface between these concepts, including attention to the absence of cross-cutting reflections within UNHCR.

The following questions warrant additional exploration:

- What can RBA and RBM tell us about the nature of humanitarian practice?
- What are the implications of the discursive shifts produced by these technologies?

- How do RBA and RBM reflect or affect outcomes on the ground?
- What happened, in practical terms, as RBM initiatives were integrated into the everyday activities of field and sub-offices? For example, how did better Internet connectivity impact RBM implementation over time?
- As RBM has become an entrenched aspect of UNCHR management, how did that alter its relationship to RBA?
- As RBA has lingered on, seemingly largely as a rhetorical device, what challenges to RBA have been posed by the humanitarian resort to remote management?

By following the implementation of particular instruments, procedures or software applications (such as Focus), the crafting of UNHCR's comprehensive needs assessment and the development of documents, such as the Global Strategic Priorities, it will be possible to learn more regarding the types of governance exercised through technical and moral accountability technologies and the ways in which these technologies shape international protection efforts.

Notes

1 The writing of this chapter was funded by the Norwegian Research Councils AID EFFECT programme. I am grateful to Katja Lindskov Jacobsen, Maral Mirshahi and Kjersti Lohne for their comments.
2 'International protection' is a fluid concept that means many things to many actors, both within and outside the realm of refugee management, and is commonly understood as some sort of composite of legal standards, humanitarian sensibilities, bureaucratic routines and technological innovations. As pertinently observed by Stevens (2015, p. 17), 'there is no single, uniform response that can be labelled "protection". Rather, "protection" is a fluid concept with a tempo-spatial and human dimension – that is, what constitutes protection will be dependent on time, geography and personal circumstances. The nature of protection will differ in the short term (say, 0–2 years), the mid-term (say, 2–5 years), and the long-term (5+ years). Likewise, spatial factors, such as region, country, urban or rural setting, family or local host, or camp, will also have a significant bearing'.
3 Humanitarian governance occurs primarily in the so-called humanitarian emergency zone, where a global system of international organizations, donor and troop-contributing nations, and NGOs operate similarly with as well as across domestic state structures to respond to a permanent condition of crisis (Ferguson 2006; see also Janmyr and Kinchin in this volume).
4 According to Zetter (2015, p. 15, n 13), the term 'protection gap' has no official meaning; however, it is typically used to refer to cases in which national or international normative and legal protection instruments fail to adequately address specific situations or needs or in which protection capacity is limited by the failure to apply (or to consistently apply) standards and norms for refugee protection.
5 This framework includes, but is not limited to, the Universal Declaration of Human Rights, and the International Covenants on Civil and Political Rights; Economic, Social and Cultural rights; the Convention on the Elimination of All Forms of Discrimination against Women); the Convention on the Rights of the Child (CRC); and the Convention against Torture and the Convention on the Elimination of All Forms of Racial Discrimination.
6 International media picked up the donor countries' discontent with UNHCR's accounting practices. See, for example, Burns and Williams (1998).

References

Benelli, P. (2013) 'Human rights in humanitarian action and development cooperation and the implications of rights based approaches in the field'. Available online at www.atha.se/content/human-rights-humanitarian-action-and-development-cooperation-and-implications-rights-based (accessed 22 September 2015).

Burns, J. and F. Williams. (1998) 'United Nations High Commissioner for Refugees: special report; refugees' agency lost in wilderness of bungling and waste', *Financial Times* 29 July, p. 7.

Chandler, D. (2001) 'The road to military humanitarianism: how the human rights NGO's shaped a new humanitarian agenda', *Human Rights Quarterly*, 23(3): 678–700.

Darcy, J. (2004) *Human Rights and Humanitarian Action: a Review of the Issues, HPG Background Paper 12*. London and Geneva: Humanitarian Policy Group Overseas Development Institute.

Darcy, J. (2013) 'Have we lost the plot, humanitarian accountability report'. Available online at //www.hapinternational.org/pool/files/2013-har.pdf (accessed 22 September 2015).

Davis, K., B. Kingsbury and S. E. Merry. (2012) 'Indicators as a technology of global governance', *Law & Society Review*, 46(1): 71–104.

DuBois M. (2010) 'Protection: fig-leaves and other delusions', *Humanitarian Exchange*, Issue 46. London: ODI. Available online at http://www.odihpn.org/humanitarian-exchange-magazine/issue-46/protection-fig-leaves-and-other-delusions (accessed 22 September 2015).

Duffield, M. (2001) *Global Governance and the New Wars: The Merging of Development and Security*. New York: ZED Books.

Ebrahim, A. and V. K. Rangan. (2010) 'The limits of nonprofit impact: a contingency framework for measuring social performance', Working paper. Available online at http://hbswk.hbs.edu/item/6439.html (accessed 22 September 2015).

Espinoza, V. M. (2009) 'The relation between the UNHCR and main donors: challenges to global governance'. Available online at http://dspace2.conicyt.cl/bitstream/handle/10533/91227/VERA_MARCIA_1506M.pdf?sequence=1 (accessed 22 September 2015).

Ferguson, J. (2006) *Global Shadows: Africa in the Neoliberal World Order*. Durham, NC: Duke University Press.

Flint, M. (2003) *Easier Said than Done: a Review of Results-Based Management in Multilateral Development Institutions*. Herefordshire, UK: Wernddu Pontrilas.

Fox, F. (2001) 'New humanitarianism: does it provide a moral banner for the 21st century?', *Disasters*, 25(4): 275–289.

FRA. (2009) 'Developing indictors for the protection, respect and promotion of the rights of the child in the European Union'. Available online at http://fra.europa.eu/sites/default/files/fra_uploads/358-RightsofChild_summary-report_en.pdf (accessed 27 September 2015).

Hammerstad, A. (2014) *The Rise and Decline of a Global Security Actor: UNHCR, Refugee Protection, and Security*. Oxford: Oxford University Press.

Hastrup, K. (2003) 'Violence, suffering and human rights: anthropological reflections', *Anthropological Theory*, 3(3): 309–323.

Hofmann, C. A., et al. (2004) "Measuring the impact of humanitarian aid: A review of current practice: Humanitarian Policy Group." *HPG Report 17*. London: Overseas Development Institute.

HRBA Portal (UN Practitioners Portal on Human Rights Based Approaches to Programming). (n.d.) 'The human rights based approach to development cooperation: towards a common understanding among UN agencies'. HRBA Portal. Available online at http://hrbaportal.org/the-human-rights-based-approach-to-development-cooperation-towards-a-common-understanding-among-un-agencies (accessed 22 September 2015).

Human Accountability Partnership. (n.d.) 'The 2010 HAP standard'. Available online at www.hapinternational.org/what-we-do/hap-standard.aspx (accessed 22 September 2015).

JIU. (2004/5) *Overview of the Series of Reports on Managing for Results in the United Nations System*. Geneva: JIU/REP/2004/5.

JIU. (2004/6) *Implementation of Results-Based Management in the United Nations Organizations.* Geneva: JIU/REP/2004/6.

Kelley, N., P. Sandison and S. Lawry-White. (2004) *Enhancing UNHCR's Capacity to Monitor the Protection, Rights and Well-Being of Refugees.* Geneva: United Nations High Commissioner for Refugees EPAU/2004/06.

Kenny, K. (2000) 'When needs are rights: an overview of UN efforts to integrate human rights in humanitarian action', *The Watson Institute*, Occasional paper. Providence, RI: Watson JR Institute for International Studies.

Kindornay, S., R. James and C. Carpenter. (2012) 'Rights-based approaches to development: implications for NGOs', *Human Rights Quarterly*, 34(2):472–506.

Kjaerum, M. (2002) 'Refugee protection between state interests and human rights: where is Europe heading?', *Human Rights Quarterly*, 24(2): 513–536.

Klasing, A., S. Moses and M. L. Satterthwaite. (2011) 'Measuring the way forward in Haiti: grounding disaster relief in the legal framework of human rights', *Health and Human Rights: An International Journal*, 13(1): 15–35.

Larner, W. (2000) 'Neo-liberalism: policy, ideology, governmentality', *Studies in Political Economy*, 63: 5–25. Available online at http://spe.library.utoronto.ca/index.php/spe/article/view/6724/3723 (accessed 22 September 2015).

Leebaw, B. (2007) 'The politics of impartial activism: humanitarianism and human rights', *Perspectives on Politics*, 5(2): 223.

Minear, L. (2002) *The Humanitarian Enterprise, Dilemmas & Discoveries.* Bloomfield, Conn.: Kumarian Press.

MOPAN 2014 (2014) 'Multilateral Organisation Performance Assessment Network Synthesis report United Nations High Commissioner for Refugees (UNHCR)'. Available online at www.mopanonline.org/fr/publications/MOPAN2014UNHCR-Fullreport.htm?hf=5&b=0&sl=mopan_publications&s=desc(t4_datepublished) (accessed 22 September 2015).

Morris, C. (2014, December 12). *Investigating evaluation as an accountability mechanism by international non-governmental organizations working in humanitarian relief* (T). University of British Columbia. Retrieved from https://open.library.ubc.ca/cIRcle/collections/24/items/1.0166082 (Original work published 2014).

OIOS. (2007) 'Office of the United Nations High Commissioner for Refugees: inspection on results-based management practices (INS-07-005)'. Available online at https://wikileaks.org/wiki/Office_of_the_United_Nations_High_Commissioner_for_Refugees:_Inspection_on_Results-Based_Management_practices_(INS-07-005),_21_Dec_2007 (accessed 22 September 2015).

OIOS. (2008) *Review of results-based management at the United Nations.* New York: Office of Internal Oversight Services.

OIOS. (2010) Audit of Focus system. Assignment No. AR2010/166/02.

Ortiz, A. and P. Taylor. (2009) 'Learning purposefully in capacity development: why, what and when to measure'. Available online at unesdoc.unesco.org/images/0018/001869/186984E.pdf (accessed 26 November 2015).

Ramalingam, B., J. Mitchell, J. Borton, & K. Smart, (2009) 'Counting what counts: performance and effectiveness in the humanitarian sector', in Alnap (ed.), *8th Review of Humanitarian Action. Performance, Impact and Innovation.* 1–90. London: ODI.

Sandvik, K. B. (2008) *On the Everyday Life of International Law: Humanitarianism and Refugee Resettlement in Kampala.* Cambridge, MA: Harvard Law School SJD.

Sandvik, K. B. (2009) 'The legitimacy of humanitarian governance: on the relationship between indicators, law and rights', Annual Meeting of the Law and Society Association (LSA), Denver, CO, 30 May 2009.

Sandvik, K. B. (2010) 'Rapprochement and misrecognition: humanitarianism as human rights practice', in C. C. Eriksen and M. Emberland (eds.), *The New International Law: An Anthology*, Vol. 36. pp. 139–57, Leiden, Netherlands: Martinus Nijhoff Publishers.

Sandvik, K. B. (2011) 'Blurring boundaries: refugee resettlement in Kampala – between the formal, the informal, and the illegal', *PoLAR: Political and Legal Anthropology Review*, 34(1): 11–32.

Sandvik, K. B. (2013) 'UNHCR reforms revisited: rights-based versus results-based', The World Conference on Humanitarian Studies, Istanbul, 24–27 October 2013.

Slaughter, A. and J. Crisp. (2009) 'A surrogate state? The role of UNHCR in protracted refugee situations', UNHCR New Issues in Refugee Research, Paper 168.

Slim, H. (2002) 'Not philanthropy but rights: the proper politicization of humanitarian philosophy in war', *The International Journal of Human Rights*, 6(2): 1–22.

Stevens, D. E. (2015) 'Rights, needs or assistance? The role of the UNHCR in refugee protection in the Middle East', *International Journal of Human Rights*, Available online at http://www.tandfonline.com/doi/abs/10.1080/13642987.2015.1079026?journal Code=fjhr20, DOI:10.1080/13642987.2015.1079026.

Türk, V. (2013) '64th session of the Executive Committee of the High Commissioner's programme'. Available online at www.refworld.org/docid/524d6ade9.html (accessed 22 September 2015).

Türk, V. and E. Eyster. (2010) 'Strengthening accountability in UNHCR', *International Journal of Refugee Law*, 22(2): 159–172.

UNHCR. (1995) *Human Rights and Refugee Protection (RLD 5)*. Geneva: UNHCR. Available online at www.unhcr.org/3ae6bd900.pdf (accessed 22 September 2015).

UNHCR. (2004) 'Registration project improves profile of refugees', *Mozambique News Stories*, 30 December. Available online at www.unhcr.org/41d42e904.html (accessed 22 September 2015).

UNHCR. (2005) UNHCR community manual. Adapted from J. Theis, 'Promoting rights-based approaches' and 'Child rights programming: handbook for Save the Children alliance members', 2002, p. 22; J. Theis, 'Challenges for a rights-based approach', p. 28, in *Children's Rights Information Newsletter*, No. 18, March.

UNHCR. (2005b) 'Statement by Ms. Wendy Chamberlin, Acting United Nations High Commissioner for Refugees', 32nd Standing Committee of the Executive Committee of the High Commissioner's Programme (ExCom), Geneva, 8 March 2005.

UNHCR. (2006) *Practical Guide to the Systematic Use of STANDARDS & INDICATORS in UNHCR Operations*. Geneva: UNHCR.

UNHCR. (2008) 'UN High Commissioner for Refugees (UNHCR), Note on International Protection', 30 June, A/AC.96/1053. Available online at www.refworld.org/docid/48690 2122.html (accessed 22 September 2015).

UNHCR. (2008b) 'UNHCR manual on a community based approach in UNHCR operations', March. Available online at www.refworld.org/docid/47da54722.html (accessed 22 September 2015).

UNHCR. (2009) 'UN General Assembly, note on international protection', 26 June, A/AC.96/1066. Available online at www.refworld.org/docid/4a5c594d3c.html (accessed 22 September 2015).

UNHCR. (2010) 'UN General Assembly, note on international protection', 30 June, A/AC.96/1085. Available online at www.refworld.org/docid/4caaeabe2.html (accessed 22 September 2015).

UNHCR. (2010b) 'Measure for measure: a field-based snapshot of the implementation of results based management in UNHCR', PDES/2010/13, November. Available online at www.unhcr.org/4cf3ad8f9.pdf (accessed 22 September 2015).

UNHCR. (2013) 'The world turned upside down: a review of protection risks and UNHCR's role in natural disasters', PDES/2013/03. Available online at www.refworld .org/docid/5142d4652.html (accessed 22 September 2015).

Wigley, B. (2005) 'The state of UNHCR's organization culture', Geneva: UNHCR.

Wigley, B. (2006) 'The state of UNHCR's organization culture: what now?' EPAU/2006/01, January 2006.

Zetter, R. (2015) *Protection in Crisis: Forced Migration and Protection in a Global Era*. Washington, DC: Migration Policy Institute.

9 UNHCR, accountability and refugee biometrics

Katja Lindskov Jacobsen

As argued in this book and elsewhere, 'accountability is an important principle for the United Nations High Commissioner for Refugees (UNHCR)' (Turk and Eyster 2010; Kinchin 2013). Yet, the issue of accountability continues to be surrounded by much controversy. On the one hand, critics have argued that UNHCR pays too little attention to *downward accountability* (Sleiman 2012; Poole 2014) and that UNHCR is more concerned with ensuring accountability to the states rather than the beneficiaries (Lee 2010, p. 7). On the other hand, donors have raised a number of accountability concerns, e.g. regarding inflated UNHCR population figures as an issue of insufficient downward accountability to the donors who provide funding based on such figures (US Embassy 2003). This donor concern is indicative of a more general concern, namely, that 'counting refugees is at best an approximate science' (US Bureau for Refugees, cited in Crisp 1999). Although the refugee population data are indeed important (in relation to funding, the planning of specific programmes, etc.), this importance should not preclude a critical appreciation of 'the politics of refugee numbers' (Crisp 1999), including the ways in which political considerations 'impinge upon refugee statistics' (Crisp 1999). In the current political landscape, one consideration that 'impinges upon' refugee numbers is the on-going Global War on Terror, which for example has entailed a more pronounced donor focus on *individual* refugee data (as different from *aggregate population* figures). This political context is important to bear in mind as we consider the use of biometrics as a tool through which UNHCR seeks to improve accountability. More specifically, this chapter zooms in on the question of *how UNHCR's adoption of new biometric registration technologies (such as fingerprinting and iris scans) in an ever-increasing range of refugee contexts may affect upward and downward accountability* in the context of UNHCR's refugee protection activities.

Such questions regarding the politics of technology have arguably been largely overlooked in debates about UNHCR's current accountability measures, a gap that this chapter addresses by drawing on critical insights from International Relations as well as from Science and Technology Studies. Indeed, to better appreciate several challenges that UNHCR confronts in relation to the task of ensuring upward and downward accountability – also certainly insofar as accountability is sought improved through the introduction of new biometric technology – this chapter argues that it is crucial to be aware of the complex political landscape in which

UNHCR manoeuvres. One important feature of this political landscape, which places UNHCR in a difficult position, is its relation to donor states. As has been argued: 'one of UNHCR's most significant weaknesses is its dependence on *voluntary* contributions to carry out existing and new programs' (Loescher 1997, p. 367) and more recently, critics have identified a tendency for donors to increasingly seek 'closer involvement in humanitarian action' (Macrae 2002, p. 5). Others again have called attention to the effects of 'donor dictates' on specific UN refugee activities (Misselwitz and Hanafi 2010, p. 371). Although states undeniably play an important role vis-à-vis the activities of UNHCR, this situation should not lead us to conclude too readily that UNHCR does not have any degree of independent agency (Loescher 2001; Betts 2012). Rather, UNHCR is best understood as being in 'an ambiguous position of, on the one hand, representing states' interests and being dependent upon donor state funding, and, on the other hand, needing to influence states in order to persuade them to fulfil their humanitarian obligations towards refugees' (Betts, Loescher and Milner 2008, p. 2). *This 'ambiguous position' is important to bear in mind when considering UNHCR's turn to biometric registration technologies* (primarily fingerprints and iris scans) with reference to how such technology can improve accountability.

Biometric technologies include more familiar examples, such as fingerprinting, iris scanning and voice recognition as well as less well-known examples, such as gait and vein recognition. The key point concerning biometrics is that it refers to a bodily or behavioural feature, which is unique to each individual and which therefore can be used to identify that individual; once you have 'captured' the fingerprint or another biometric feature of an individual, you will subsequently be able to recognize this biometric feature and thus the specific individual again. Biometrics has a long history of use in prisons and in the colonial periphery (Pugliese 2010). What is 'new' regarding the biometric technologies that have been used for the last two decades is that the recognition process has been automated such that large amounts of digitalized biometric data can be processed, for example, in search of a 'match' between a 'stored' biometric template and the 'live' biometric of a person whose identity is sought to be verified.

Despite the seeming newness of biometrics in refugee contexts, UNHCR has already used various biometric registration technologies for more than 10 years (Jacobsen 2015a). Since initial projects in the early 2000s, including the use of iris recognition in the repatriation of refugees from Pakistan back to Afghanistan (initiated in October 2002) and the use of fingerprint technology in refugee camps in Tanzania and Kenya a few years later, UNHCR has deployed biometrics in an increasing number of contexts, most recently as a central component of its response to the Syrian refugee crisis. Indeed, UNHCR has been deploying biometric registration systems for such a long time that a need for an updated version of the system has now been identified and this new system has recently been tested in a refugee camp in Malawi (2014). Yet, from the perspective of accountability, one of the important things to note regarding this development is that after more than a decade of refugee biometrics, UNHCR still does not have a publicly available policy that sets the terms and conditions for its use of biometrics. In the absence of such a policy, it is difficult to know UNHCR's official stance on important questions, such as data protection, data retention and data sharing. This is an important point that we shall return to later in the chapter. Obviously, such challenges have not been at the forefront of UNHCR's official representations of its use of biometric technology. Rather, UNHCR has formulated a variety of arguments regarding the ways in which biometrics can help improve UNHCR's accountability (upward as well as downward).

Three perspectives on biometrics and UNHCR accountability

UNHCR has stressed a number of reasons why it sees biometrics as a favourable technology in the context of its refugee protection practices. In several cases, arguments regarding efficiency and accuracy have been stressed, whereas in other cases 'improved accountability' has been stressed more explicitly – this was, for example, the case in relation to the use of biometrics in the Kakuma refugee camp in Kenya. In a recent article from *Kakuma News* (an independent news magazine produced by regional journalists),[1] which describes a new collaboration between UNHCR and the World Food Programme (WFP) concerning the use of biometric registration technology in this refugee camp, we were informed that '*accountability remains the main reason for implementing the Biometrics System*, as a measure to ensure that the food given by WFP reaches its intended subjects' (italics added) (September 2013). Indeed, the article concluded that this new system of 'food distribution through biometric assessment [...] is believed to foster accountability and transparency in food monitoring' (*Kakuma News* 2013).[2] But has the soundness of such assumptions been explored in any detail? How can we, for example, trust that biometrics will help ensure that aid gets to 'the correct people'? Have the last 10 years of deploying biometrics in refugee camp contexts given rise to any counter-narratives, lessons, debates etc. that may challenge such assumptions? We shall return to these questions, as we shall now look at *how UNHCR itself represents this link between the use of biometrics and improved accountability.*

UNHCR on biometrics and improved accountability

Speediness as improved accountability: faster food and faster registration

One context in which UNHCR has introduced biometric refugee registration is at various sites in South Sudan, including the Maban camp (UNHCR 2013), the Nimule camp (*Sudan Tribune* 2014) and the Yida camp (*Relief Web* 2015). According to a UNHCR news article, one of the benefits of using this new technology is that it can improve accountability. As Tunzaw Oo (UNHCR Registration Officer) explained when asked about the new 'food distribution tool' that uses biometrics, this new tool was '*designed to improve* efficiency and *accountability*' (italics added) (UNHCR 2013). In what sense the use of biometric technology helps UNHCR improve accountability in its distribution of food to this refugee population is, however, not explained in any further detail. What is mentioned is only that the new biometrically endowed system has helped speed up the delivery of food aid to refugees – yet, it remains unspecified in what sense this biometric system was *designed to improve accountability*, unless 'improved accountability' simply means 'faster food aid' to refugees. In a different account of the same biometric system, we are further informed that biometrics does not only help speed up the delivery of food aid, more generally, biometrics will also 'help to identify refugees more quickly so they can receive better assistance' (UNHCR 2012). Indeed, this emphasis on how biometric technology can help speed up otherwise cumbersome refugee assistance processes has been stressed by UNHCR in numerous contexts. Recently, this benefit was emphasized in UNHCR accounts of how the use of biometrics has helped speed up the registration of large numbers of Syrian refugees fleeing into Jordan, which has a population size that the old system was ill-prepared to manage: 'The time that Syrians need to register as refugees in Jordan has been slashed from up to eight months to zero after the UN refugee agency rolled out new technology [biometric iris scanning]' (Alsalem and Riller 2013).

Although biometrics may in several cases help speed up refugee registration processes as described above, it should be mentioned that in other cases, this claim has indeed confronted counter-narratives. In Afghanistan, 'hundreds of Afghans waiting in long queues for registration attacked the Verification Centre in protest against the slow pace of repatriation' (Ghufran 2006), and in the Dadaab camp in Kenya, the use of biometrics was characterized by 'occasional delays, disruption or cancellation of the food distribution in the camps; contributing to long queues and crowd control challenges' (Otieno and Gazarwa 2014, p. 18). Later in this chapter, we shall return to this issue of challenges to UNHCR's expectations regarding the ability of biometrics to act as an accountability-improving technology. Now, in addition to these accounts of how biometrics can bring greater accountability through a 'speedier' delivery of assistance to and processing of refugees, UNHCR has highlighted other ways in which biometrics can help improve accountability.

Fraud prevention as improved accountability

With limited resources available to fulfil its mandate and protect refugees, being accountable to refugees also implies making sure that the scarce assistance deliveries are distributed fairly among the affected communities. Yet, in the Registration Handbook from 2003, UNHCR noted that in certain environments, UNHCR has experienced 'widespread abuse and fraud (recycling, multiple registrations, [and] "borrowing" children [...] from local community to inflate family size)' (UNHCR 2003), p. 98). Such abuse and fraud ultimately imply an unfair distribution of limited resources – potentially leaving several refugees without sufficient aid because others have illegitimately received 'too much'. Being accountable to *all* of the refugees entails ensuring that available resources are distributed fairly (Harrell-Bond 1992). Thus, when UNHCR highlights how biometrics helps UNHCR prevent fraud and 'double-dipping' (UN News 2004) and how the technology thus becomes important in helping ensure a fair distribution of resources among refugees, this situation can be understood as a way in which biometrics helps improve accountability. This type of accountability benefit was, for instance, emphasized in UNHCR's first use of iris recognition technology in a refugee context, namely, in the repatriation of Afghan refugees living in Pakistan (Jacobsen 2015b). As UNHCR stated in a Briefing Note: 'It was believed that some wily Afghans might be "recycling" older kids through the verification centres in order to collect their assistance package more than once', and to tackle that problem, 'We opted to use this biometric recognition system in order to prevent identification fraud' (UNHCR August 2003). The ability of the technology to serve as a solution to this problem was also stressed by the selected technology provider: 'Iris recognition is vital to helping the UN refugee agency […] avoid potential fraudulent use of the program through repeated claims for assistance' (Iridian 2003). A similar argument was also stressed in relation to the above-mentioned use of biometrics in South Sudan (as well as in numerous other contexts). Several refugee camps in South Sudan are close to the border and UNHCR has observed that 'it is not unusual for refugees to risk their lives by returning home to escort other family members to safety' (UNHCR, December 2012). Such movements make it difficult for UNHCR to maintain 'accurate population figures' and UNHCR has then emphasized how 'biometrics is a critical way for UNHCR to […] prevent multiple registrations' (UNHCR, December 2012).

Whereas faster registration and food aid delivery would seem to improve UNHCR's accountability to refugees, the issue of fraud prevention is closely related to the representation of biometrics as an accountability measure geared more towards improving upward accountability.

More accountable use of donor resources

The accountability benefits of introducing biometric technologies into various refugee contexts have also been explained with reference to improvements in upward accountability. In a review of UNHCR's response to the refugee emergency in South Sudan, it has been stressed that implementing biometrics 'increases the credibility of the operation with donors' (2013, p. 24). But how, more specifically, does UNHCR see that biometrics has helped increase credibility and accountability towards donors? In many accounts, it is difficult to gather precisely how UNHCR sees the link between biometrics and accountability because we are merely informed in general terms that biometrics has, for example, 'improved […] accountability in the distribution process' (2014, p. 18), without further explanation of what this means in practice. Yet, the focus of this 'improved accountability' was recently described in an official job advertisement for a position on a WFP/ UNHCR biometric project. In this job description, we are, for example, informed in the following manner: 'the new procedures will *utilize biometric* (fingerprint) ID checks' *to promote* 'efficient and *accountable use of donor resources*' (2013). In other words, it would seem that – as understood by UNHCR – one aspect of the link between biometrics and accountability has to do with the ability of biometrics to ensure a more accountable use of donor resources. In summary, from the perspective of

UNHCR, these three arguments, thus, seem to suggest that the use of biometric technology can help improve both upward and downward accountability.

Donor perspectives on biometrics and accountability: more reliable numbers

Donors also stress the link between biometrics and improved accountability. The U.S. has, for example, urged UNHCR to prioritize biometrics. In a recent opening statement by U.S. Ambassador Lane, she stressed that 'an area of increasing importance to the United States [...] is the use of biometrics to best ensure that scarce food goes to food insecure households' and that, therefore, the U.S. urges UNHCR to prioritize the use of biometrics (November 2014). Ten years earlier, a similar focus on urging UNHCR to implement biometrics was evident in a report from U.S. DoS on *Reforms for a New Era of Refugee Resettlement*, which urged UNHCR 'to go further and do all it can to require the routine inclusion of biometric identifiers at the appropriate stage of registration' (2004). Looking closely at this interest in urging UNHCR to use biometrics, two main reasons are related to two types of concerns that donors have raised, i.e. questions concerning the accuracy of the population figures presented by UNHCR in its appeals for funding and the question of how funding is spent once provided. Let's look more closely at each of these concerns.

Accountability, biometrics and more reliable population data

One of the benefits being stressed by donors is that biometric registration can help deliver more accurate population data. A 2003 document from the U.S. Embassy in Rome, for example, expressed concerns over the accuracy of the population figures presented by UNHCR regarding refugee protection needs in Tanzania and noted that inflated numbers 'questionable refugee population figures could leave some WFP food aid donors with a stomachache' (WikiLeaks (2003)). In view of such concerns, it has been suggested that biometrics can prove to be helpful. Because biometric characteristics are unique to every individual, the same individual cannot be registered twice and, thus, inflated numbers as a result of double-registration can be minimized. Since the implementation of biometric refugee registration, this benefit has been stressed in a number of reports, e.g. in a review by the UK Department for International Development (DFID) on its 'support for refugees in Kenya'. Before the use of biometrics, there was concern that 'ration cards [were] being used illegitimately', e.g. because refugees had 'left the camps and sold their ration cards' (2014, p. 11). Other examples can also be mentioned: In the aforementioned Joint Assessment Mission report on UNHCR and WFP's use of biometrics in the Kakuma camp, more reliable refugee population data were stressed as an important benefit; and in relation to the influx of Malian refugees in Mauritania, we observed a similar focus on the ability of biometrics to curb inflated refugee population data (Hussain 2014; Hussain 2013). With the implementation of biometrics, concerns about inflated refugee population figures appear to have lessened; donors are presented with results so they can see how, since the introduction of biometrics, 'the number of people receiving assistance from the GFD [General Food Distribution] has dropped significantly' (2014, p. 11). Indeed, DFID highlighted a '17% reduction between October-December 2013 [...] following the start of the biometrics programme in October 2013' – an achievement, which 'substantially exceeded expectations' (2014, p. 10). In short, biometric 'verification of genuine recipients' seems to have contributed to making donors feel that their funds are being used in a more accountable manner and in this sense 'the introduction of iris scanning at voluntary repatriation centres [...] have been important in securing the support and *confidence* of donors' (Troger and Tennant 2008, p. 3). In addition to this focus on how biometrics can deliver trustworthy population figures, UNHCR's use of biometrics has been linked to another 'benefit'.

Positive identification: accountability, biometrics and the use of funding

To appreciate this 'benefit', it is necessary first to say a few additional words concerning the political landscape in the context of which decisions to implement biometrics were being made. UNHCR's very first use of biometrics was on the Afghan-Pakistan border in 2002 (UNHCR 2013d; Jacobsen 2010). Since 9/11, various humanitarian agencies, including UNHCR, 'have been hard hit by allegations of links to terrorism' (Metcalfe-Hough *et al.* 2015) and various reports have argued that terrorists have infiltrated refugee camps in places, such as Kenya (Garvelink and Tahir 2012) and Algeria (Vogler 2012). Such allegations are not only difficult to verify but also to disprove. Certainly, an important implication has been a renewed focus on defining who is a refugee (and who is a terrorist). This focus is part of a broader phenomenon of post-9/11 security considerations having affected humanitarian practices in a number of ways. Donors have, for example, increasingly called on UNHCR to assure them that the funds they provide are spent on feeding and *only* protecting 'genuine' refugees, *not* on aiding the cause of 'terrorists'. In other words, accountability demands from donors have increasingly become focused on the question of *who* receives assistance (e.g. with a view to ensuring that suspected terrorists do not receive humanitarian assistance).[3]

Using biometrics as a technology to verify whether a person is a 'genuine refugee' by matching his or her biometric image against a database of biometrics from 'known' identities is different from using biometrics in the ways explained above (that is, 'to ensure that a refugee cannot be registered multiple times' (UNHCR 2015) or to ensure that a person who turns up to collect food items is the same person who was originally recognized as a genuine refugee (and was given a ration card). Now, to illustrate the difference between these uses of biometrics and the use of the technology to verify that the fingerprint of a refugee does not match that of another 'known' identity, it is helpful to examine the use of biometrics in the Dadaab camp complex. In the Dadaab camp in Kenya, biometrics has not only been used by UNHCR to offer more reliable refugee population data but biometric registration has also been used to ensure that refugees who receive assistance *were not local Kenyans* claiming to be refugees (to receive food aid from UNHCR). As explained earlier, in order for biometrics to serve this purpose, it is necessary to match the fingerprint or iris scan of that individual not 'just' against UNHCR's own database of refugee biometrics but also against Kenya's national biometric database (created by using biometric voter registration).

In the case of Kenya, this data exchange is described in various documents that refer, for example, to the 'cross-referencing biometric data against Kenya's national database to avoid registration of Kenyan nationals seeking assistance in the camps' (Human Rights Watch 2009, p. 17). However, such matching processes – where the aim is not to prevent that refugees are registered and receive assistance twice but rather to ensure that the biometric identity of a refugee does not match that of other known biometric identities, in this case Kenyan nationals – may not 'only' take place vis-à-vis host state databases but *possibly* also through processes of cross-checking refugee biometrics against 'known identities' in other databases, identities that are not to be mistaken for 'genuine refugees' deserving of UNHCR assistance. For not only have the host states expressed interest in the use of biometric refugee data for such verification purposes, the donor states have expressed similar interests. The United States, for example, emphasizes the 'assurance of positive identification via biometrics throughout the refugee assistance process', noticing that in a post-9/11 context, refugee management processes, including resettlement, 'would carry enormous advantages' from such positive biometric identification (U.S. DoS 2004). Such positive identification is also the function that would be necessary if biometrics was to be used as a technology to ensure donors that no 'known' terrorists were hiding as refugees. Even if it is impossible to find out whether cross-matching of refugee and terrorist biometrics have occurred, the important point to stress in the context of this chapter is that this type of 'biometric accountability benefit' is different from the above-mentioned concerns with inflated population figures. Unlike 'population figures' in the form of *aggregate* biometric data, this other use of biometrics for positive identification moves UNHCR's use of biometric technology to the level of the individual and, thus, to the delicate question of *who* qualifies for UNHCR assistance and protection. In short, this move towards a more pronounced focus on *individual* rather than aggregate refugee data seems to be an important aspect of the politics of refugee numbers anno 2015, which is an aspect with important implications for the use of biometrics as an accountability technology. Although this move from aggregate to individual data is presented as an important part of the way in which biometrics can provide improved upward accountability, the implications of this move may not necessarily be considered to be an improvement when we turn to the question of downward accountability. Indeed, there is arguably a need to evaluate how the use of biometrics has affected downward accountability because the reports published so far offer no thorough analysis of this question. As we shall see in the following section, various critics have voiced concerns regarding UNHCR's use of biometrics, i.e. concerns that challenge the above expectations regarding how biometrics will improve accountability.

Critical reflections on biometrics and downward accountability

Critical voices within: accountability in the case of failure?

It seems that UNHCR and donors, to a certain extent, agree about the potential accountability benefits of using biometrics in various refugee contexts. However, not all parts of the UN system agree with the links between biometrics and downward accountability that UNHCR stresses in the above-mentioned statements. Interestingly, criticism has been raised from within the UN system, more specifically, from the United Nations Office of Internal Oversight Services. In a report from May 2006, the Internal Oversights Office evaluated 'Project Profile' – the name of the first version of UNHCR's biometric refugee registration system (see Ashley's chapter) – and noted the following: 'Senior management are not always available which results in infrequent meetings, while *the accountability for the success or failure of the project cannot be clearly assigned*' (2006, pp. 3, 11). In other words, critical voices from within the UN have thus (nearly 10 years ago) pointed to what they saw as a lack of attention to the important question of how the use of biometrics may *challenge* downward accountability if the technology fails to perform as expected and if refugees have no ways of holding UNHCR accountable for such failures. Regarding this critical comment, it should be added that UNHCR has itself referred to its use of biometrics as 'experimental' on the note that, for example, with iris recognition in Afghanistan, this was 'the first use of the technology in such a challenging environment' (UNHCR 2003; Jacobsen 2010). Despite this point being raised in the above-mentioned report from the Internal Oversight Services, we still find no official guidelines or policies that detail how UNHCR will ensure that refugees have ways of holding accountable UNHCR for technical failures, which may potentially have a significant impact on their safety (Hosein and Nyst 2013). Such failures have indeed occurred (Jacobsen 2010; Muller 2004; Hosein and Nyst 2013). When sensitive iris recognition cameras are, for example, deployed in the Afghan-Pakistan borderland where they are exposed to heat and dust, this situation affects the ability of the technology to capture a useable iris image (Jacobsen 2015b).

External criticism: biometrics, accountability and well-informed refugees

The absence of guidelines and official policies and the lack of mechanisms to ensure that potential failures can be clearly assigned arguably conflict with UNHCR's own description of how a crucial part of downward accountability is about UNHCR's responsibility to ensure that 'assisted people [are] informed about the programme (who is included, what people will receive, where people can complain)' (UNHCR/WFP). From this perspective, accountability is about delivering assistance in ways that the intended recipients are informed about, have ways of complaining about and ways to hold UNHCR liable. Indeed, various critics have indicated how UNHCR has often failed on this point not only in relation to biometrics but also more generally. A report from a follow-up mission to the Dadaab camp complex in Kenya conducted by Humanitarian Accountability Partnership (HAP), for example, pointed to a lack of accountability measures designed to ensure that affected communities were informed about 'their right to complain, without fear of harm or retaliation' as well as to 'assist them on how to raise a complaint in a safe and confidential manner' (2011).[4] In the case of biometrics, we arguably seem to find a similar lack of information given to refugees. On the one hand, 'information campaigns' are conducted 'with all registration events in the camp' (Malawi, UNHCR External Relations Officer). However, simultaneously, it is difficult to know exactly what type of information refugees are given when biometric technologies are being introduced. At least two things seem to indicate a certain paucity of information regarding the technology and the data being collected. First, in several of the refugee contexts where a trial of biometric refugee registration has been conducted, the use of this new technology has given rise to considerable frustration among the refugees, which in several cases has evolved into violent confrontations. One example was a violent clash between internally displaced persons (IDPs) and aid workers in South Sudan, which resulted in 'a consolidated incident report of the physical security threats received from the IDP leaders on the fifth day of the IDP biometric registration exercise' (UNHCR 2014). Another example was an upheaval in Malaysia – one of the first countries in which UNHCR introduced biometric fingerprint technology in its registration of refugees on the note that this would mark 'a new direction in refugee registration' (UNHCR 2006). Yet, the use of biometrics in Malaysia has not been without complications; critics have argued that these upheavals, which emerged as refugees discovered 'that, after having their fingerprints taken, some were being issued letters stamped: *Return to Home Country*' (Needham 2011), are illustrative of a critical 'lack of transparency and accountability' in relation to the use of this new biometric registration technology (*ReliefWeb* March 2012). Such examples are arguably indicative of a broader problem concerning the level of information given to refugees by UNHCR regarding crucial questions, such as biometric data ownership and usage. Indeed, this is an issue that we shall return to later in relation to UNHCR's use of refugee biometrics in the Syrian refugee crisis. Another notable point is that not only refugees but also privacy rights groups, technology vendors and other interested persons seem to be unable to find answers from UNHCR to crucial questions, such as *who is accountable for failures* (as was pointed out by the Internal Oversight Services) and *what* the biometric data will be used for. We shall elaborate on this latter point in the following section.

Biometrics and protection: refugee privacy as a challenge to downward accountability

Although measures have been taken to address a number of accountability challenges (e.g. UNHCR has a new policy on sexual violence), an important point to stress in this chapter is how the use of biometrics may give rise to *new* accountability challenges, notably concerning the use and storage of biometric refugee data, e.g. What happens to the biometric data collected by UNHCR? With whom is it shared and in what form? These are the types of questions that UNHCR has not provided refugees with clear answers.[5] Indeed, after more than a decade of refugee biometrics, UNHCR still does not have a publicly available policy that sets the terms and conditions for its use of biometrics concerning sensitive questions, such as with whom the biometric data that UNHCR collects will be shared.[6] In a 'response to bidders', UNHCR replied as follows: 'Biometrics will be used at UNHCR's discretion. Whether or not UNHCR exchanges data with partners, is not relevant' (UNHCR). Thus, with the introduction of biometrics, it arguably becomes important to explore what measures UNHCR is taking to ensure downward accountability, especially in view of how refugee biometrics is being rolled out in an increasing number of refugee contexts.

Such data protection challenges have, indeed, been stressed by a number of international privacy experts, who have for example said the following about UNHCR's use of refugee biometrics: 'there are serious questions about accountability, transparency and avenues for recourse for beneficiaries' (Privacy International 27). In a similarly critical vein, technology expert Simon Davies has published an article in which he explained how on a previous mission for UNHCR he had found a number of critical points to which he alerted UNHCR; however, the result simply was that the study was abandoned and that he was not allowed to publish it. What he then revealed In this article, he revealed the way in which UNHCR used biometrics, which 'gave rise to substantial risk to life and liberty of hundreds of thousands of the most vulnerable people in the world' and how they, on that note, 'urged a radical shift in the way it viewed the security risks to the people whose safety was its responsibility' (Davies 2012). After having visited a number of refugee settings in which UNHCR was using biometric refugee registration, the two technology experts noted the following:

> Had the UNHCR's system been implemented in any of these countries, it would have been declared illegal. The UNHCR's Automated Fingerprint Identification System (AFIS) operated in the absence of protections, lacked even the most basic safeguards, and most importantly, lacked the necessary framework of policy. (Davies 2012)

Several of the more specific risks that Davies highlighted were the following:

- 'Data falling into the wrong hands could result in persecution, discrimination or even imminent threat to liberty and life';
- 'Data are acquired by host governments which then use the information to assist efforts to imprison or persecute populations'; and
- 'Stolen or lost files become associated with an act of genocide or execution'.

Such warnings from technology experts (appointed by UNHCR itself) were neglected. Indeed, it seems that the likelihood of negative implications for refugee safety has not been given much consideration in UNHCR accounts of how biometrics can *improve* accountability by speeding up registration and food delivery processes. In this sense, UNHCR's representation of biometrics and accountability arguably suffers from a weakness that has also been pointed out in earlier accountability debates, namely, that 'accountability is skewed in the direction of the donors' (Harrell-Bond 2002, p. 15), in this case given the focus on how biometrics may improve upward accountability at the expense of neglecting the likelihood of negative implications for downward accountability. Indeed, if we consider the above-mentioned remarks, it seems that the link between biometrics and accountability is more complex than what we can gather from the official representations offered by UNHCR.

All of the above perspectives, understandings, expectations and warnings have been formulated in relation to UNHCR's use of refugee biometrics as carried out for the last 10 years (Jacobsen 2015a), that is, primarily in refugee camp contexts. However, UNHCR has most recently announced that camps are not 'ideal settings' and have instead placed emphasis on urban refugee settings. Since the contemporary Syrian refugee crisis, UNHCR has been using biometric registration technologies in several of the main urban refugee settings hosting Syrian refugees. In view of this new application context, the following section turns to the important question of how specific characteristics of urban refugee settings may pose particular challenges to the use of biometrics in refugee protection practices, i.e. challenges that come *in addition to* the issues raised above in relation to the use of biometrics in refugee camps, and challenges that may call for a revision of initial expectations regarding the ability of biometrics to improve upward accountability.

Refugee biometrics in urban settings

In July 2014, UNHCR published their stand in a new revised version 'Alternatives to Camps'; here it was noted that camps are not necessarily the preferred option — and UNHCR makes a move to acknowledge cities as legitimate areas of refugees and to maximize refugee protection within urban areas (UNHCR 2009, p. 6). Concerning biometrics, UNHCR's 2009 policy on 'refugee protection and solutions in urban areas' stated that 'UNHCR will record the special needs of individual refugees in ProGres', the name of UNHCR's biometric registration system (see Ashley's chapter). However, this shift begs an important question: *Does the use of biometrics in urban settings come with the same accountability benefits as those mentioned above, by donors as well as by UNHCR? How about the challenges pointed out by critics, do they persist and/or do new ones emerge as UNHCR thus expands its use of biometrics into various urban refugee settings?*

General limitations, context specific challenges and risks from successful applications

The use of biometrics in refugee contexts comes with a general set of challenges, such as reliable connectivity and usability of the technology in challenging conditions of dust, heat and humidity and with individuals whose fingerprints may be more difficult for the technology to capture, but importantly, many of the challenges that emerge as biometrics is being implemented are context specific (Jacobsen 2010; Hosein and Nyst 2013). UNHCR is also aware of such challenges; regarding the use of biometrics in the Afghani-Pakistan borderland, UNHCR noted that this was a particularly 'challenging environment' where heat, humidity and dust would challenge the performance of biometric technology (UNHCR, 2003). Another context-specific challenge concerns the difference in bodies rather than surroundings; the Western-developed technology is less adept at capturing biometrics from people of colour and, therefore, when used in refugee contexts in Africa and Asia, biometric technology is prone to various 'failures to enrol', e.g. if fingerprints or iris patterns of a specific population are difficult to capture (Pugliese 2010; Jacobsen 2010).[7] Finally, in addition to general and context-specific challenges, protection issues may arise even if biometric technology performs as expected. As mentioned above, the production and storage of large amounts of digitalised biometric refugee data entail a number of privacy and protection issue that – as critics have suggested – can affect accountability towards refugees who are, for example, not informed about the purposes for which these sensitive data may be used by UNHCR, including with whom it may be shared. We shall return to this point later, but for now we emphasize that all of these different challenges to the technology also become potential challenges to the accountability of UNHCR when deploying this technology in different refugee contexts. What must be added to this is that as UNHCR has expanded its use of biometrics into various urban refugee settings, new challenges can be expected to arise and confront particularly vulnerable urban refugee populations who 'unlike those in camps […] often find it difficult to gain access to aid and protection' (UNHCR 2013). To better understand how the specifics of urban settings may challenge the performance of biometrics in ways that may potentially have unforeseen protection consequences, it is necessary to detail these context-specific characteristics.

The urban issue: registering a dispersed refugee population

One of the most obvious differences between a refugee camp and an urban refugee setting, which can be expected to affect UNHCR's use of refugee biometrics, is that the refugee population in an urban context is far more scattered and difficult to access. Indeed, it has proven for UNHCR and other stakeholders/humanitarian actors to get access to urban refugees. In a recent review of its own progress on the Urban Policy, UNHCR offers an overview of 'a range of reason for difficulties in community outreach'; however, as critics have pointed out, UNHCR does not mention 'the suspicion that many urban refugees harbour towards UNHCR' (Morris and Ben Ali). Indeed, dispersed urban refugee populations may pose specific challenges to the use of biometrics as an accountability tool, i.e. challenges that arguably need to be addressed more systematically by UNHCR as well as by donors whose presumptions regarding biometric data have influenced the decision to deploy this technology in new contexts, but perhaps without fully grasping what challenges this expansion may entail.

Negative implications for mobility: how biometric registration may affect refugee mobility

Various features of the current situation with urban Syrian refugees in Lebanon illustrate how the use of refugee biometrics in urban settings can affect refugee mobility in ways that, in turn, may have a significant impact on the livelihood and safety of refugees. One challenge is, of course, that UNHCR has little experience with the use of biometrics in urban refugee contexts because biometrics has thus far primarily been used in camp settings. Yet, there are at least two types of refugee mobility that the use of biometrics may have an impact on, namely, refugee movements *within* the host country and refugee movements *across borders*.

Crossing internal checkpoints

'Secondary movement is significant in Lebanon' (MapAction 2013) and there are different reasons why urban refugees may need to move *within* the host country. One reason is that initially, refugees may have 'anticipated residing in Lebanon for only a limited time and therefore remained near the northern and eastern borders. With the prolonged situation refugees are moving towards urban areas [...] in search of accommodation and employment' (MapAction 2013, p. 6). Another reason is that 'the work Syrians find is mostly in the construction and agriculture sector, which is seasonal'; hence, to stay, employed refugees need to move from one location to another (MapAction 2013, p. 2). A third reason for secondary movement is access to health care (NRC 2014). Yet, biometric refugee registration may affect such refugee mobility in different ways. For example, for refugees who 'due to *security considerations* [have] not entered Lebanon through an official border crossing' (NRC 2014, p. 6), the use of biometric identification may increase an already prevalent fear that they may be arrested when crossing an internal checkpoint. We should not expect such fears to fade in the face of government statements, such as the Turkish Interior Ministry's recent proclamation that the very same biometric data that will be 'used in the provision of aid' will also 'be used to identify those who have been involved in criminal activity' (12 January 2015). In other words, the use of refugee biometrics may intertwine with and likely exacerbate an existing 'fear of movement' in ways that can have negative implications for the safety of Syrian refugees if this situation, for example, causes difficulties and fears among refugees who need to access health care or who seek employment opportunities.

Cross-border movements

Context-specific challenges, such as limited access to health care for Syrian refugees in Lebanon, do not only produce a need for mobility *within* the host country but also imply that several refugees may need to go back to Syria to access lifesaving medical treatment. As indicated by the Norwegian Refugee Council (NRC), four of 21 interviewed refugees 'had problems accessing medical services [in Lebanon]' (NRC 2014, p. 19) and for several refugees, the consequence of this situation has been a need to return to Syria momentarily to seek medical treatment: 'the situation is so desperate that in some cases refugees have resorted to returning to Syria to receive the treatment they need' (Amnesty 2014). What must be added to this is that the use of biometric refugee registration may aggravate this difficulty *if* the technology is applied in ways that hinder Syrian refugees in returning to Syrian when they need to access medical assistance. Thus, one issue to consider more carefully in urban refugee settings is the question of how UNHCR's use of biometric refugee registration may affect cross-border movements in ways that could, in this case, have implications for the ability of Syrian refugees to access lifesaving medical assistance or feed into a more general fear of how biometric refugee data will be used in this highly political and sensitive context. In Lebanon, refugees have, for example, expressed concerns about the implications of potential data sharing between UNHCR and the government of Lebanon, whose Minister of Social Affairs has stated that 'General Security was working with UNHCR to access the agency's biometric data' (*The Daily Star Lebanon,* May 2014), and whose interior minister has 'announced that Syrian refugees registered with the U.N. would have their status revoked if they returned to their home country, even for brief spells' (The Daily Star Lebanon, October 2014). Indeed, Syrian refugees in Lebanon have expressed concerns about how UNHCR will use their biometric data (Knutsen and Lutz 2014). Thus, in addition to various context-specific challenges surfacing as biometrics is rolled out in urban settings, 'old' challenges persist and one such challenge concerns the question of how UNHCR will use the biometric refugee data that they collect.[8] In addition to how such concerns may result in refugees deciding not to register with UNHCR (as biometric registration is *mandatory*), which in turn challenges the argument that biometrics will enhance accountability by providing donors with more accurate population statistics, this issue sheds light on a more profound challenge: UNHCR has thus far not managed to ensure transparency regarding its use of biometrics in urban settings, which is arguably at odds with a definition of accountability that UNHCR endorses, namely, a definition in which downward accountability is about ensuring that 'assisted people [are] informed about the programme' (here the use of biometrics) and about 'where people can complain' (see, for example, WFP 2014). This brings us back to the important point that it is difficult for refugee populations to obtain clear information about how UNHCR uses the biometric data that the institution has collected. As mentioned in the beginning of this chapter, UNHCR has replied in an answer to a query from a potential technology provider that how UNHCR will use the biometric data that are being collected on an increasing number of refugees is 'up to the discretion of UNHCR' (UNHCR).

Concluding remarks

The current focus on humanitarian accountability, combined with the securitization of humanitarian practices, is creating pressures for the humanitarian world to take on new methods and tools, such as to live up to new accountability expectations. One such 'tool' has been biometric registration technologies. More than a decade ago, UNHCR began using biometrics, primarily in refugee camps (Jacobsen 2015a). What we see today is that in addition to continued debates and concerns regarding biometric data protection in refugee contexts, including UNHCR's accountability towards an ever-increasing number of biometrically registered refugees, an exploration of urban refugee contexts seems to indicate a new set of challenges to the use of refugee biometrics. For example, large numbers of unregistered refugees challenge the assumption that biometrics can deliver more accurate refugee population data and thus improve upward accountability. Concerning downward accountability, the ways in which biometrics may feed into existing fears of movement and hinder refugee mobility is but one example of the specific challenges that the use of biometrics confronts in urban refugee settings. Arguably, these challenges require us to revise the assumption that biometrics can help improve accountability in UNHCR's refugee protection practices.

What the above analysis illustrates is that, on the one hand, donors stress a number of ways in which biometrics can *improve upward accountability* (more reliable numbers), whereas simultaneously critics stress how biometrics may have *negative implications for downward accountability*, for example, because refugees (and others) are not informed about how exactly UNHCR will use this biometric refugee data. As such, it seems that an old critique re-emerges as biometrics is being implemented as a new accountability tool, namely, the critique that an effect of this could be an increasing 'gap between financial accountability and moral accountability' (Harrell-Bond 1992, p. 219). Biometrics may enhance UNHCR's accountability vis-à-vis donors and the use of funding. Yet, if UNHCR does not inform refugees regarding its stance on data sharing and protection, and if UNHCR does not find ways to identify – let alone resolve – a variety of context specific challenges (e.g. implications for lifesaving refugee mobility), then there is a risk that the improved upward accountability that biometrics is expected to deliver will come at the expense of serious challenges to UNHCR's accountability to the affected refugee populations.

With UNHCR's commitment to effective and rapid registration (Registration Handbook), it seems that biometrics in refugee protection practices has come to stay; i.e. we have already observed the use of biometrics for more than 10 years, it is now being expanded into new contexts, and UNHCR has recently completed a pilot test of a new and updated version of its biometric registration system (Malawi). To ensure that the use of biometrics in refugee assistance does not compromise refugee safety, UNHCR needs to follow its own definition of accountability, which would entail being more transparent regarding its use not only of the biometric registration technology but also of its use in the biometric refugee data being collected by the agency. Indeed, one could argue that because UNHCR is mandated to protect several of the most vulnerable people, UNHCR should lead the way on how to deploy such new technology in a responsible, transparent and accountable manner. As the chapter also showed, not only are transparency and information to refugees important in ensuring a responsible use of biometrics in refugee contexts, UNHCR also needs to provide more information and engage in a closer dialogue with implementing partners and technology providers regarding its use of biometrics. More open dialogue concerning the use of biometrics could also serve as a way for UNHCR to gain important information regarding the challenges that emerge as biometrics is being rolled out in different settings; implementing partners may, for example, have valuable information regarding how refugees experience the use of biometrics. Yet, such information is not currently collected in any systematic manner. Such initiatives may be needed if UNHCR is to improve on an old point of critique, namely, an 'inconsistency with regard to the extent that beneficiary voices have been solicited' (Kaiser 2004, p. 10).

Now, insofar as the reasons for urging UNHCR to use biometrics are motivated by political and security concerns, it must of course be acknowledged that donor influence and interests could hinder such transparency. Yet, at the same time UNHCR has previously been able to exert a degree of institutional autonomy vis-à-vis placing demands on the institution by donors, for example, in the discussion of how to interpret UNHCR's mandate and the scope of UNHCR's activities. Emphasizing that the use of biometrics must adhere to certain standards should be a matter of priority to UNHCR because the framework that defines how biometrics is being deployed will have important consequences for the safety of biometrically registered refugees. In other words, biometric registration technology will not *automatically* improve accountability. Certainly, as the technology is now being deployed in urban contexts, it is not clear what negative consequences this situation could entail, which further increases the need for transparency and discussion regarding the use of biometric technology (although it should also be stressed that transparency will not automatically lead to accountability). In order for these assumptions regarding biometrics and accountability to hold, a number of issues need to be addressed and among the most important is the question of how biometric refugee data are being used – a question that UNHCR should define a clear stance on, clearly stated in a publicly available policy.

Notes

1 Available online at http://kanere.org/about-kanere/ (accessed 23 September 2015).
2 According to this article, 'the initiative was aimed to improve accountability between the implementing agencies and the donors because abuse of food resources has been frequently reported' (*Kakuma News* 2013).
3 Indeed, with recent changes in counter-terror legislation, UNHCR (and other humanitarian actors) is not only expected to live up to a new set of accountability measures but UNHCR now risks facing criminal prosecution if they violate the new and more extensive counter-terror laws that several main donors have put in place (Mackintosh and Duplat 2013; Pantuliano *et al.* 2011).
4 It should, of course, be mentioned that there has recently been a shift from HAP to the new *Core Humanitarian Standards* and the accountability implications of this shift have yet to be explored, for example, how these new Core Humanitarian Standards compare with the HAP certification's emphasis on complaint and response mechanisms and the process of making complaints publicly accessible.
5 From interviews and e-mail exchanges, it seems that an important point to consider is perhaps also that UNHCR staff may not themselves know exactly what the answers to all of these questions are. This point may be due to limited technical knowledge and

lack of knowledge regarding the details of the agreements that have been made with the companies who set up the biometric infrastructure in a given camp.

6 The question asked was: 'Are there plans to exchange biometric data with their partners (NGO, governments, etc.)? If yes, have the legal implications of sharing biometric data among foreign countries/governments been considered?'

7 Rather than talking of a failure of the technology, it is framed as 'lower quality' of fingerprints (Pugliese 2010, p. 64).

8 Indeed, in other contexts, scholars have been critical of a similar inability to assure refugees that their biometric data will not be shared with a third country or even their country of origin (Faraj 2011, pp. 920–921).

References

Alexander, M. (1999) 'Refugee status determination conducted by UNHCR', *International Journal of Refugee Law*, 11(2): 251–289.

Alsalem, R. and F. Riller, (2013) "UNHCR slashes waiting time, clears backlog of Syrian registrations in Jordan" UNHCR news story, Making a Difference, 3 October 2013 [http://www.unhcr.org/524d5e4b6.html]

Amnesty International (2014) 'Lebanon: Agonizing choices: Syrian refugees in need of health care in Lebanon.' *Amnesty International*, 21 May 2014.

Betts, A. (2012) 'The United Nations High Commissioner for refugees: autonomy and mandate change', Chapter 4, in J. E. Oestreich (ed.), *International Organizations as Self-Directed Actors: A Framework for Analysis*, London: Routledge.

Betts, A., G. Loescher and J. Milner. (2008) *UNHCR: The Politics and Practice of Refugee Protection Into the 21st Century*, New York, NY: Routledge.

Boehler, P. (2012) "Burmese Migrants in Malaysia Face Registration Woes" ReliefWeb, 2 March 2012 [http://reliefweb.int/report/malaysia/burmese-migrants-malaysia-face-registration-woes] (Accessed September 22).

Crisp, J. (1999) 'A state of insecurity: the political economy of violence in refugee-populated areas of Kenya', Working Paper.

Crisp, J. (1999) 'Who has counted the refugees? UNHCR and the politics of numbers', Working Paper no. 12, June 1999.

Davies, S. (2012) 'How a United Nations agency buried a security report that warned of potential genocide', *The Privacy Surgeon* [http://www.privacysurgeon.org/blog/incision/how-a-united-nations-agency-buried-a-security-report-that-warned-of-potential-genocide/] (Accessed September 22).

Faraj, A. (2011) 'Refugees and the biometric future: the impact of biometrics on refugees and asylum seekers', *Columbia Human Rights Law Review*, 42.3(Spring): 891–941.

Farmer, A. (2006) 'Refugee responses, state-like behavior, and accountability for human rights violations: a case study of sexual violence in Guinea's refugee camps', *Yale Human Rights and Development Journal*, 9(1): 44–84.

Garvelink, W.J. and F. Tahir (2012) "The Dadaab Refugee Complex: A Powder Keg and It's Giving Off Sparks" 1 March 2012, The Center for Strategic and International Studies [http://csis.org/publication/dadaab-refugee-complex-powder-keg-and-its-giving-sparks]

Ghufran, N. (2006) 'Afghan refugees in Pakistan current situation and future scenario', *Policy Perspectives*, 3(2), July 2006. Available online at www.ips.org.pk/the-muslim-world/1023-afghan-refugees-in-pakistan-current-situation-and-future-scenario (accessed 23 September 2015).

Harrell-Bond, B., E. Voutira and M. Leopold (1992) 'Counting the refugees: gifts, givers, patrons and clients', *Journal of Refugee Studies*, 5(3–4): 205–225.

Harrell-Bond, B. E. (1986) *Imposing Aid: Emergency Assistance to Refugees*, Oxford: Oxford University Press.

Harrell-Bond, B. E. (2002) 'Can humanitarian work with refugees be humane?, *Human Rights Quarterly*, 24(1): 51–85.

Hosein, G. and C. Nyst, (2013) "Aiding Surveillance," Privacy International, October 2013 [https://www.privacyinternational.org/sites/default/files/Aiding%20Surveillance.pdf]

Humanitarian Accountability Partnership. (2011) 'Follow-up mission report of the HAP 2010 deployment to Dadaab refugee operations'. Humanitarian Accountability Partnership (HAP) [http://www.alnap.org/resource/7768.aspx] (Accessed September 22 2015).

Human Rights Watch (2009) " From Horror to Hopelessness: Kenya's Forgotten Somali Refugee Crisis". Washington, DC: Human Rights Watch.

Hussain, M. (2013) 'Slaves, fake refugees and lentils: the Mbera camp in Mauritania', *Reuters*. Available online at http://www.trust.org/item/20131009133413-snelw/?source =dpagetopic (accessed 9 October 2013).

Hussain, M. (2014) 'Ghost' Malian refugees show abuse of U.N. registration system', *Reuters*. Available online at http://www.reuters.com/article/2014/03/21/us-burkina-refugees-idUSBREA2K13Y20140321 (accessed 21 March 2014).

IRIDIAN. (2003) 'Iridian announces expansion of iris use in UN repatriation program for afghan refugees', 26 March. Available online at www.businesswire.com/news/ home/20030326005505/en/Iridian-Announces-Expansion-Of-Iris-Repatriation-Program-Afghan#.VOSFM3l0zAU (accessed 23 September 2015).

Jacobsen, K.L. (2010) 'Making design safe for citizens: a hidden history of humanitarian experimentation', *citizenship studies*, 14(1): 2010.

Jacobsen, K.L. forthcoming 'More than a decade of humanitarian refugee biometrics', *Disasters Journal*, Special Issue, Forthcoming.

Jacobsen, K.L. (2015) 'Experimentation in humanitarian locations: UNHCR and biometric registration of Afghan refugees', *Security Dialogue*, April 2015, 46(2): 144–164.

Kakuma News. 'Refugees grumble as the biometrics system for food collection rolls out', The Refugee Newsletter, September 2013. Available online at http:// therefugeekakuma.blogspot.dk/2013/09/refugees-grumble-as-biometrics-system.html (accessed 23 September 2015).

Kinchin, N. (2013) 'UNHCR as a subsidiary organ of the UN: plurality, complexity and accountability', IRPA Research Paper No. 4.

Knutsen, E. and M. Lutz (2014) 'Lebanon seeking refugee biometric data: Derbas', *The Daily Star Lebanon*, 30 May. Available online at www.dailystar.com.lb/News/Lebanon-News/2014/May-30/258268-government-has-refugee-eye-scans-derbas.ashx (accessed 23 September 2015).

Lee, C. "Humanitarian assistance as containment: new codes for a new order". Oxford University, Refugee Studies Centre, Working Paper Series, No. 72.

Loescher (1997) "The United Nations High Commissioner for Refugees in the Post-Cold War Era," chapter 9 in *The Politics of International Humanitarian Aid Operations* E. Belgrad, and N. Nachmias. (eds) (1997), Westport, Connecticut, London: Greenwood Publishing House.

Loescher, G. (2001) "The UNHCR and world politics: state interests vs. institutional autonomy". *International Migration Review*, 2001, pp. 33–56.

Macrae, J. (2002) 'The bilateralization of humanitarian response: implications for UNHCR', UNHCR Evaluation and Policy Analysis Unit. EPAU/2002/15. December 2002.

Mackintosh, K. and P. Duplat (2013) 'Study of the impact of donor counter-terrorism measures on principled humanitarian action', Independent study commissioned by United Nations Office for the Coordination of Humanitarian Affairs and Norwegian Refugee Council, July 2013. Available online at https://docs.unocha.org/sites/dms/Documents/ CT_Study_Full_Report.pdf (accessed 23 September 2015). The Assessment Capacities Project (ACAPS) and MapAction "Regional Analysis Syria" 28 March 2013 [http:// www.mapaction.org/component/mapcat/download/2929.html? fmt=pdf]

Metcalfe-Hough, V., T. Keatinge, and S. Pantuliano, (2015) "UK humanitarian aid in the age of counter-terrorism: perceptions and reality" HPG Working Paper, March 2015. Overseas Development Institute, London.

McSweeney, D. (2012) 'Conflict and deteriorating security in Dadaab', *Humanitarian Exchange Magazine*. Available online at www.odihpn.org/humanitarian-exchange-magazine/issue-53/conflict-and-deteriorating-security-in-dadaab (accessed 23 September 2015).

Morris, T. and S. Ben Ali, (2013) "UNHCR reviews its urban policy: an air of complacency?" 10 June 2013, urbanrefugees.org [http://urban-refugees.org/debate/unhcr-reviews-urban-policy-air-complacency/]

Misselwitz, P. and S. Hanafi (2010) "Testing a New Paradigm: UNRWA's Camp Improvement Programme" *Refugee Survey Quarterly (2009)*, 28(2-3): 360–388.

Milner, J. (2009) 'The consequences of limited legal status for Syrian refugees in Lebanon', *Refugees, the State and the Politics of Asylum in Africa*. Basingstoke: Palgrave Macmillan. NRC (Norwegian Refugee Council) (April 2014).

Muller, B. (2004) "(Dis)qualified Bodies: Securitization, citizenship and identity management," *Citizenship Studies*, 8(3): 279–294.

Needham, K. (2011) "Refugee unrest in Malaysia after deportation bungle" 26 August 2011, *The Sydney Morning Herald* [http://www.smh.com.au/national/refugee-unrest-in-malaysia-after-deportation-bungle-20110825-1jcj2.html]

Norwegian Refugee Council (NRC) (2014) "The Consequences of Limited Legal Status for Syrian Refugees in Lebanon," NRC Lebanon Field Assessment. NRC Lebanon, March 2014.

Otieno, P. and D. Gazarwa, (2014) "Joint Assessment Mission - Kenya Refugee Operation Dadaab (23-27 June 2014) and Kakuma (30 June - 1 July 2014) Refugee Camps" UNHCR/WFP [http://reliefweb.int/sites/reliefweb.int/files/resources/Final%20Version_2014%20WFP-UNHCR%20Kenya%20Joint%20Assessment%20Report.pdf]

Pantuliano, S., K. Mackintosh and S. Elhawary with V. Metcalfe. (2011) 'Counter-terrorism and humanitarian action: tensions, impact and ways forward', *HPG Policy Brief*, 43: 9.

Poole, L. (2014) 'Bridging the needs-based funding gap: NGO field perspectives', Independent Study Commissioned by Norwegian Refugee Council (NRC Lebanon).

Pugliese, J, (2010) *Biometrics: Bodies, Technologies, Biopolitics*, New York and London: Routledge.

Vogler, S. (2012) "Security Challenges in Libya and the Sahel" Workshop Report, December 2012. CNA Strategic Studies [https://www.cna.org/CNA_files/PDF/DCP-2012-U-003450-Final.pdf]

Sleiman, N. F. (2012) 'Accountability of international non-governmental organizations'. U.S. Ambassador Lane (2014) Available online at http://usunrome.usmission.gov/news/second-regular-session-wfp.html (accessed 23 September 2015).

Sudan Tribune (2014) "UNHCR, S. Sudan launch biometric registration of IDPs" Sudan Tribune, 20 September 2014 [http://www.sudantribune.com/spip.php?article52475]

Troger, F. and V. Tennant, (2008) "The use of cash grants in UNHCR voluntary repatriation operations" Report of a 'lessons learned' workshop, September 2008. UNHCR Policy Development and Evaluation Service (PDES) and Division of Operational Services (DOS). PDES/2008/09.

Turk, V. and E. Eyster, (2010) "Strengthening Accountability in *UNHCR*" *International Journal of Refugee Law*, Vol. 22, Issue 2, pp. 159–172.

UNHCR 2012 "Modern technology helps meet the needs of refugees in South Sudan" UNHCR *News Stories*, 29 December 2012 [http://www.unhcr.org.uk/news-and-views/news-list/news-detail/article/modern-technology-helps-meet-the-needs-of-refugees-in-south-sudan.html]

UNHCR (2003) "Iris testing of returning Afghans passes 200,000 mark" *UNHCR News Stories*, 10 October 2003 [http://www.unhcr.org/3f86b4784.html]

UN News Centre (2004) "Afghans living in Iran and Pakistan will be able to vote in elections - UN Mission" UN News Centre [http://www.un.org/apps/news/story.asp?NewsID=11406&Cr=afghanistan&Cr1=#.VinTxHkcTZ4].

UNHCR (2009a) 'UNHCR policy on refugee protection and solutions in urban areas'. Available online at www.unhcr.org/4ab356ab6.pdf (accessed 26 November 2015).

UNHCR (2003) "UNHCR Handbook for Registration. Procedures and Standards for Registration, Population Data Management and Documentation" Provisional Release (September 2003), UNHCR [http://www.unhcr.org/4a278ea1d.html]

UNHCR (2012) 'The implementation of UNHCR's policy on refugee protection and solutions in urban areas', Global Survey – 2012, M.B. Morand, (PDES), K. Mahoney, with S. Bellour, and J. Rabkin, – Independent Consultants. UNHCR [http://www.unhcr.org/516d658c9.pdf]

UNHCR (2013) 'Update on emergency response operations in south Sudan – week ending 4 March 2013' UNHCR Refugee Weekly Update 04.03.2013.

UNHCR (2013b) 'Request for proposals'. Available online at www.unhcr.org/50c85dd69.pdf (accessed 23 September 2015).

UNHCR (2013c) 'UNHCR slashes waiting time, clears backlog of Syrian registrations in Jordan', *Making a difference*, 3 October. Available online at www.unhcr.org/524d5e4b6.html (accessed 23 September 2015).

UNHCR (2013d) 'Iris testing of returning Afghans passes 200,000 mark', *News Stories*, 10 October 2013.

UNHCR (2014a) 'Living in the shadows. Jordan home visits report 2014'. Available online at http://unhcr.org/jordan2014urbanreport/home-visit-report.pdf (accessed 23 September 2015).

UNHCR Global Trends Report (2010) Available online at www.unhcr.org/516d658c9.pdf (accessed 23 September 2015).

UNHCR (August 2003). Available online at www.unhcr.org/3f3378c44.html (accessed 23 September 2015).

U.S. DOS (2004) "The United States Refugee Admissions Program: Reforms for a New Era of Refugee Resettlement" U.S. State Department, Under Secretary for Democracy and Global Affairs [http://2001-2009.state.gov/g/prm/refadm/rls/rpts/36066.htm]

Al Arabiya News. (2015) 'Turkey provides 1.5 million Syrian refugees with ID cards', *Al Arabiya News, staff writer*, 12 January 2015. Available online at http://english.alarabiya.net/en/News/middle-east/2015/01/12/Turkey-provides-1-5-million-Syrian-refugees-with-ID-cards-.html (accessed 23 September 2015).

WFP (World Food Programme). (2014) 'Projects for executive board approval. Protracted relief and recovery operations', WFP/EB.2/2014/8-B/4, 17 October 2014.

WikiLeaks (2003) "wfp's collaboration with unhcr in providing food assistance to refugees in tanzania joint mission assessment", 24 September 2003. Available online at https://wikileaks.org/plusd/cables/03ROME4340_a.html.

Index

For Product Safety Concerns and Information please contact our EU
representative GPSR@taylorandfrancis.com
Taylor & Francis Verlag GmbH, Kaufingerstraße 24, 80331 München, Germany

www.ingramcontent.com/pod-product-compliance
Ingram Content Group UK Ltd.
Pitfield, Milton Keynes, MK11 3LW, UK
UKHW021611240425
457818UK00018B/495